Consuming Music

Eastman Studies in Music

Ralph P. Locke, Senior Editor
Eastman School of Music

Additional Titles of Interest

*The Art of Musical Phrasing in the Eighteenth Century:
Punctuating the Classical "Period"*
Stephanie D. Vial

Beyond "The Art of Finger Dexterity": Reassessing Carl Czerny
Edited by David Gramit

Dance in Handel's London Operas
Sarah McCleave

Marching to the Canon: The Life of Schubert's "Marche militaire"
Scott Messing

Marianna Martines: A Woman Composer in the Vienna of Mozart and Haydn
Irving Godt
Edited by John A. Rice

Mendelssohn, the Organ, and the Music of the Past: Constructing Historical Legacies
Edited by Jürgen Thym

Music in Print and Beyond: Hildegard von Bingen to The Beatles
Edited by Craig A. Monson and Roberta Montemorra Marvin

The Music of Carl Philipp Emanuel Bach
David Schulenberg

Rossini and Post-Napoleonic Europe
Warren Roberts

Sacred Song and the Pennsylvania Dutch
Daniel Jay Grimminger

A complete list of titles in the Eastman Studies in Music series may be found
on the University of Rochester Press website, www.urpress.com

Consuming Music

Individuals, Institutions, Communities, 1730–1830

Edited by Emily H. Green
and Catherine Mayes

UNIVERSITY OF ROCHESTER PRESS

First published 2017

University of Rochester Press
668 Mt. Hope Avenue, Rochester, NY 14620, USA
www.urpress.com
and Boydell & Brewer Limited
PO Box 9, Woodbridge, Suffolk IP12 3DF, UK
www.boydellandbrewer.com

ISBN-13: 978-1-58046-577-9
ISSN: 1071-9989

Library of Congress Cataloging-in-Publication Data

Names: Green, Emily, editor. | Mayes, Catherine, 1979– editor.
Title: Consuming music : individuals, institutions, communities, 1730–1830 / edited by Emily H. Green and Catherine Mayes.
Other titles: Eastman studies in music ; v. 138.
Description: Rochester : University of Rochester Press, 2017. | Series: Eastman studies in music ; v. 138
Identifiers: LCCN 2016038663 | ISBN 9781580465779 (hardcover : alk. paper)
    Subjects: LCSH: Music publishing—History—18th century. | Music publishing—History—19th century.
Classification: LCC ML112 .C72 2017 | DDC 780.9/033—dc23 LC record available at https://lccn.loc.gov/2016038663

A catalogue record for this title is available from the British Library.

This publication is printed on acid-free paper.
Printed in the United States of America.

An online supplement to this book is available at consumingmusic.lib.utah.edu.

Contents

Acknowledgments

We have long wanted to collaborate on a book about the consumption of music in the eighteenth and early nineteenth centuries, and we are therefore grateful to all those who have helped to make this volume a reality. The University of Utah's University Research Committee supported the publication of this book through a Faculty Research and Creative Grant. George Mason University's School of Music, College of Visual and Performing Arts, and Office of Research, as well as the University of Utah's College of Fine Arts and J. Willard Marriott Library, also underwrote the project. In addition, we would like to thank those affiliated with the University of Rochester Press and the Eastman Studies in Music series—including but not limited to Ralph Locke, Sonia Kane, Julia Cook, Ryan Peterson, Tracey Engel, the manuscript's anonymous reviewers, and especially Cheryl Carnahan—for helping the volume come to fruition in its best possible form. Finally, our interest and immersion in this topic would not have been possible without the support and encouragement of early mentors James Webster and David Rosen; current colleagues Linda Monson, Tom Owens, and the participants in the College of Fine Arts Scholars group at the University of Utah; Stephen, Matt, and the boys at home (especially when they were napping!); and each other as the dearest of friends.

Introduction

Emily H. Green and Catherine Mayes

In a print by Carl Schütz from 1786, a rather large crowd gathers in front of Artaria's shop in Vienna (fig. I.1). Among the roughly two dozen well-dressed individuals, some inspect the shop window, while others try to peer into the store itself, presumably to gather an impression of its offerings beyond those on display. The *Kunsthandlung*, as the shop billed itself, might be advertising engraved pictures, maps, or even music; Schütz's faint scribblings obfuscate the exact nature of the wares exhibited. Based on available evidence, we can't know what curious onlookers might have seen, either in the window or beyond. Like the viewers on the street, we are left, rapt, with an incomplete picture of the contents of the store and its windows.

A later print, Franz Weigl's aquarelle of Steiner and Haslinger's shop ca. 1835 (fig. I.2), takes us inside a Viennese *Kunsthandlung*, but again no music is visible. Rather, one sees shop attendants, customers, prints of visual art, books one can assume to be shop registers, and commemorative busts. The only sounds in the room presumably emanate from the conversations among the buyers and attendants in the room. A transaction might be taking place, but it likely concerns a picture of some sort rather than anything musical.

These two prints are vivid reminders that the successful sale and distribution of music depended on much more than the quality of the ideas on the page: musical commerce involved both a physical and a social infrastructure. Though the existence of that infrastructure is most likely obvious, its organization and participants are among the least well-preserved and thus least-understood elements of the musical culture of the common-practice period: who bought music, and how did those consumers know what music was available? Where was it sold and by whom? How did the consumption of music affect its composition? How was consumers' musical taste shaped and by whom? The documentary difficulty one encounters when attempting to answer such questions has been an impediment to engaging in more complex historical inquiries about consumers' tastes, publishers' promotional strategies, celebrity

Figure I.1. Carl Schütz, *Ansicht vom Kohlmarkt* (1786), detail. © Wien Museum, Vienna, Austria.

Figure I.2. Franz Weigl, *Musikalienhandlung von Sigmund Anton Steiner und Tobias Haslinger in Wien* (1835/1840), photograph of a watercolor. Reproduced by permission of the Beethoven-Haus Bonn, Germany.

culture, and the wider communities that were fundamental to these and many more aspects of musical life in the eighteenth and nineteenth centuries. Though we can identify the major music publishers in nearly every European city at this time based on their catalogs and advertisements in periodicals, their clientele has often remained opaque, as have, moreover, the motivations of these purchasers.

Indeed, the musical consumer is underdocumented, underresearched, and undertheorized. Musicologists have done considerable archival legwork to establish the means of musical producers, particularly in the eighteenth century—from extensive work on publishers and their wares to studies of Carl Philipp Emanuel Bach and Telemann and other musical entrepreneurs—but the identities and activities of music's consumers are still unclear.[1] Relying mainly on data from subscription lists, Bianca Maria Antolini has divided this group into social and professional categories—"aristocracy, citizens (employees, lawyers, merchants), clergymen, musicians, entrepreneurs in the musical domain such as impresarios, book-sellers, and publishers, and people related to the author"—as well as female amateurs and institutions, including music societies.[2] In his investigation, Axel Beer has separated consumers by their modes of access: those who read periodicals, attended concerts, and participated in music-making.[3] Furthermore, despite their otherwise thorough and foundational work, neither author has fully investigated the role of publishers in the consumption of music, especially the ways publishers modeled consumption for each other and for their customers. And consumers—to whose ranks dancers also belonged, although Beer left them out of his classification—and publishers are only two groups who participated in the consumption of music; other notable producers include performers (who are also consumers), impresarios, instrument makers, and composers themselves. The goal of this volume is therefore to provide a more thorough framework within which to understand the activity and proliferation of musical consumption during the century spanning approximately the years 1730–1830.

Undoubtedly at least part of the reason why the consumption of music during this time has received relatively little scholarly attention is that the mid- to late nineteenth century has commonly been acknowledged as the period during which consumerism in general blossomed in Europe, nurtured by the Industrial Revolution and its infrastructure for the mechanical reproduction, transportation, and distribution of accumulated wealth and income across a large segment of the population. For some writers, including John Benson, the resulting consumer society identifies itself as one "in which choice and credit are readily available, in which social value is defined in terms of purchasing power and material possessions, and in which there is a desire, above all, for that which is new, modern, exciting, and fashionable."[4] For others, from Thorstein Veblen to Peter Stearns, the key ingredient of full-blown consumerism is widespread and enthusiastic participation in leisure activities, such as shopping, sporting events, resort travel, numerous toys and games for children, and indeed musical entertainment.[5] Another crucial step in the formation of a consumer society, at least in the eyes of Karl Marx and his ideological descendants, is the moment in which all of these activities and objects become fetishized upon entering the marketplace, sloughing off any whiff of the labor and social relations required to produce them. A great amount of nonmusicological work on this topic focuses on London—and to some degree Paris—as the birthplace and breeding ground of these consumer habits, exemplifying commodity fetishism, for instance, in the marketing of English fashion and tracing the concept of leisure to the Parisian department store later in the nineteenth century.[6] In fact, scholarship that explores the early stages of consumerism in Europe focuses on London almost exclusively.

It may seem misplaced, therefore, to set a discussion of continental musical culture predating the mid-nineteenth century against the backdrop of so-called consumerism, but we believe the origins of the modern marketplace are clearly evident in the period in question in this volume. Music became, particularly in its printed form, a luxury leisure item (as argued by Emily H. Green and Rupert Ridgewell); the marketplace offered increasing options for individuals to buy, quite literally, into a community of ideas (as demonstrated by Steven Zohn, Patrick Wood Uribe, and Peter Mondelli); and the broad consumption of music fostered both emulation (as explored by Marie Sumner Lott, Catherine Mayes, and Glenda Goodman) and diversity (as suggested by Roger Mathew Grant) in musical style, notation, and performers' self-presentation.

Moreover, we are not alone in our desire to search for the origins of modern consumerism in an earlier period. In particular, aside from a number of sociological studies, Nicholas Vazsonyi has argued for the rather loose application of "consumer" to the characters in and spectators of Wagner's mid-nineteenth-century works, because the term captures both the relation of certain characters to the objects they encounter and audiences' approach to those works as leisure items.[7] Studies of self-publishing in the eighteenth century have laid a more convincing groundwork for ours by outlining the entrepreneurship typical of a more robust modern market economy.[8] In fact, entrepreneurship is the focus of a collection of essays—*The Musician as Entrepreneur, 1700–1914*, edited by William Weber—that addresses consumerism in all but name, examining the ways individuals embodied and drove changes in the musical marketplace.[9] Weber's volume emphasizes the roles of composers, performers, and patrons in the formation of a new musical economy, with particular attention to the mid- to late nineteenth century. Here, we expand on Weber's important work and that of his contributors as we highlight the efforts of similar types in an earlier period, adding publishers, theorists, impresarios, and critics to the individuals and groups under consideration.

The present study of eighteenth- and early nineteenth-century music, in its printed and sounding forms as well as in the communities that fostered it, further contributes to the existing scholarship on consumerism in at least three ways. First, it highlights an interesting impulse toward the mundane. Because of the difficulty of measuring the effect of commodification on the content—rather than the packaging—of a product, particularly an artistic one, it is significant that three of the chapters in this volume offer insights in that regard. Both Sumner Lott and Mayes present evidence that the process of commodification led to the simplification of music destined for a wide market, and Goodman explores how some female performers also presented themselves in a very basic and simple guise to ensure their social acceptability. Second, the studies in this collection bring into focus the mechanisms of consumerism across the continent and beyond, as they deal with the German-speaking lands (Green, Ridgewell, Zohn, Grant, Sumner Lott, Mayes, and Wood Uribe), Paris (Mondelli), and the United States (Goodman)—areas whose musical marketplaces (unlike London's) have not been broadly studied in this period. Finally, the research presented here offers new ways of characterizing the activities of producers and consumers as individuals and as groups.

The temporal scope of the chapters in this volume ranges from the late 1720s to the mid-1830s. This period of roughly one hundred years encompasses the latter two portions of what James Webster has posited as the "long" eighteenth century (ca. 1670–1830), analogous to the now familiar concept of a "long" nineteenth century, commonly accepted as the period spanning the years 1789–1914.[10] As Webster reminds us, periods are constructions, and what we call a century need not accord with the calendar, much less can the end of one period (or century, in the broader construal of the term) and the beginning of the next be narrowed down to a precise year. Rather, a period is coherent by virtue of turning points at each of its extremes important enough to outweigh potential partitions within it. Webster's own reading of the long eighteenth century relies on a tripartite division of the period into spans of approximately equal duration: 1670–1720, 1720–80, and 1780–1830. The early portion of the long century (what Webster terms the "late Baroque") was marked particularly by the dominance of Italian opera—especially *opera seria*, which was born from the Arcadian reform of ca. 1690—and French *tragédie*, as well as by the emergence of instrumental genres that would be lastingly influential (the keyboard suite, solo concerto, and trio sonata) and the rise of major-minor tonality. The importance of Italian opera continued throughout the central part of the period, with the eventual rise of *opera buffa* and wane of *opera seria*, the advent of what Webster has termed "Enlightened–galant aesthetics," and the cultivation of sensibility after ca. 1760. The final portion of the long century witnessed the dominance of the Viennese style throughout Europe and the dawning of Romanticism on the heels of the French Revolution.

The chapters in this collection do not engage with the first part of Webster's long eighteenth century simply because it was relatively insignificant with respect to musical consumerism, especially compared with developments that took place during the latter two portions of the period.[11] Despite the star status cultivated by castrati, for example, *opera seria* was essentially a court genre supported by the aristocracy, whereas *opera buffa* and other national genres of comic opera that arose during the central portion of the long century were sustained by a growing middle-class public. Similarly, keyboard and chamber music of the early part of the century was enjoyed by a relatively small number of musicians; only during the middle and final portions of the period was a substantial quantity of such music composed for and marketed to a specifically middle-class, largely amateur audience. The rapid expansion of this segment of society during the time period under investigation in this volume accounts in large part for the unprecedented proliferation of printing technologies and publication infrastructure, improvements in the design and availability of musical instruments, and the importance of large-scale public performance spaces that characterized it. These developments in turn allowed for the publication, distribution, and enjoyment of previously unheard-of quantities of music and writings about music in books and periodicals of various sorts.

These changes took place over the course of years and continued well beyond 1830. Nonetheless, the musical landscape changed markedly after the first three decades of the nineteenth century: the deaths of Beethoven and Schubert marked the end of Vienna's position as the undisputed musical center of Europe, and the mythologizing of Beethoven after his death largely fostered the rise of the concept and ideal of autonomous musical works. Moreover, in the second half of the nineteenth century, the consumption of music was revolutionized by the advent of sound-recording technology, forever changing how music was preserved, distributed, and enjoyed.

The century spanning ca. 1730–1830, furthermore, is coherent by virtue of the dominance of Austro-German—and especially of Viennese—music throughout Europe. Indeed, the "mixed" style of composition of the early part of this century, which blended elements of French, Italian, English, and Polish music, was none other than the German style, which eventually rose to international prominence over its Italian and French rivals.[12] For this reason, seven of the nine chapters in this volume (all except those by Goodman and Mondelli) are devoted to the consumption of music in Austro-Germany, with a special emphasis on Vienna in the contributions by Ridgewell and Mayes. Furthermore, as many of the essays in this collection attest, studying the consumption of music in the eighteenth and early nineteenth centuries leads to an engagement with purchasers, producers, and repertoires that have frequently received little attention from scholars, in part because they have long been overshadowed by the reception of Haydn, Mozart, and Beethoven (among other figures of the period under investigation here) and of their music as "great." Yet Václav Veit's string chamber-music compositions and numerous Hungarian-Gypsy–inspired contredanses for keyboard were popular and successful because of—not in spite of—their simplicity (Sumner Lott and Mayes); Mary Ann Wrighten Pownall cultivated a celebrity persona in the United States that depended on mundaneness (Goodman); and Telemann (whose writings are taken up here by Zohn) was in many ways more significant in his own day than was Johann Sebastian Bach.

We have organized the nine chapters in this volume into four parts, although each individual contribution addresses more topics than a single subheading can adequately capture. First, in "Selling Variety," Green and Ridgewell probe how publishers cultivated and demonstrated a preference for wide-ranging products, both musical and nonmusical, thereby subtly guiding consumers' purchases. In her consideration of the ways readers may have been enticed to purchase printed music, Green argues that publishers advertised their habits of consumption publicly and served as models for their nascent communities of customers. Ridgewell investigates the activities of one Viennese publisher in particular—Artaria—through a close examination of its earliest surviving ledger from 1784, which reveals not only the full spectrum of Artaria's activities as a *Kunsthändler* but also the relative importance of music to the firm and the degree to which it attempted to anticipate demand for its products.

In part 2 of the collection, "Edifying Readers," Zohn and Grant explore how writings about music, in periodicals and books, attempted to educate readers and encourage consensus among them. Zohn interprets Telemann's journal *Der getreue Music-Meister* in light of other contemporaneous German and English moral weeklies, arguing that it enlightened and entertained a broad audience while fostering women's education and constructing a German national identity through a shared literary and musical language. Conversely, Grant suggests that representations of meter in music-theoretical treatises ultimately failed to mediate the realms of print and sound because they could not properly transmit precise information about tempo and affect to readers through notated musical examples.

The third part of the volume, "Marketing the Mundane," includes chapters by Sumner Lott, Mayes, and Goodman, all three of whom respond in different ways to David Gramit's appeal to consider "specific, music-producing relationships not as the context for great works, but as elements of a musical practice that was in itself meaningful for its participants."[13] Through a close analysis of one of Veit's string quartets, Sumner Lott argues that much string chamber music from the 1830s was consciously composed and published for upper-middle-class men to play in domestic settings, and the accessible style and formal regularity of this music, interspersed with novel harmonic and melodic turns, allowed it to flourish. Similarly, Mayes offers a case study of the marketplace's

influence on music, suggesting that stylistic changes in Viennese representations of Hungarian-Gypsy music in the early nineteenth century can be convincingly attributed to changing fashions in social dance in the Habsburg
capital at this time. Finally, Goodman presents a case study of the British singer
and actor Mary Ann Wrighten Pownall, who established a successful career in
Philadelphia and New York in the 1790s by carefully crafting her image as a
generous and maternal woman to whom her audiences could readily relate.

Lastly, in "Cultivating Communities," Wood Uribe and Mondelli explore
strategies for encouraging shared tastes and political views in communities of
readers and spectators in the early nineteenth century. Taking the *Berliner allgemeine musikalische Zeitung* as his primary focus, Wood Uribe draws attention to
the important function of periodicals in generating business for their publishers, who also issued large quantities of sheet music. Far from only advertising
this music, periodicals included reviews that guided readers' understanding
and appreciation of these works, influencing their aesthetic tastes. Mondelli
argues that in spite of the transformation of opera into a commercial enterprise in Paris in the 1820s, the art form continued to express and create a sense
of communal good.

We offer these contributions as a way of enriching the methodologies, repertoires, and cast of characters often associated with music of the eighteenth
and early nineteenth centuries. The reader will find little mention of "major"
composers or their works in these pages; instead, the focus is on commercialized collections of Hungarian-Gypsy music and music-theoretical explanations
of meter, the public personae of Austro-German publishers and American
female theatrical singers, periodicals and performance venues that sought to
cultivate their audiences and build consensus, and the ways records of sales
and wares reflected consumers' tastes in music and other media. In other
words, the reader will encounter individuals and communities of a type and
class typically considered to be merely supporting in the story of musical cre-
ativity and reception. By focusing on the means by and purposes with which
those individuals and communities published, performed, read, and wrote, we
hope to help redefine the received notion of musical culture itself with respect
to a period associated since the nineteenth century with a more absolute conception of the art form.

Notes

1. Examples include Alexander Weinmann's thorough compilations of publishers' catalogs, the encyclopedic work of Donald Krummel and Anik Devriès,
   as well as more specific scholarship on subscription lists by a number of
   individuals. See, for instance, Klaus Hortschansky, "Pränumerations- und

Subskriptionslisten in Notendrucken deutscher Musiker des 18. Jahrhunderts," *Acta Musicologica* 40, nos. 2–3 (1968): 154–74; Alexander Weinmann, *Johann Traeg: die Musikalienverzeichnisse von 1799 und 1804* (Vienna: Universal Edition, 1973); Alexander Weinmann, *Vollständiges Verlagsverzeichnis Senefelder, Steiner, Haslinger* (Munich: Musikverlag Katzbichler, 1979); Anik Devriès and François Lesure, *Dictionnaire des éditeurs de musique français* (Geneva: Minkoff, 1979, 1988); Donald Krummel, *Music Printing and Publishing* (London: Macmillan, 1990); Peggy Daub, "The Publication Process and Audience for C. P. E. Bach's 'Sonaten für Kenner und Liebhaber,'" *Bach Perspectives* 2 (1996): 65–83; William Weber, "From the Self-Managing Musician to the Independent Concert Agent," in *The Musician as Entrepreneur, 1700–1914: Managers, Charlatans, and Idealists*, ed. William Weber (Bloomington: Indiana University Press, 2004), 105–29; Steven Zohn, "Telemann in the Marketplace," *Journal of the American Musicological Society* 58, no. 2 (2005): 275–356.

2. Bianca Maria Antolini, "Publishers and Buyers," in *Music Publishing in Europe 1600–1900: Concepts and Issues, Bibliography*, ed. Rudolf Rasch (Berlin: Berliner Wissenschafts-Verlag, 2005), 229–35.

3. Axel Beer, *Musik zwischen Komponist, Verlag und Publikum: die Rahmenbedingungen des Musikschaffens in Deutschland im ersten Drittel des 19. Jahrhunderts* (Tutzing: Hans Schneider, 2000), 97–153.

4. John Benson, *The Rise of Consumer Society in Britain, 1880–1980* (New York: Longman, 1994), 4; quoted in Peter Stearns, "Stages of Consumerism: Recent Work on the Issues of Periodization," *Journal of Modern History* 69, no. 1 (March 1997): 105.

5. Thorstein Veblen, *The Theory of the Leisure Class: An Economic Study of Institutions* (London: George Allen and Unwin, 1925); Peter Stearns, *Consumerism in World History: The Global Transformation of Desire* (New York: Routledge, 2006).

6. See, for instance, Michael Miller, *The Bon Marché: Bourgeois Culture and the Department Store, 1869–1920* (Princeton: Princeton University Press, 1981); Neil McKendrick, Colin Brewer, and J. H. Plumb, *The Birth of a Consumer Society: The Commercialization of Eighteenth-Century England* (Bloomington: Indiana University Press, 1982).

7. Nicholas Vazsonyi, *Richard Wagner: Self-Promotion and the Making of a Brand* (Cambridge: Cambridge University Press, 2012). Studies outside of music that push the emergence of consumerism into the eighteenth century or earlier include Gordon Vichert, "The Theory of Conspicuous Consumption in the Eighteenth Century," in *The Varied Pattern: Studies in the Eighteenth Century*, ed. Peter Hughes and David Williams (Toronto: A. M. Hakkert, 1971), 253–67; Joan Thirsk, *Economic Policy and Projects: The Development of a Consumer Society in Early Modern England* (Oxford: Clarendon, 1978); Walter Minchinton, "Convention, Fashion and Consumption: Aspects of British Experience since 1750," in *Consumer Behaviour and Economic Growth in the Modern Economy*, ed. Henri Baudet and Henk van der Meulen (London: Croom Helm, 1982), 207–30; McKendrick, Brewer, and Plumb, eds., *Birth of a Consumer Society*; Carole Shammas, *The Pre-Industrial Consumer in England and America* (Los Angeles: Figueroa, 1990).

8. Barry S. Brook, "Piracy and Panacea in the Dissemination of Printed Music in the Late Eighteenth Century," *Journal of the Royal Musical Association* 102 (1975): 13–36; Klaus Hortschansky, "The Musician as Music-Dealer," in *The Social Status of the Professional Musician from the Middle Ages to the Nineteenth Century*, ed. Walter Salmen, Herbert Kaufman, and Barbara Reisner (New York: Pendragon, 1993), 189–218; Daub, "The Publication Process and Audience for C. P. E. Bach's Sonaten für Kenner und Liebhaber," 65–83; Stephen L. Clark, "C. P. E. Bach as a Publisher of His Own Works," in *Carl Philipp Emanuel Bach: Bericht über das internationale Symposium vom 8. März bis 12. März 1994 im Rahmen der 29. Frankfurter Festtage der Musik an der Konzerthalle "Carl Philipp Emanuel Bach" in Frankfurt (Oder)*, ed. Hans-Günter Ottenberg (Frankfurt an der Oder: Konzerthalle "Carl Philipp Emanuel Bach," 1998), 199–211; Zohn, "Telemann in the Marketplace," 275–356; Stephen Rose, "The Mechanisms of the Music Trade in Central Germany, 1600–1640," *Journal of the Royal Musical Association* 130 (2005): 1–32.

9. Weber, ed., *The Musician as Entrepreneur*.

10. James Webster, "The Eighteenth Century as a Music-Historical Period?" *Eighteenth-Century Music* 1, no. 1 (March 2004): 47–60. This paragraph as a whole is heavily indebted to Webster's article.

11. Furthermore, as Webster has noted (ibid., 53), Carl Dahlhaus did not even consider what Webster has identified as the first portion of the period to be part of the eighteenth century: "Dahlhaus, who was relatively little interested in the seventeenth century, was correspondingly uncertain as to when it shaded into the eighteenth; he estimated this date variously as 'around 1720,' 'in the 1720s,' 'around 1730' and even 'around 1740.'"

12. For a sustained discussion of the "mixed" style, with particular reference to Telemann, see Steven Zohn, *Music for a Mixed Taste: Style, Genre, and Meaning in Telemann's Instrumental Works* (Oxford: Oxford University Press, 2008).

13. David Gramit, "Musicology, Commodity Structure, and Musical Practice," in *Crosscurrents and Counterpoints: Offerings in Honor of Bengt Hambraeus at 70*, ed. Per F. Broman, Nora A. Engebretsen, and Bo Alphonce (Gothenburg: University of Gothenburg, 1998), 27–28.

Part One

Selling Variety

Chapter One

Music's First Consumers

Publishers in the Late Eighteenth Century

Emily H. Green

In a Prague newspaper's assessment of culture in the Rheinland in 1820, Johann Anton André stands out as the prime merit of Offenbach: "[In Offenbach], nothing interests me more than André, the famous lithographer, the famous composer, the famous virtuoso, the famous music-printer, who is also, in addition to [having] many good qualities, a very pleasant associate [*Gesellschafter*] and a very cultured man."[1] For the writer, André is an exemplary citizen of the greater Frankfurt area. Not only is the music publisher competent in his professional capacity as a lithographer, he is also worthy of praise in a host of other surprising ways. He is hailed as a composer, virtuoso (presumably as a performer, as André came from a family of musicians), and generally educated member of society. While publishers were rarely afforded any descriptive adjectives as individuals in the press, here André is painted as a skilled and well-rounded person. Inasmuch as it praises André for his fame and character, this short passage recalls the language used to describe patrons in dedications of the mid- to late eighteenth century.

Around the same time, and following in the tradition of his predecessors and contemporaries, André issued a catalog of wares (fig. 1.1)—a document that presented his activities as a publisher somewhat differently. Printed on the back of the title page of a violin concerto by C. F. LaFont, the list demonstrates a thoughtful, thorough, and possibly excessive hand at collecting, advertising many genres of interest to an individual who might purchase a string concerto and demonstrating a careful alphabetic approach to each category. The depth and breadth of the offerings within a limited range of string genres—including sonatas, duos, quartets, quintets, concertos, works for orchestra, etudes, and cello works—seem designed to demonstrate the publisher's versatility and taste. In fact, one could argue that the list was intended to highlight those qualities explicitly: the catalog is a public display of André's habits in acquiring new music, and thus it is a conspicuous record of the firm's purchasing power.

Axel Beer has written of the "Doppelnatur" of publishers both as individuals with musical ability and taste and as businessmen, citing as an example a letter from the Leipzig Bureau de Musique to the organist Eucharius Florschütz in Rostock: "As composers we confess to you that we are happy with your four-hand sonata; as merchants, however, we must remark that the payment [*Debit*] is meager because the amateur usually does not know how to judge intrinsic quality [*das Innere*]."[2] To establish themselves and survive as musical businessmen, publishers in the eighteenth century had to take on a different dual role in their dealings with composers as well as with the public; they not only produced but also bought and advertised music, acting both as quasi-patrons and as music's first conspicuous consumers. Though this duality is borne out in several places and times, including in London at the beginning of the century and in Paris around the middle of the century, my focus here is Germany toward the end of the century, primarily because of the richness of its musical marketplace, to which a relative lack of scholarly attention has been paid.

Echoes of Old Domains

The narrative of the late eighteenth-century musical economy as typically told is one in which publishers filled a void created by the flagging support of patrons across Europe. Leaving aside the difficulty of generalizing about economies on the continent at that time, the constructed binary between patronage and publishing is also overly simplistic, and it has been questioned in recent musicological scholarship as well as in the work of cultural historians like Mary Poovey, who emphasizes the ways modernity is "inconsistent and ineffective at disaggregating cultural spheres," pointing out that "new domains carry echoes of old ones."[3]

One echo of an old domain immediately apparent in Germany in the late eighteenth century was the status of manuscript circulation. Whereas London had supported a thriving and centralized market economy and print industry for the entire eighteenth century, Germany in particular supported a kind of musical economy wherein manuscripts were still dominant and prints were a particularly special and scarce commodity.[4] Beer has hypothesized that the entire German publishing marketplace before 1750 consisted of only approximately 10 percent printed music, a low figure because of the large number of manuscripts in circulation.[5] There is ample evidence, furthermore, that the

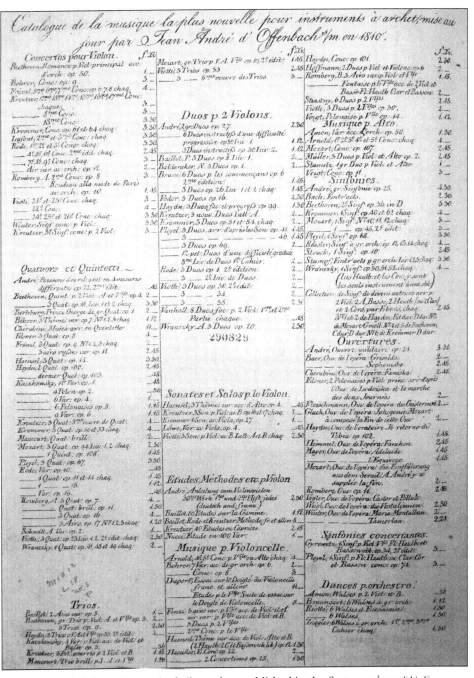

Figure 1.1. Johann Anton André's catalog, published in the first opening of C. F. LaFont's Third Violin Concerto (ca. 1810). Courtesy of the Library of Congress, Music Division, Washington, DC.

importance of manuscripts did not wane in the second half of the eighteenth century. Christian Gottfried Thomas in Leipzig noted in 1778 that "everybody indeed prefers handwritten music to even the best print or engraving,"[6] while several German composers and publishers are known to have complained about the under-the-table manuscript-copying business to which they felt they were losing income.[7] Manuscript circulation had an impact on other European marketplaces as well. Greger Andersson has demonstrated similarities between Germany and Sweden, where more than 90 percent of the repertoire of the university ensembles in Lund in the second half of the eighteenth century consisted of manuscripts prepared by the director.[8] Even in Paris, a city with a healthy engraving industry, an advertisement in the *Journal de musique* from 1777 claimed that most Italian music was distributed in manuscript.[9] These data, however, do not diminish the importance of printed music in the late eighteenth century but rather suggest the very opposite: if we understand the role of printed music, particularly within the broader context of the musical marketplace at large, to comprise only part of the landscape of circulating music, then it becomes clearer that printed music was a scarce, luxury item.[10] German publishers would have had reason to suspect that their marketing of that kind of item would be met with similar interest at home and abroad.

While publishers advertised their handwritten wares in opposition to printed music, they simultaneously adopted a different characteristic of an older economy in their reliance on the well-established behaviors of patrons. In fact, the complex means by which late eighteenth-century publishers acquired music situates them on the cusp between patronage and market economies in a way that is emblematic of a system in transition. On the grand scale, a comparison of the roles of publishers and patrons in 1800 and in 1900 reveals that the behavior of publishers gradually converged upon that of patrons; the Esterházy family's 1761 contract with Haydn remanded all his compositions to Prince Paul much in the way Durand and Ricordi had exclusive contracts with Ravel and Puccini, respectively. Many cultural and economic factors are responsible for this change, including the institutionalization and streamlining of publishing itself. A publisher around 1900 likely had a larger budget and was therefore able to finance greater and more varied print runs; employ in-house typesetters or engravers, printers, and distributers; and monitor international copyright violations. Publishers around 1800, by contrast, did not have the resources to demand exclusive long-term contracts, as they were only recently capable of paying composers in advance for their works, particularly in Germany.[11] They sold their wares to each other with great frequency to aid in distribution, partly because their competition was fierce and frequently changing; booksellers published, composers sold on subscription, and works were pirated. The late eighteenth-century print economy was one of pervasive multifarious activity for its participants. As Klaus Hortschansky has demonstrated, one could subsist at this time in Germany as both a composer and a part-time music dealer, and individuals commonly adopted many different roles.[12]

In fact, one of the factors that precipitated the gradual convergence of the behavior of publishers and patrons was the adventurous entrepreneurship of composers themselves: publishers acted like patrons because composers treated them as such. For example, as is well-known to anyone who has studied the livelihood of late eighteenth-century composers, publishers acquired a great deal of their wares by virtue of direct solicitation from composers. Dittersdorf, for example, sent a set of string quartets to Artaria in 1788, hoping to entice the publisher with a comparison to Mozart's earlier set: "I offer you the original manuscript or, more accurately, my own score of [the quartets] for the same price you paid for Mozart's and in addition for the first 10 prints or copies, and I am certain that you will do better with mine than you did with Mozart's."[13] Dittersdorf's plea worked, and Artaria bought the set, though under different terms. Many similar examples abound in this period, including Leopold Mozart's numerous attempts to secure publication on behalf of his son throughout the 1760s and 1770s.[14] While less often solicited than publishers in Paris and London, those in Germany were approached by composers with increasing frequency in the last decades of the eighteenth century.[15] The similarities between this kind of solicitation and the ways composers engaged with patrons are likely immediately apparent.[16]

For further evidence of the parallel between publishers and patrons, let us compare the passage, quoted above, that praises André's skill and reputation with any number of descriptions of patrons and patron-like figures in dedications from a slightly earlier generation. In 1783, Ignaz Pleyel described his patron, Joszéf Erdödy, as "a true connoisseur and amateur of the noble art of music." Jean-Baptiste Canavas named one Monsieur Barbaut de Glatigny as "among the protectors of talents . . . who, in encouraging them with zeal, cultivate themselves with success" (1773). Carlo Graziani (1760) attributed to his patron "the most profound knowledge," while Pachelbel credited his organist-dedicatees, Ferdinand-Tobias Richter and Dietrich Buxtehude (1699), with "universal renown" and as "very worthy and excellent, very venerable sirs, and very honorable benefactors." Jean Barrière (1733) praised Madame Jourdain's "discernment, insight, not only in music, but even [more] in the most sublime sciences."[17] To be sure, these texts have different contexts from the André description, as they are attached to a variety of types of works; they also have different modes of interaction with their publics, included as they are in front matter and title pages of engraved editions and only sometimes transcribed in full in periodical advertisements. But they do not, I argue, have different purposes. Both the description of André and these dedications seek to flatter and promote an individual who sponsors music, and they accomplish that flattery in similar terms, praising taste and experience in the arts (*gebildeter Man*), reputation (*berühmte*), and social virtue (*angenehmer Gesellschafter*).

Publishers as Consumers

The parallel between publishers and patrons is plausible not least because it reinforces long-held beliefs about the late eighteenth-century musical economy. Any analogy between publishers and consumers, in contrast, might seem redundant, false, or—worse—meaningless. Redundant, because publishers are middlemen by definition; Karl Marx, after all, who focused on production rather than consumption, long ago pointed out that suppliers consume goods in order to produce them. False, because of the possibility that publishers couldn't *really* consume in the ways musicians could; they did not exhibit the same habits of performance. And meaningless, because of the suspicion that such a parallel doesn't tell us anything new about publishers. The first two of these objections, in fact, depend on one's definition of consumption itself, and the last I ask the reader to suspend for a few more paragraphs.

In the broader field of cultural studies, consumers constitute a category of individual whose behavior has been described in a host of ways: they purchase goods preferred by those above them in the social hierarchy (Veblen); they purchase en masse (Baudrillard); they thrive on a system of credit (Brewer); they act on latent desires to acquire goods (McKendrick); they are manipulated by producers (Packard); they engage in "autonomous imaginative hedonism" (Campbell); they are compelled by ideology (Zizek).[18] All of these models establish a kind of abstract consumer behavior seeking far beyond utility; consumers are recognized as those who purchase not merely to use goods but also because of a social habitus. While it might seem odd to consider publishers to be consumers because they were not the most obvious "users," that is, players, of music, they did consume it in many of these more abstract and socially driven ways.

These models, furthermore, are primarily designed to explain the *why* of consumerism first and the *how* second (with the exception of McKendrick, Brewer, and Plumb, who set out the first attempt at a comprehensive consideration of the means of consumption in late eighteenth-century England). Few studies in music, aside from those of Axel Beer and Bianca Maria Antolini (discussed in the introduction), consider the elusive *who*, primarily, I imagine, because of its historic and geographic contingency.[19] Moreover, little of the musicological work on musical print culture considers the status of music as a marketable, desirable commodity or the ways that status might affect the fundamental motives for musical participation. If my reconsideration of publishers under the heading of consumers is inspired by any model in particular, it would be Igor Kopytoff's recognition of the role consumers play in the recommoditization of goods; he understands that in many economies, goods can circulate repeatedly as they are put to initial and secondary uses—sold and resold. Consumers are, he argues, fundamentally both buyers and sellers.[20]

Late eighteenth-century German publishers acted as consumers in ways that would satisfy many models. Though they engaged in activities similar to those of patrons, their ultimate means were entirely different economically; whereas patrons' operations were governed by an underlying system of gift exchange, publishers participated as middlemen and as buyers in a market economy.[21] They purchased goods using a variety of means, as we shall see below. The most obvious abstract kind of consumption they demonstrated is more than a little Veblenesque: they engaged in conspicuousness and excess. For Thorstein Veblen, consumption becomes conspicuous when it is not only public but a "waste of time and effort" (associated with leisure) or a "waste of goods" (excessive).[22] A number of scholars, including Colin Campbell, and Ben Fine and Ellen Leopold, have critiqued Veblen's model as both historically inaccurate and implicitly classist, as it speaks to a top-down view of taste and cultural production in which individuals model their purchasing habits on those of the leisure class.[23] In fact, Catherine Mayes's work in this volume might be interpreted to provide evidence for that well-deserved critique. But for all its faults in capturing the activities and desires of consumers in this period, Veblen's model does adequately explain the attraction to luxury goods, particularly in an age in which leisure was clearly defined, as argued by Andrew Trigg.[24] Conspicuous consumption may not have been the only kind of consumption in this period, but it was one common way of demonstrating cultural capital and achieving distinction—and it was an approach in which publishers engaged, as we shall see below.[25]

What qualifies late eighteenth-century publishers as conspicuous consumers is not only the fact that they purchased music in the sorts of direct ways detailed above. Conspicuous consumers are not mere buyers: they are excessive and public buyers operating within a market economy. The ways publishers show themselves to be excessive are actually well-known to us, as they are evident in the kinds of documents scholars already use to study the distribution of music: their advertisements and catalogs. Both types of documents, particularly at this time, were designed to demonstrate not only the wide variety of wares on offer but also their quantity.

The advertisement of excess among German publishers around 1800 was evident even earlier in Paris and London, as one might expect. Paris's *Journal de musique*, which dipped its toe into the music printing, publishing, and dealing business in the 1770s, advertised a collection of Italian songs (mentioned above) with this language: "We believe, therefore, that we do music-lovers a service and give them interesting news by announcing that a valuable collection of Italian scores and over 400 arias of the best masters, such as Anfossi, Piccini, Maïo, Sacchini, Paisiello, etc., has been established at the office of the *Journal de musique*, rue Montmartre, next to that of the Vieux Augustins."[26] While the number four hundred is certainly meant to assure readers of the variety available, it is also unfathomably large. It communicates the same information as the well-placed "etc.," signaling to the reader that the options are many—too many to list. Not wishing to engage in my own trope of excess, I will simply indicate that other examples can be found in many advertisements and reviews from the late eighteenth century.

A similar exuberant surplus was evident slightly later in Germany in catalogs transcribed in periodicals—certainly a type of document familiar to many scholars of this era.[27] Figure 1.2 shows Hoffmeister and Kühnel's Bureau de Musique's catalog from the *Intelligenzblatt*, a supplement to the *Zeitung für die elegante Welt*, published in Leipzig beginning in 1801. The stream-of-consciousness listings, one right after another with no line breaks, make it difficult to parse composers, genres, instruments, and titles. The goal seems to be to overwhelm the reader with unbounded possibilities rather than to inform her of the publication of particular pieces. A close look at the listings in this catalog demonstrates an astonishing variety of works, including exercises, Lieder, potpourris, marches, divertissements, quartets, symphonies, and sonatas. This collection is also advertised in a publication devoted to the "elegant world," further confirming the suggestion that a great deal of published music around 1800 was a luxury item in Germany.

In 1795, as Beer has discovered, Ernst Ludwig Gerber suggested that publishers sought "to make their various things [*Siebesachen*] known through diligent distribution of their catalogues from all angles."[28] Part of their diligence was demonstrated in their distribution of catalogs to other publishers and individual buyers by mail, as discussed below; toward the end of the eighteenth century, they began to publish their catalogs in periodicals and at the backs of editions. Beer has found evidence that the Leipzig Bureau de Musique ordered one thousand copies of the catalog of its Mozart editions from a printer to distribute to 170 merchants and individuals.[29] That these catalogs served many purposes simultaneously is evident from a variety of sources. Publishers themselves used catalogs to purchase music from one another, often from quite a distance and at a discounted rate. Luigi Marescalchi, a publisher in Venice and Naples, for example, wrote to the Leipzig publisher August Kühnel in 1807:

> I have therefore studied your catalogue and your conditions, and found them quite different from our publishers', because they generally give the music-sellers a discount of 50%, and payments within six months. . . . And although the music in my Naples catalogue is much cheaper than the music of all the others . . . I have always allowed a discount of 50% with payment within six months, 45% within ten months and 40% within fifteen months for the remote countries, such as Saint Petersburg, Moscow, Riga, and so on.[30]

This passage could inform a rich discussion of the international arrangements and aspirations of individuals in the music publishing industry, but for the

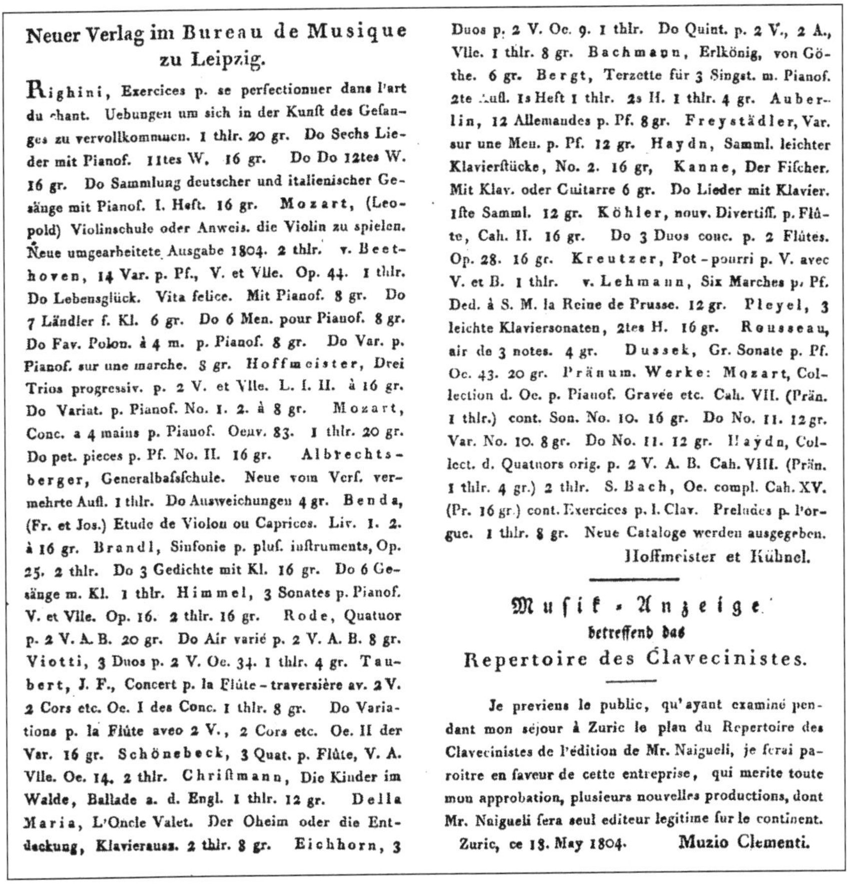

Neuer Verlag im Bureau de Musique zu Leipzig.

Righini, Exercices p. se perfectionner dans l'art du chant. Uebungen um sich in der Kunst des Gesanges zu vervollkommnen. 1 thlr. 20 gr. Do Sechs Lieder mit Pianof. 11tes W. 16 gr. Do Do 12tes W. 16 gr. Do Sammlung deutscher und italienischer Gesänge mit Pianof. I. Heft. 16 gr. Mozart, (Leopold) Violinschule oder Anweis. die Violin zu spielen. Neue umgearbeitete Ausgabe 1804. 2 thlr. v. Beethoven, 14 Var. p. Pf., V. et Vlle. Op. 44. 1 thlr. Do Lebensglück. Vita felice. Mit Pianof. 8 gr. Do 7 Ländler f. Kl. 6 gr. Do 6 Men. pour Pianof. 8 gr. Do Fav. Polon. à 4 m. p. Pianof. 8 gr. Do Var. p. Pianof. sur une marche. 8 gr. Hoffmeister, Drei Trios progressiv. p. 2 V. et Vlle. L. I. II. à 16 gr. Do Variat. p. Pianof. No. 1. 2. à 8 gr. Mozart, Conc. a 4 mains p. Pianof. Oeuv. 83. 1 thlr. 20 gr. Do pet. pieces p. Pf. No. II. 16 gr. Albrechtsberger, Generalbaßschule. Neue vom Verf. vermehrte Aufl. 1 thlr. Do Ausweichungen 4 gr. Benda, (Fr. et Jos.) Etude de Violon ou Caprices. Liv. I. 2. à 16 gr. Brandl, Sinfonie p. pluß. instruments, Op. 25. 2 thlr. Do 3 Gedichte mit Kl. 16 gr. Do 6 Gesänge m. Kl. 1 thlr. Himmel, 3 Sonates p. Pianof. V. et Vlle. Op. 16. 2 thlr. 16 gr. Rode, Quatuor p. 2 V. A. B. 20 gr. Do Air varié p. 2 V. A. B. 8 gr. Viotti, 3 Duos p. 2 V. Oe. 34. 1 thlr. 4 gr. Taubert, J. F., Concert p. la Flûte-traversière av. 2 V. 2 Cors etc. Oe. I des Conc. 1 thlr. 8 gr. Do Variations p. la Flûte avec 2 V., 2 Cors etc. Oe. II der Var. 16 gr. Schönebeck, 3 Quat. p. Flûte, V. A. Vlle. Oe. 14. 2 thlr. Christmann, Die Kinder im Walde, Ballade a. d. Engl. 1 thlr. 12 gr. Della Maria, L'Oncle Valet. Der Oheim oder die Entdeckung, Klavierauss. 2 thlr. 8 gr. Eichhorn, 3

Duos p. 2 V. Oe. 9. 1 thlr. Do Quint. p. 2 V., 2 A., Vlle. 1 thlr. 8 gr. Bachmann, Erlkönig, von Göthe. 6 gr. Bergt, Terzette für 3 Singst. m. Pianof. 2te Aufl. 1s Heft 1 thlr. 2s H. 1 thlr. 4 gr. Auberlin, 12 Allemandes p. Pf. 8 gr. Freystädler, Var. sur une Men. p. Pf. 12 gr. Haydn, Samml. leichter Klavierstücke, No. 2. 16 gr, Kanne, Der Fischer. Mit Klav. oder Cuitarre 6 gr. Do Lieder mit Klavier. 1ste Samml. 12 gr. Köhler, nouv. Divertiss. p. Flûte, Cah. II. 16 gr. Do 3 Duos conc. p. 2 Flûtes. Op. 28. 16 gr. Kreutzer, Pot-pourri p. V. avec V. et B. 1 thlr. v. Lehmann, Six Marches p. Pf. Ded. à S. M. la Reine de Prusse. 12 gr. Pleyel, 3 leichte Klaviersonaten, 2tes H. 16 gr. Rousseau, air de 3 notes. 4 gr. Dussek, Gr. Sonate p. Pf. Oe. 43. 20 gr. Pränum. Werke: Mozart, Collection d. Oe. p. Pianof. Gravée etc. Cah. VII. (Prän. 1 thlr.) cont. Son. No. 10. 16 gr. Do No. 11. 12 gr. Var. No. 10. 8 gr. Do No. 11. 12 gr. Haydn, Collect. d. Quatuors orig. p. 2 V. A. B. Cah. VIII. (Prän. 1 thlr. 4 gr.) 2 thlr. S. Bach, Oe. compl. Cah. XV. (Pr. 16 gr.) cont. Exercices p. l. Clav. Preludes p. l'orgue. 1 thlr. 8 gr. Neue Catalogue werden ausgegeben.

Hoffmeister et Kühnel.

Musik-Anzeige betreffend das **Repertoire des Clavecinistes.**

Je previens le public, qu'ayant examiné pendant mon séjour à Zuric le plan du Repertoire des Clavecinistes de l'édition de Mr. Naigueli, je ferai paroitre en faveur de cette entreprise, qui merite toute mon approbation, plusieurs nouvelles productions, dont Mr. Naigueli sera seul editeur legitime sur le continent.

Zuric, ce 18. May 1804. **Muzio Clementi.**

Figure 1.2. Catalog of Hoffmeister and Kühnel's Bureau de Musique, published in the *Intelligenzblatt für die Elegante Welt* (June 2, 1804). Courtesy of the Houghton Library, Harvard University, Cambridge, MA.

purposes of this argument we should observe that Marescalchi confirms the existence of a healthy and widespread purchasing system between publishers around 1800—a system so commonplace that he took its arrangements for granted.[31] Moreover, this use of catalogs suggests that publishers consulted them to model their own consumption on that of their peers.

Catalogs were also the gateway for many individuals on the marketplace. Beer details one consumer's interaction with these documents: Antoinette von Wilcke from Gera, who ordered specific works from the Leipzig Bureau de Musique. Instead of simply asking for "guitar music with string accompaniment" or "twelve new waltzes," as some orders did, Wilcke's requests included a great deal of information, such as "*Rondeau en G pour le P. F. comp. et dediee a*

Mlle la Comtesse Henriette de Lichnowski par L. v. Beethoven" and "*Walze en forme de Rondeau pour le Pianoforte comp. p. L. Abeille.*" The detail of her orders, alongside the discovery that she had previously requested that the firm send her a catalog, suggests that she arrived at her choices as a result of contact with the catalog itself.[32]

One could further argue that the turn toward "complete" editions of composers' works at the beginning of the nineteenth century was an outgrowth of this tendency to offer an extensive catalog—a way of focusing excess on a single (new) object of cultural fascination: the genius composer. The successful early nineteenth-century attempts at such comprehensive collections are well-known (Artaria's *Collection complette* of Haydn's string quartets, published from 1803 to 1808, for instance). Less well-known are genre-specific collections, such as Simrock's *Collection complète de toutes les œuvres de musique pour le piano-forte* of Mozart (1803–7), as well as editions of piano works of Domenico Scarlatti and Johann Baptist Cramer produced by the Bureau des arts et d'industrie in the first decade of the nineteenth century and Carl Zulehner's unauthorized edition of Beethoven's piano works.[33] We might find amusement in the fact that some of these "complete" works were by definition incomplete because their authors were still living and composing. In the context of excessive and public consumption, though, we can take "complete" to mean something else: immeasurably extensive.

It is also possible that publishers' advertisement of their consumption habits transmitted something more fundamental to their readers: not merely the desire to consume excessively but the excessive desire to consume. New catalogs appeared in the *Intelligenzblatt für die Elegante Welt* almost monthly, communicating an insatiable appetite for collecting on the part of the publishers. Those who buy music, we are meant to believe, are never finished buying music. This deep and necessarily unfulfilled appetite for purchasing has, of course, become one of the hallmarks of the market economy as a whole. As far as musical consumption is concerned, the seeds were planted in the eighteenth century.

Publishers as Prosumers

I conclude by going out on a limb to suggest one further model for the behavior of publishers at this time. Certainly, publishers were producers, a basic identity I have aimed to expand because it does not explain the entirety of their behavior in late eighteenth-century Germany and in Western Europe in general, where they acted as individuals rather than as institutions. It fails to explain their approach to marketing (aside from the obvious fact that they thought their behaviors and activities would sell music) or how their tastes might have affected their stock of wares. As mentioned in the context of Kopytoff's theory of commoditization as a continuous process, however, it can be difficult to draw an exclusive distinction between sellers and buyers. If the reader accepts my argument, publishers were also consumers—a facet of their identity that helps to explain the establishment of a healthy musical marketplace in Germany and beyond. To take a broader, more holistic view of their role in the musical marketplace, in the end, requires a fundamental recognition of the parallelism between production and consumption. While the recognition of that overlap is neither a revolutionary nor a new contribution to cultural historiography, it is unique in the study of music production.

Nearly every significant thinker on the topic of consumption has recognized that the dichotomy between production and consumption is false.[34] Baudrillard generally, across his more and less Marxist work, recognized how consumers are "workers," producers of their own economies.[35] Many other scholars have similarly recognized this dual role, including George Ritzer, Paul Dean, and Nathan Jurgenson, who have described the "coming of age" of the consumer (or prosumer, in their conception) in the 1990s.[36] In fact, they anthologize the many other terms invented to describe this overlap; "prosumption," the one with the most staying power despite its awkwardness on the tongue, was coined by Alvin Toffler in 1980.[37] The concept of prosumption has its roots in the ways consumers have become active creators of their own commercial experiences in the late twentieth and early twenty-first centuries, including self checkout, the creation of knowledge on wikis, and the style of table bussing at McDonald's. It is fair to say that all of the work related to prosumption regards the twilight of the twentieth century in the United States as the ideal incubator for this kind of behavior. Particularly for music, the late eighteenth century, however, was an economy of similar instability and growth. The ways of distributing musical wares were changing rapidly, and fewer institutions existed to provide artistic support than had previously been the case; publishers were an emblem of the heterogeneity of roles inherent in that musical economy.

Publishers might be considered prosumers because of the ways they affected the content of musical products. It is evident from surviving correspondence that they influenced generic designations and dedications as well as the ordering of sets; they determined a great deal of both the notes themselves and the significant packaging that colored a user's experience of the music. In fact, this particular creative behavior was operative long before the late eighteenth century. Jane Bernstein, for example, has documented the ways publishers and typesetters in sixteenth-century Venice determined both layout and paratextual content, including some dedications.[38] In late eighteenth century Germany, this habit persisted and deepened. Leopold Mozart, for instance, tried, unsuccessfully, to secure a contract with Immanuel Breitkopf in 1772 by promising that the young Wolfgang would compose in any genre that pleased him: "Should you wish to deliver something by my son to the press, the best time would be soon. . . . In short, it may be a composition of any genre that seems to suit you; he will do anything if you only ask it quickly."[39] One year later, C. P. E. Bach changed the order within a set of works to suit the same publisher's taste,[40] and in 1789, Haydn told Artaria that he had written the Piano Trio in C Minor, Hob. XV:13, with variations "to suit [the publisher's] taste."[41] Similarly, there is evidence that other composers sought to entice their publishers with the possibility of dedications to prominent individuals, as in Andreas Romberg's declaration to Simrock in 1801 that an offering to Haydn would "promote the sale" of his string quartets.[42]

⁊⁊ ⁊⁊ ⁊⁊

Publishers were the most public purchasers of music in late eighteenth-century Germany, Paris, London, and Vienna. While courts and sacred institutions had long histories of keeping private libraries, publishers actively advertised the breadth and depth of their own collections. Taking advantage of a marketplace in flux, they established themselves as models of taste, thorough and careful purchasing, and cultural influence and distinction—as models of consumption itself. Because the general musicological public considers publishers in this period to be at best conduits for the decisions of composers and at worst (because they sometimes introduced mistakes into musical texts) hindrances in the communication of composers' intent, I have tried to demonstrate the ways they contributed to the creation of musical culture. My goal has not been merely to deconstruct the binary between the supply of and demand for musical goods but to posit new methods of thinking about the multiplicity of roles available to an individual participating in the long transition from a patron-centered to a market economy.

Notes

1. "Andrée [sic], der berühmte Lithograph, der berühmte Componist, der berühmte Virtuose, der berühmte Musikalien-Verleger, der außer noch mehreren guten Eigenschaften auch ein sehr angenehmer Gesellschafter und sehr gebildeter Mann ist." *Hesperus. Encyclopädische Zeitschrift für gebildete Leser* (Prague) 25, no. 13 (March 1820) (Supplement), 95; quoted in Axel Beer, *Musik zwischen Komponist, Verlag und Publikum: Die Rahmenbedingungen des Musikschaffens in Deutschland im ersten Drittel des 19. Jahrhunderts* (Tutzing: Hans Schneider, 2000), 90. The copy of *Hesperus* I consulted is held in the Bayerische Staatsbibliothek (http://www.mdz-nbn-resolving.de/urn/resolver. pl?urn=urn:nbn:de:bvb:12-bsb10531398-4). Interestingly, the journal was edited

by Christian Carl André, who was not a close relation of Johann Anton as far as I can tell.

2. "Als Tonkünstler gestehen wir Ihnen, daß wir mit Ihrer Son. à 4 m. zufrieden sind; als Kaufleute aber müssen wir bemerken, daß der Debit gering ist; denn—der Musikliebhaber weiß meist das In[n]ere nicht zu beurtheilen etc." Ambrosius Kühnel to Eucharius Florschütz, Leipzig (April 17, 1805); quoted in Beer, *Musik zwischen Komponist, Verlag und Publikum*, 248.

3. Mary Poovey, *Genres of the Credit Economy: Mediating Value in Eighteenth- and Nineteenth-Century Britain* (Chicago: University of Chicago Press, 2008), 14. For arguments questioning the straightforwardness of the shift from patronage to a market economy, see, for instance, Rudolf Rasch, "Introduction," in *The Circulation of Music in Europe, 1600–1900*, ed. Rudolf Rasch (Berlin: Berliner Wissenschaftsverlag, 2008), 1–6; Rupert Ridgewell, "Mozart's Music on Sale in Paris and Vienna," in Rasch, ed., *The Circulation of Music in Europe*, 121–42; Tia DeNora, *Beethoven and the Construction of Genius: Musical Politics in Vienna, 1792–1803* (Berkeley: University of California Press, 1995).

4. See Rosamund McGuinness, "External and Internal Factors in the Circulation of Music in London around 1700," in Rasch, ed., *The Circulation of Music in Europe*, 33–46.

5. Some publishers sold music by manuscript as well. Bianca Maria Antolini notes that Breitkopf's catalogs between 1762 and 1787 offered manuscripts alongside prints. See Antolini, "Publishers and Buyers," in *Music Publishing in Europe, 1600–1900*, ed. Rudolph Rasch (Berlin: Berliner Wissenschaftsverlag, 2005), 214. See also Axel Beer, "Composers and Publishers: Germany, 1700–1830," in Rasch, ed., *Music Publishing in Europe*, 164.

6. "[dass] jederman doch die geschriebenen Noten dem besten Druck oder Stich vorzieht." Christian Gottfried Thomas, *Praktische Beyträge zur Geschichte der Musik, musikalischen Litteratur und gemeinen Besten* (Leipzig: Christian Gottfried Thomas, 1778), 13; quoted and translated in Beer, "Composers and Publishers," 164.

7. Beer, "Composers and Publishers," 169. See also Barry S. Brook, "Piracy and Panacea in the Dissemination of Music in the Late Eighteenth Century," *Proceedings of the Royal Musical Association* 102 (1975–76): 13–36.

8. Greger Andersson, "Music from Abroad in Eighteenth-Century Sweden," in Rasch, ed., *The Circulation of Music in Europe*, 162.

9. *Journal de musique* (1777): 2151–52; quoted in Sarah Adams, "International Dissemination of Printed Music during the Second Half of the Eighteenth Century," in *The Dissemination of Music: Studies in the History of Music Publishing*, ed. Hans Lenneberg (Lausanne, Switzerland: Gordon and Breach, 1994), 26.

10. Furthermore, more research is needed on the relationship between manuscript and print circulation in Europe in this period.

11. See Beer, "Composers and Publishers," esp. 174.

12. On the multifariousness of this musical economy, see Klaus Hortschansky, "The Musician as Music-Dealer," in *The Social Status of the Professional Musician from the Middle Ages to the Nineteenth Century*, ed. Walter Salmen, Herbert Kaufman, and Barbara Reisner (New York: Pendragon, 1993), 189–218.

13. Transl. in Cliff Eisen, ed., *New Mozart Documents: A Supplement to O. E. Deutsch's Documentary Biography* (London: Macmillan, 1991), 54; quoted in Ridgewell, "Mozart's Music on Sale in Vienna and Paris," 124.

14. Christian Broy, "Leopold Mozarts Kontakte zum Verlag Breitkopf," *Acta Mozartiana* 58, no. 2 (2011): 132–48.

15. Sarah Adams provides evidence in "International Dissemination of Printed Music," 25.

16. Solicitation is a habit of the patronage economy, and considering it to be part of consumption highlights the ways patrons supported music for more abstract, socially driven reasons as well. This parallel is, of course, one of the premises behind Tia DeNora's work on Beethoven's Vienna, cited in note 3.

17. Pleyel, String Quartets op. 1; reprinted in Rita Benton, *Ignaz Pleyel: A Thematic Catalogue of His Compositions* (New York: Pendragon, 1977), 100. Canavas, Sonatas op. 2; reprinted in *Late Eighteenth-Century Cello Sonatas*, ed. Myron Lutzke (New York: Garland, 1991), x. Graziani, Sonatas op. 2; reprinted in *Mid-Eighteenth-Century Cello Sonatas*, ed. Jane Adas (New York: Garland, 1991), xi. Pachelbel, *Hexachordum Apollinis* (Nuremburg: Pachelbel, 1699); reprinted in Pachelbel, *Hexachordum Apollinis* (Courlay, France: Éditions J. M. Fuzeau, 1996). Jean Barrière, Sonatas op. 2 (Paris: Boivin, 1733), whose original language describing Madame Jourdain's qualities is "discernement, pénétration, non seulement dans la musique, mais encore dans les sciences les plus sublimes."

18. Thorstein Veblen, *The Theory of the Leisure Class: An Economic Study of Institutions* (London: George Allen and Unwin, 1925); Jean Baudrillard, *The Consumer Society: Myths and Structures*, transl. Chris Turner (London: Sage, 2004); Neil McKendrick, John Brewer, and J. H. Plumb, *The Birth of a Consumer Society: The Commercialization of Eighteenth-Century England* (London: Europa, 1982); Vance Packard, *The Hidden Persuaders* (London: Longmans, 1957); Colin Campbell, *The Romantic Ethic and the Spirit of Modern Consumerism* (Oxford: Basil Blackwell, 1987); Slavoj Zizek, *The Sublime Object of Ideology* (London: Verso, 1989).

19. Beer, *Musik zwischen Komponist, Verlag und Publikum*, 97–153; Antolini, "Publishers and Buyers," 229–35.

20. Igor Kopytoff, "The Cultural Biography of Things: Commoditization as Process," in *The Social Life of Things: Commodities in Cultural Perspective*, ed. Arjun Appadurai (Cambridge: Cambridge University Press, 1986), 64–93.

21. See Rob Wegman, "Musical Offerings in the Renaissance," *Early Music* 23 (2005): 425–37; as well as Emily H. Green, "A Patron among Peers: Dedications to Haydn and the Economy of Celebrity," *Eighteenth-Century Music* 8, no. 2 (2011): 215–37; Emily H. Green, "Dedications and the Reception of the Musical Score, 1785–1850" (PhD diss., Cornell University, Ithaca, NY, 2009), 19–48.

22. Veblen, *Theory of the Leisure Class*, 85.

23. This critique is outlined in a number of places, including Colin Campbell, "The Sociology of Consumption," in *Acknowledging Consumption*, ed. Daniel Miller (New York: Routledge, 1995), 95–124; Ben Fine and Ellen Leopold, *The World of Consumption* (London: Routledge, 1993).

24. Andrew B. Trigg, "Veblen, Bourdieu, and Conspicuous Consumption," *Journal of Economic Issues* 35, no. 1 (2001): 103.

25. For more on the role of cultural capital on the formation of taste, see Pierre Bourdieu, *Distinction: A Social Critique of the Judgement of Taste* (Cambridge: Harvard University Press, 1984).

26. *Journal de musique* (1777): 2151–52; quoted in Adams, "International Dissemination of Printed Music," 26.

27. Catalogs were not new items in the musical marketplace. They were used as early as the mid-fifteenth century in Venice, though they were usually distributed ephemerally and locally. See Jane Bernstein, *Print Culture and Music in Sixteenth-Century Venice* (New York: Oxford University Press, 2001), 91.

28. "Durch fleißige Verbreitung ihrer Catalogen in alle Winkel, ihre Siebesachen bekannt zu machen." Ernst Ludwig Gerber, "An Kenner und Liebhaber der Musik; auch einige Worte an Nichtkenner und Gleichgültige gegen diese Kunst," *Berlinisches Archiv der Zeit und ihres Geschmacks* 1 (1795): 139; quoted in Beer, *Musik zwischen Komponist, Verlag und Publikum*, 298.

29. Beer, *Musik zwischen Komponist, Verlag und Publikum*, 299.

30. Quoted and transl. in Luca Aversano, "The Transmission of Italian Musical Articles through Germany and Austria to Eastern Europe around 1800," in Rasch, ed., *The Circulation of Music in Europe*, 152.

31. Sarah Adams has documented this kind of arrangement between Pleyel and Hofmeister. See Adams, "International Dissemination of Printed Music," 32–35. Rupert Ridgewell discusses Artaria's business with foreign publishers in Ridgewell, "Economic Aspects: The Artaria Case," in Rasch, ed., *Music Publishing in Europe*, 92.

32. Beer, *Musik zwischen Komponist, Verlag und Publikum*, 331–32.

33. Ibid., 261.

34. See, for instance, Karl Marx, *Capital: A Critique of Political Economy*, transl. Ben Fowkes (New York: Penguin Books, 1977), esp. 125–77; Baudrillard, *Consumer Society*; also Daniel Miller, "Consumption as the Vanguard of History," in Miller, ed., *Acknowledging Consumption*, 22–24.

35. Baudrillard acknowledges that "the truth of consumption is that it is not a function of enjoyment but *a function of production* and, hence, like all material production, not an individual function, but an *immediately and totally collective one*" (italics original). See Baudrillard, *Consumer Society*, 78. This conception of consumption reminds one, for instance, of George W. Bush's exhortation to shop after 9/11, an implicit confirmation of the belief that consumption is the producer not only of tangible items but also of community and public health.

36. George Ritzer, Paul Dean, and Nathan Jurgenson, "The Coming of Age of the Prosumer," *American Behavioral Scientist* 56, no. 4 (2012): 379–98.

37. See ibid., 379–81. Alvin Toffler's monograph on the concept is *The Third Wave* (New York: William Morrow, 1980).

38. Bernstein, *Print Culture and Music in Sixteenth-Century Venice*, esp. 29–72.

39. "Wollten sie etwas von meinem Sohne zum Druck befördern, so wäre bis dahin die beste Zeit. . . . Kurz, es mag seyn von einer Gattung Composition als es immer ihnen verträglich scheinet, alles wird er machen, wenn sie es nur

bald melden." Leopold Mozart to Breitkopf and Sohn, Salzburg, February 7, 1772; quoted in Otto Erich Deutsch, ed., *Mozart: Die Dokumente seines Lebens* (Kassel: Bärenreiter, 1961), 126; quoted and transl. in Beer, "Composers and Publishers," 170.

40. Beer, "Composers and Publishers," 170.
41. Letter to Artaria, March 29, 1789, published in *Joseph Haydn: Gesammelte Briefe und Aufzeichnungen*, ed. Dénes Bartha (Kassel: Bärenreiter, 1965), 202; transl. and discussed in Elaine Sisman, "Haydn's Solo Keyboard Music," in *Eighteenth-Century Keyboard Music*, ed. Robert Marshall (New York: Routledge, 2003), 270.
42. Kurt Stephenson, *Andreas Romberg: ein Beitrag zur hamburgischen Musikgeschichte* (Hamburg: H. Christian, 1938), 70; quoted in Horst Walter, "Haydn gewidmete streichquartette," in *Joseph Haydn Tradition und Rezeption*, ed. Georg Feder (Regensburg, Germany: Gustav Bosse Verlag, 1985), 31–32: "Bernhard hat drei Quartetten an Haydn dediziert, die in diesen Tagen hier [in Paris] erscheinen werden. Auch ich will drei Quartete an Haydn dedizieren, und das sollen die Eurigen sein. Fanget den Stich nur gleich an und lasset bei der ersten Violine eine Seite frei für die Dedikation, die ich Euch schon zur rechten Zeit schicken werde. Diese Dedikation wird Euch gewiß nicht unlieb sein, da sie den Abgang der Werke ohne allen Zweifel befördert. Sagt nun einmal, ob wir das Publikum nicht kennen—oder vielmehr die Welt?"

Chapter Two

Inside a Viennese
Kunsthandlung

Artaria in 1784

Rupert Ridgewell

In Vienna around the turn of the nineteenth century, sales of various forms of print media—sheet music, engravings, books, and maps—were prominent and closely interconnected features of the commercial landscape. The relationship between media was easily articulated in the use of the word *Kunsthandlung* to describe many of the shops that printed and sold music. The literal translation "art shop" hardly conveys the broader meaning that would have been understood at the time, encompassing not only art but also everything regarded as "cultural," including books, maps, music, and scientific gadgets like telescopes and geometric instruments. Thus the contemporary chronicler of Viennese life, Johann Pezzl (1756–1823), identifies fifteen *Kunsthändler* active in the city in 1822, selling "prints, drawings, maps, music, mathematical and optical instruments, colored inks, drawing materials, stitch and knitting patterns, visiting cards, games, books concerned primarily with prints, as well as paintings and busts."[1] In this way, one might say that the *Kunsthändler* sought to provide nourishment for the enlightened sensibility, in which the cultivation of music was but one strand in a portfolio of interests that also encompassed the desire to decorate one's home with engravings and curiosities and to view the world through both maps and topographical landscapes.

To what extent did this intermingling of the arts and sciences have an impact on the production, marketing, and sale of printed music? Were the different trades pursued entirely separately within each shop, or were they integrated to some degree? How did the *Kunsthändler* manage competing priorities and engage with different constituencies of consumers associated with different media? These questions have not been addressed in histories of music publishing or indeed in discussions of the art, book, and cartographic trades, which have largely pursued independent narratives without considering influences or dependencies in the wider commercial sphere. In part, this is a result of deficiencies in the evidential record: very few such establishments continued to trade beyond the nineteenth century, and in most cases their archives have simply not survived. Thus it is rarely possible to step beyond the threshold to explore the inner workings of a particular shop or to engage more deeply with the mechanics of the trade, beyond enumerating the items that were produced and sold.

Certainly, the most visible sign of crossover is found in the area of title page engraving. Many Viennese editions published in the 1780s and 1790s are noted for their decorative title pages, often with engravings specially commissioned from such prominent local practitioners as Johann Ernst Mansfeld (1739–96) and Carl Schütz (1745–1800). This aesthetic enhancement made it possible, in theory at least, to present music as part of an ensemble of visually pleasing objects offered for sale. Whether topical or subjective associations between different media were promoted within the physical space of the *Kunsthandlung* is difficult to say, since we have no knowledge of the way music was physically marketed in relation to other products in any particular shop. Specific connections at least were not made explicit in public advertisements, even if music, prints, books, and maps were occasionally juxtaposed in the regular notices placed by various shops in the Viennese press in the late eighteenth and early nineteenth centuries.

In terms of production, the rationale for pursuing art engraving, music, and cartography in one business was clear: all three were, in Vienna, based on the process of printing from engraved copper or pewter plates. The alternative process of printing music from type, which was still common in Germany around 1800, required a very different set of skills and equipment. Viewed in this context, it is not difficult to imagine a situation in which the production of music was contingent on demand in other areas, depending on the staffing and capacity of the printing workshop and the way conflicting priorities were managed.

The publisher would also need to develop workflows and supply chains that reflected the characteristics and materials needed for different products. Whereas maps and prints required particular care at the press to ensure a minimum standard and clarity of presentation, engraved music was rather less intricate in terms of the surface design of the plate but often much more complicated and labor-intensive with regard to assembling the printed copy. Editions of symphonies, concertos, and string quartets published in parts, for example, might cover up to one hundred pages or more, with each part consisting of varying numbers of pages and therefore a different collation. Each edition was typically assembled from nested bifolios with up to four printed pages on each sheet, requiring considerable forethought about the final makeup of the copy to ensure consistent pagination from beginning to end. Engravings and maps, by contrast, were normally printed on one side of a sheet of paper only.

In other respects, it is quite possible that the different branches of the publishing business could have benefited from close integration. Contacts with dealers and publishers in different towns and countries formed in the pursuit of one trade, for example, could have led to new opportunities for other parts of the business. Conversely, it is also likely that different trades were more or less profitable at different times, leading to varying degrees of emphasis on certain activities. All these factors potentially impinge on our understanding of the way music was published, depending on the extent to which the various strands of business activity were interrelated and the way in which such tensions or correlations played out within a particular firm.

The Artaria *Kunsthandlung* offers a good case study for exploring these issues in some depth. The firm was established in Vienna in 1768 by three members of the Artaria family (Carlo, Francesco, and Ignazio), which was active in the art trade in Germany and Italy from at least the early eighteenth century and continued to trade uninterrupted until the 1920s (a successor shop bearing the same name closed only in 2013). The firm was a pioneer in the introduction of music engraving to Vienna, initiating a development that had far-reaching implications for the technology of music appreciation and composition in the city into the nineteenth century. For this reason, the context in which music was produced and marketed in the earliest years of the firm's existence merits detailed investigation.

A series of inventory ledgers deriving from the Artaria archive and now held by the Wienbibliothek im Rathaus offers a unique window on the firm in the late eighteenth century. The firm compiled inventory ledgers periodically to account for its stock and assess its overall financial position and in turn to determine the profit due to each partner in the business. At least until 1796, all the partners were members of the extended Artaria family, each period of ownership typically lasting three or four years. The ledgers that resulted from the first two periods of ownership are not known to survive, which means the third ledger represents our earliest opportunity to investigate their role in Artaria's business practice and the extent to which they shed light on the inner workings of the firm.

Ledger 3 was initiated at the end of a term of ownership among four partners in the firm (Carlo, Francesco, Ignazio, and Pasquale Artaria) covering the period from 1780 until March 1, 1784.[2] The bulk of the ledger was compiled around the time the partnership came to an end, and it gives an extensive inventory of the firm's assets and liabilities, with entries successively reporting the firm's stocks of unsold goods (including books, prints, frames, pastels, maps, musical instrument strings, and paper), cash, and fixed assets such as engraving plates and furniture. As well as commissioning work from engravers, artists, and composers in Vienna, the firm also imported goods from major centers throughout Europe, notably London and Paris. The inventory therefore includes entries for both items published by the firm and items imported from abroad. The extent of the trade with French publishers and dealers at this time may help to explain why the main currency used in the inventory for asset valuation is the French livre tournois rather than the Austro-Hungarian gulden.[3]

Assets were held in two locations. The principal shop was located on the Kohlmarkt in Vienna, a key commercial thoroughfare at the center of the trade in books, music, and prints in the city, while the firm also operated an outpost in the town of Mainz in central Germany, a strategic location within striking distance of the important Frankfurt book fairs and on the trade routes to Paris and Berlin. The inventory is accordingly divided into two parts: an account of assets held in Mainz followed by those held in Vienna together with lists of balances drawn from the firm's account books in each location divided between credit (money owed to the firm) and debt (money owed by the firm), and a final balance sheet that records the total value of the business and the profit due to each partner.[4] Judging by the handwriting, a single bookkeeper was responsible for entering the majority of the entries into the ledger in the first instance, no doubt copying from subsidiary lists to produce a fair copy of the full inventory. The remaining pages in the ledger (from fol. 40r) were later used to document payments made to the firm to settle accounts that were in debt when the inventory was compiled. This section was written in several stages and by various bookkeepers between 1787 and 1796.

In previous studies, I have discussed the method by which music-related stock and printing equipment is reported in the ledgers.[5] Here, by contrast, I shall place music in the context of other strands of business activity, with a view to illustrate the full spectrum of the firm's commercial interests and to seek evidence of the different characteristics associated with each branch of the business. A full description of the ledger is beyond the scope of this chapter, as is a comprehensive treatment of the multimedia aspects of the trade. I instead restrict my comments to assets reported in the Vienna inventory of Ledger 3, where the largest volume of stock was held and where many products are reported in sufficient detail to make it possible to identify them with a reasonable degree of confidence. Limited internal evidence, discussed below, implies that some entries refer to the physical arrangement of the stock or appear to reflect the way items were stored. It seems likely, therefore, that at least some parts of the inventory were compiled by physically working through the storeroom rather than being copied from stock books that were kept up-to-date over time. The accuracy with which this information was assembled is, of course, difficult to gauge with any certainty, although there are signs that the inventory was subject to a process of checking, auditing, and updating. Clearly, the inventory reports only the level of stock available at the time of compilation and not the movement of stock over time, which means we cannot chart sales of individual items or second-guess changes in consumer behavior or shifts in taste over time. But the breadth and depth of Artaria's stock and the methods by which it was organized and documented can potentially tell us much about how the firm mediated consumer expectation and positioned itself in relation to the market.

Prints

Carlo Artaria first announced his presence in Vienna by placing a notice in the *Wiener Zeitung* for July 28, 1770: "Connoisseurs and amateurs are hereby informed that the dealer Karl Artaria has acquired a notable assortment of the newest and finest English and French prints, as well as the rarest antiques, and is willing to offer them at a very cheap price. He is lodging on the first floor of the Tatenriederischen Haus in the kleiner Dorothegasse."[6] As the advertisement makes clear, the prime commercial interest at this time was the trade in prints, an activity that had been the core of the business pursued by itinerant members of the family for many years. The precise circumstances that led the family to settle in Vienna are unknown, but the city clearly offered a fertile ground for pursuing the art trade at that time. As the administrative seat of the Habsburg Empire, Vienna presented a propitious market encompassing the Imperial Court and various levels of the aristocracy, as well as the ecclesiastical community and a comparatively strong professional class, not to mention a significant volume of passing trade resulting from the city's geographic location at the center of Europe and as a gateway to the East. The political climate was also favorable. In 1768, the government relaxed import tariffs on luxury goods in a deliberate move to stimulate trade. Four years later, a reorganization of the institutions governing the training of artists, etchers, and engravers resulted in the foundation of a unified art academy (Vereinigte Akademie der bildenden Künste), with the explicit objective of nurturing homegrown talent to combat a perceived deficiency compared with Paris and London.

It can be no coincidence that Artaria commissioned numerous works from local engravers during the 1770s and 1780s, focusing especially on portraits of key members of the church and state, and the firm initiated important collections of engravings such as a series of Viennese topographical views titled

Sammlung von Aussichten der Residenzstadt Wien (from 1779). The firm also cultivated extensive contacts with dealers, engravers, and print publishers located in major centers of the art trade, such as Paris, London, Rome, and Berlin, and continued to import prints in significant numbers. By 1784, therefore, Artaria's stock consisted of a mixture of foreign prints plus unsold copies and engraving plates for prints issued by the firm itself.

Prints imported from France and England constituted the largest portion of the stock reported in Ledger 3.[7] For the most part, they are not identified by title or engraver but are instead valued in bulk according to their location in the firm's premises. French and English prints, for example, were held in a "large portfolio in the shop" (see fig. 2.1),[8] thus allowing customers to browse through them, rather than being stored behind the scenes. Elsewhere a distinction is made according to genre, with categories including portraits, allegorical prints, sacred historical prints, caricatures, landscapes, "English gardens," vases, and conversation pieces. Again, the extent of the stock is usually indicated simply by referring to "a portfolio" or "a large portfolio" and only rarely to the actual number of copies. Exactly how the stock was arranged or categorized within each portfolio is also not made clear. A few entries nevertheless refer to the artist, engraver, or publisher, implying that certain parts of the stock were held separately from the general run, perhaps because of their importance or because they were represented in particularly large numbers. In this category are prints by Francesco Bartolozzi (1727–1815), Johann Friedrich Bause (1738–1814), Robert Sayer (1724 or 25–94), François Chereau (1680–1729), and Giovanni Battista Piranesi (1720–78).[9]

The print market operated on several levels in the eighteenth century to cater to different demographics, and individual prints were often made available in various finishes, allowing publishers to offer them at different price brackets. Parts of Artaria's stock were accordingly valued at three levels of sophistication in Ledger 3: full color (in collore), red (in Rosso), and monochrome (in maniera nera). Although the total number of prints in each category is not specified and obviously could vary, the inventory valuations seem to reflect a sliding scale according to size and presentation. For example, "large" English prints in full color were valued in sterling at £88 7s (2,020 livres), while those colored in red came to £16 14s 6d (382 livres). "Smaller" English prints are similarly divided, with total valuations ranging from £464 for full color to £186 for monochrome.[10]

Artaria was also active in the market for antiquarian items, a more select category of stock reserved for only the richest aristocratic collectors and connoisseurs. These items are listed under the heading "Old prints and antique books" in Ledger 3 and comprise a diverse selection of Italian, Flemish, Dutch, German, and French prints dating from the seventeenth and eighteenth centuries.[11] Rather frustratingly, most of the stock is valued cumulatively rather

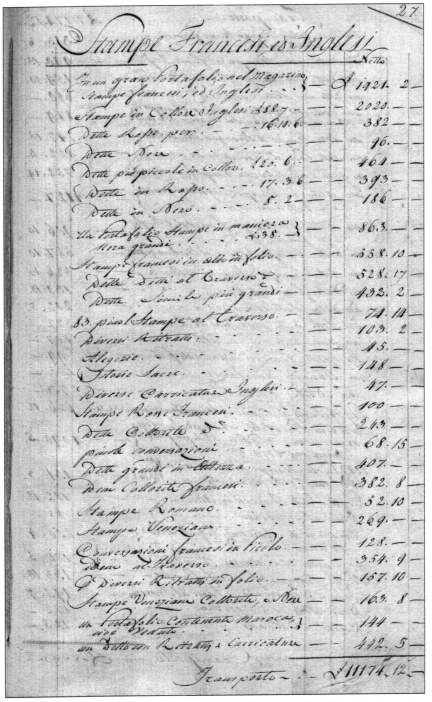

Figure 2.1. Artaria Inventory Ledger 3 (1784), 27. French and English prints in stock. Reproduced by permission of the Wienbibliothek im Rathaus, Vienna, Austria.

than being itemized or described in any detail. The first entry, for example, covers "diverse books, as well as drawings by Guercino, Bartolozzi, Galleria Gerini, books by Mulinari, by Prestel, etc.," while the stock also included a set of "original prints by Rembrandt" and "prints transferred to the library," implying that the firm maintained an internal reference library.[12]

Prints by Viennese engravers are strongly represented in Ledger 3 and are listed in more detail. One of the firm's most important ventures at this time was the publication of the *Sammlung von Aussichten der Residenzstadt Wien*, which consisted of a series of fifty-seven engravings documenting Viennese urban life produced by the local artists Carl Schütz, Johann Ziegler, and Laurenz Lanscha. By April 1784, thirty-six engravings had been published in the series, and Ledger 3 reports stocks of 327 and 676 copies of illuminated views (Prospetti) by Schütz and Ziegler, respectively. Schütz and Ziegler retained the engraving plates, at least initially, and were entitled to 24 monochrome copies, but they were not allowed to sell them either at home or abroad.[13] The comparatively large volume of stock, together with the commitment to print 1,100 more copies, seems to confirm that these were popular items the firm was confident of selling in large numbers.

The firm commissioned prints by several other notable Viennese engravers without taking ownership of the engraving plates themselves.[14] Ledger 3 reports a total of 2,903 copies of prints in this category, with works by Johann Georg Janotta, Johann Ernst Mansfeld, Quirin Marck, and Franz Anton Maulpertsch. Prints published by the firm for which it retained rights to the plates are reported separately in a section headed "Portraits of our ownership" (see fig. 2.2).[15] Each item listed here is identified by title and engraver and valued according to the number of copies held in stock, allowing a much more detailed overview of the firm's holdings. In total, there were 4,680 copies of 56 itemized prints (an average of 83 copies of each print), plus 200 copies of various prints left in Milan,[16] 3,504 "small portraits" (not itemized), 115 packets of *cartes de visite,* and 540 "Ornaments for music" (Ornamenti p[er]. Musica)—presumably decorated wrappers designed to be sold with printed music. This stock ranged from 2 copies of a small portrait by Haid to 533 copies of a monochrome engraving of Pope Pius VI (Papa in Pontificato). By far the most valuable print was a portrait of Maria Christina, Duchess of Teschen, by the preeminent London-based engraver Francesco Bartolozzi, for which the firm produced copies in three formats: in color valued at 2 gulden 30 kreutzer per copy, in monochrome at 1 gulden 30 kreutzer, or in "bad proofs" (cattive pruove) at 45 kreutzer.

The stock is dominated by portraits of prominent political, religious, and military figures of the time, notably Emperor Joseph II and members of the Imperial family, State Chancellor and Foreign Minister Prince Wenzel

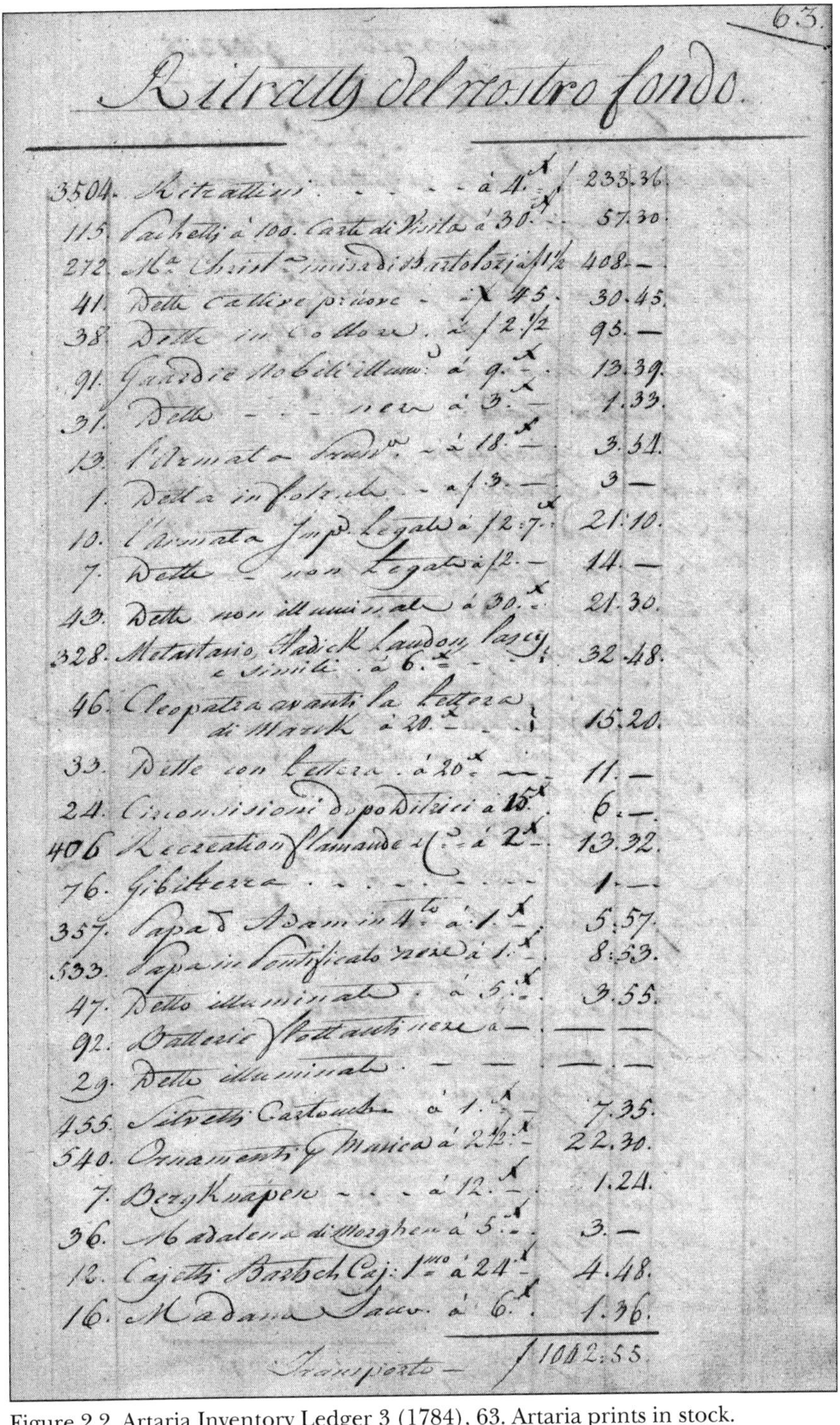

Figure 2.2. Artaria Inventory Ledger 3 (1784), 63. Artaria prints in stock. Reproduced by permission of the Wienbibliothek im Rathaus, Vienna, Austria.

Kaunitz-Rietberg, Field Marshall Baron Ernst Gideon von Laudon, the King of Sweden, Pope Pius VI, and József Cardinal Batthyány, Archbishop of Esztergom. The dominant engraver was Johann Elias Haid (1740–1809), whose subjects included Marie Antoinette, Laudon, and Maria Charlotte, as well as religious-themed works based on the Salvator Mundi, Mary Magdalene, and *La Réflexion sur la lecture d'une dame vertueuse* after Rembrandt. Contrary to the title of this section of the inventory, however, the range of genres extends beyond portraiture to encompass religious and mythological subjects, topographical views, conversation pieces, and caricature. There is, however, no indication that this portion of the firm's stock was organized in any systematic way and no evidence of its location within the premises. The same holds true for the corresponding engraving plates, which are listed separately in Ledger 3 and are identified both by title and (very often) engraver, although portrait engravings by Adam, Mansfeld, and Marck are grouped together on pages 69 and 70.[17]

Music

The first known indication that Artaria had started to sell music is an advertisement in the *Wienerisches Diarium* on October 19, 1776, in which the firm announced the recent arrival of printed music from Paris, which was available for purchase "alongside a great number of the newest and most beautiful French, English, and other engravings."[18] The consignment included "symphonies, concertos, sonatas, divertimenti, duets, trios, quartets, quintets and sextets, new minuets and contredanses for every instrument" by fifty of "the most famous composers in Europe." The trade in music grew considerably over the following years. As well as announcing details of newly arrived editions in the Viennese press, the firm periodically advertised imported music in specially produced catalogs typeset and printed by the book publisher Andreas Schmidt. No copies of the first catalog, published in 1777, are known to be extant, but various issues and supplements dating from 1779 onward have survived, giving some insight into the extent of Artaria's trade with foreign dealers and publishers. Some measure of the importance of the trade is provided by the catalog issued in 1785, which extends to 145 pages with up to thirty editions listed on each page, with symphonies and orchestral music followed by chamber music in descending order from quintets through quartets, trios, and duets to music for solo instruments. Thus a very significant range of repertoire was potentially available to the Viennese public.

The firm's first tentative steps toward establishing a music publishing business in Vienna reflect an attempt not only to develop further the burgeoning local market but also to help build reciprocal trade with foreign publishers. The first published edition, a set of string trios by Paolo Bonaga, was announced in the *Wienerisches Diarium* on August 12, 1778. It is perhaps a measure of the firm's cautious approach that the edition was initially available through subscription only: a deposit of one gulden was required in advance of publication, with the balance of one gulden payable upon collection.[19] In this way the firm could minimize financial risk by generating some advance income and by determining the size of the initial print run before publication. Confidence in the market quickly grew, however, and subsequent editions were issued directly without subscription. By the time Ledger 3 was compiled in February 1784, the firm had issued at least fifty-eight editions of music by twenty composers and built up a considerable stock of copies available for sale together with the associated plates. These assets are reported in separate itemized listings in Ledger 3, each arranged alphabetically by composer with brief title details and valuations.[20]

On the basis of these entries we can say that Artaria maintained relatively low levels of stock, typically ranging between 10 and 70 copies per edition, or 43 copies per edition on average (see appendix 2.1). In total, the firm held stocks of fifty-two editions with a total count of 2,475 unsold copies; six editions that had been published before March 1784 were no longer in stock. Haydn and Kozeluch were the most prominent composers in the firm's publishing program at this point in time, with nine editions each, and they account for 517 and 476 copies, respectively, while Mozart is represented by 54 copies of the six violin sonatas, K. 296/376–80 (issued by Artaria as op. 2), and 58 copies of the keyboard duet sonatas, K. 358/381 (op. 3). The highest individual figure relates to two books of keyboard sonatas by F. X. Riegler, of which 239 copies are reported. Two editions reported in the ledger had not yet been advertised in the press at the time the inventory was compiled; thus there were 151 copies of Haydn's Keyboard Concerto in D Major and 150 copies of Boccherini's string trios op. 35, both of which were not advertised until August 25, 1784 (although they were probably available for sale before that date).[21] In these cases, the figures are significantly higher than the average and are likely to equate to the size of the initial print run.

By printing from engraved plates, it was possible to reprint editions as new copies were required to satisfy demand. Artaria certainly reprinted editions over time, as evidenced by the different states embodied by the copies that survive today.[22] The size and frequency of such reprints are not documented, but Ledger 3 offers some tantalizing evidence that might reflect the delivery of fresh stock from the press. Two layers of handwriting are visible in the list of unsold copies (see fig. 2.3): the main body of text was written substantially by the principal bookkeeper responsible for the inventory, but the right-hand column had been left blank in anticipation that the total valuations would be entered later in the process. The totals were duly added by a different scribe, who also added to the tally of copies for eleven editions in the left-hand

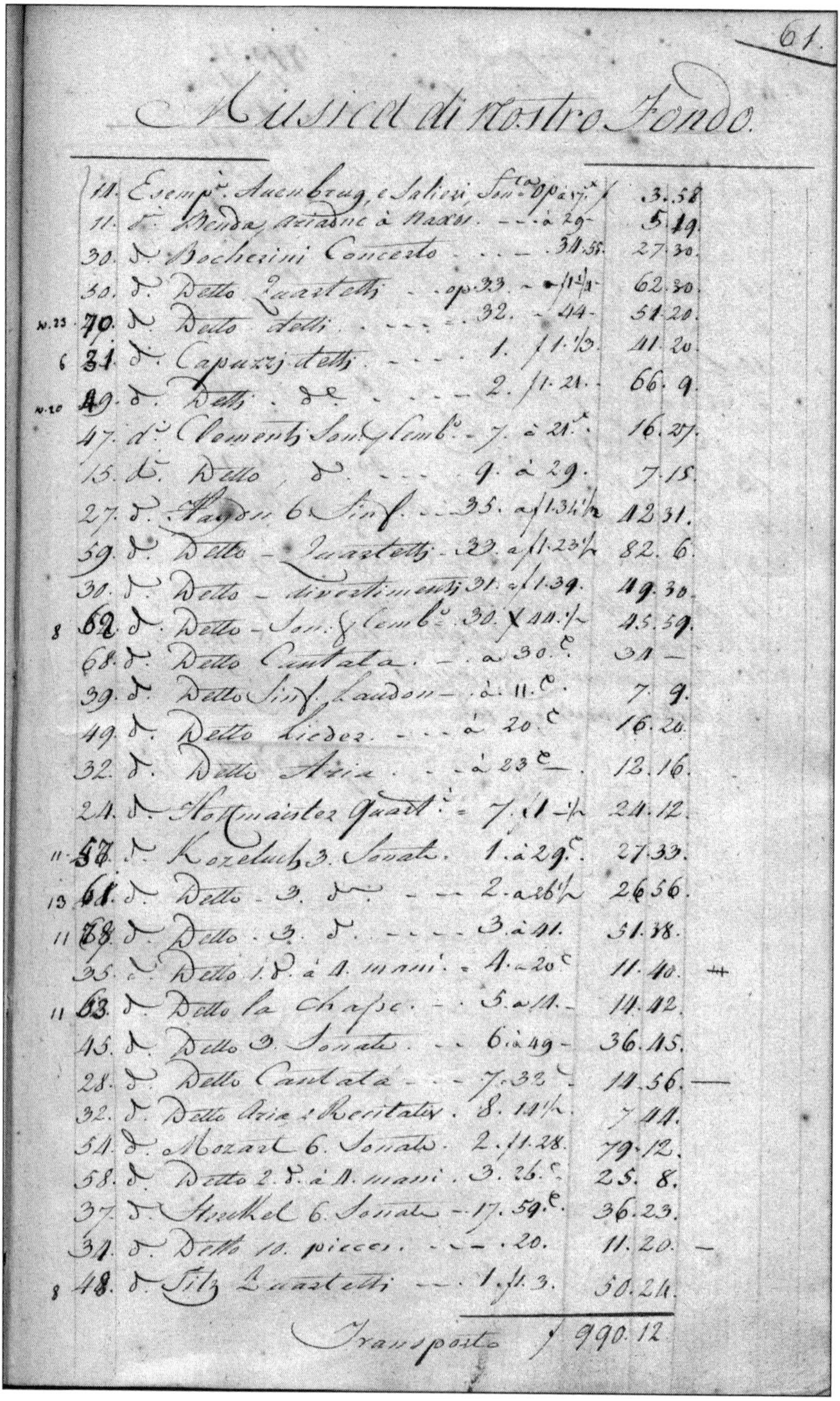

61.

Musica di nostro Fondo

	11. Esemp.ri Auenbrug, e Salieri, Sin. op. 1	3.58
	11. d.o Benda, Ariadne à Naxos . . . à 29	5.19
	30. d.o Boccherini Concerto . . . 34.55	27.30
	30. d.o Detto Quartetti . op. 33 . f1 ½	62.30
n.25	70. d.o Detto detti . . . 32. 44	51.20
6	31. d.o Capuzzi detti . . . 1. f1.½	41.20
n.20	49. d.o Detti d.o . . . 2. f1.21	66.9
	47. d.o Clementi Son. p. Cemb.o 7. à 21	16.27
	15. d.o Detto d.o . . . 9. à 29	7.15
	27. d.o Haydn 6 Sinf. . . 35. a f1.34½	42.31
	59. d.o Detto Quartetti . 33. a f1.23½	82.6
	30. d.o Detto Divertimenti 31. a f1.39	49.30
8	62. d.o Detto Son. p. Cemb.o 30. x 44½	45.59
	68. d.o Detto Cantata . . à 30	34 —
	39. d.o Detto Sinf. Laudon . à 11	7.9
	49. d.o Detto Lieder . . . à 20	16.20
	32. d.o Detto Aria . . . à 23	12.16
	24. d.o Hoffmaister Quart. 7. f1 ½	24.12
11	57. d.o Kozeluch 3 Sonate . 1. à 29	27.33
13	61. d.o Detto 3. d.o . . . 2. à 26½	26.56
11	78. d.o Detto 3. d.o . . . 3. à 41	51.38
	35. d.o Detto 1. d.o à 4. mani . 4. à 20	11.40 +
11	63. d.o Detto la Chasse . . 5. à 11	14.42
	45. d.o Detto 3. Sonate . . 6. à 49	36.45
	28. d.o Detto Cantata . . . 7. 32	14.56 —
	32. d.o Detto Aria e Recitativ . 8. 14½	7.44
	54. d.o Mozart 6. Sonate . 2. f1.28	79.12
	58. d.o Detto 2. d.o à 4. mani . 3. 26	25.8
	37. d.o Sterkel 6. Sonate . 17. 59	36.23
	34. d.o Detto 10. pieces . . . 20	11.20 —
8	48. d.o Pilz Quartetti . . 1. f1.3	50.24

Transporto f 990.12

Figure 2.3. Artaria Inventory Ledger 3 (1784), 39. Printed music in stock. Reproduced by permission of the Wienbibliothek im Rathaus, Vienna, Austria.

Table 2.1. Amendments to levels of stock reported in Ledger 3

Composer	Edition	Original number of copies reported	Additional copies	Total
Boccherini	string quartets op. 32	47	23	70
Capuzzi	string quartets op. 1	25	6	31
Capuzzi	string quartets op. 2	29	20	49
Haydn	piano sonatas op. 30	54	8	62
Kozeluch	3 piano trios op. 1	46	11	57
Kozeluch	3 piano trios op. 2	48	13	61
Kozeluch	3 piano trios op. 3	67	11	78
Kozeluch	*La chasse* for piano op. 5	52	11	63
Titz	string quartets op. 1	40	8	48
Vanhal	6 duets for 2 violins op. 28	37	5	42
Bonaga	6 string trios	10	3	13

column. These additions were relatively small, ranging from 3 to 23 copies per edition (119 copies altogether), and they mostly relate to editions for which there were already relatively healthy levels of stock (see table 2.1).

Had these copies newly arrived from the printer, and were they added to the stock while the inventory was being drawn up? On closer inspection, the eleven editions form a quite focused repertoire, with a particular emphasis on string quartets and piano trios (rather than the music of a particular composer), reflecting the genre-based approach found in Artaria's sale catalogs. This observation strengthens the case for thinking that the amendments reflect an ongoing process of stock renewal, as Artaria reprinted editions judged to be marketable either in Vienna or to foreign dealers. In this scenario, the firm did not wait until levels were at or close to zero but instead acted to ensure that relatively healthy levels of stock were maintained: on this particular occasion, a fairly homogeneous set of chamber-music editions by seven composers was prioritized for reprinting. This is a plausible explanation, although we cannot exclude the possibility that the copies were added at a late stage in the stock-taking process for other reasons. (They might, for example, simply have been overlooked before.)

The location of the stock in the firm's premises is not made clear in the ledger, but given the number of editions and the size of the holdings, it seems most likely that the music was held in a storeroom away from the shop itself, with perhaps only more recently published editions available to view. The printed sale catalogs would therefore have functioned as the main point of access for customers visiting the shop (or indeed for browsing at home) and were thus organized by genre to facilitate the selection of repertoire for performance rather than accommodating preferences for the music of particular composers. This contrasts with the alphabetical arrangement by composer found in Ledger 3, suggesting that stock management was not directly aligned with the way music was marketed.

The volume of music imported from foreign publishers and the way it was managed are difficult to establish with any certainty. Did Artaria maintain stocks of every edition listed in the sale catalogs, acting as a Viennese warehouse for foreign publishers, or did the firm instead offer an ordering service on demand? Some idea of the extent of the imported stock held is given in Ledger 3, although there is little precise detail. Imported music is accounted for separately in the ledger, in a section headed "Music by different publishers."[23] In a few cases, editions are listed individually with details of the number of copies held. These entries reflect relatively low levels of stock. Thus there were, for example, fifty-one copies of a piano tutor by Riegler (*Anleitung zum Clavier*), ten copies of a set of six divertimenti by C. B. Uber (acquired directly from the composer in Breslau at 4 gulden 14 kreutzer apiece), and eleven copies of Christian Schubart's *Etwas für Clavier und Gesang* published by Steiner in Winterthur.[24]

In general, however, Artaria made no attempt to list editions individually, and there is no indication of the physical arrangement or location of the stock in the premises. The music is instead valued with reference to the net cost of acquiring it from different countries and publishers, taking into account variable trade discounts. Editions published in England, for example, are valued at 57 pounds sterling according to catalog prices, but this figure was reduced by the trade discount of ⅓ to 38 pounds (a sum Artaria converted to 866 livres 8 sous). The same discount applied to music acquired from the publisher Van Ypen of Brussels, from the book dealer Dyck of Leipzig, from Ricci of Como, and for diverse music from unspecified dealers in Saxony (Diversa Musica di Sassonia). A discount of one quarter of catalog prices applied to music acquired from the firms Hartknoch (Riga), Korn (Breslau), Steiner (Winterthur), and Schwickert (Leipzig).

Music acquired from France accounts for the most valuable element of the stock, with a total net price of 14,042 livres 12 sous after a trade discount of 35 percent. The sale of the entire stock of French editions reported in Ledger 3 would therefore have been expected to accrue takings of about 21,588 livres over time[25] and a profit of 7,555 livres, although it is not known how quickly the stock would have been sold or how shipping costs were handled. This volume of trade allowed Artaria to proclaim in its 1785 sale catalog that music from France was available in Vienna at a price equivalent to that paid by customers in Paris or Lyon.[26] The total number of copies is not specified, but we can estimate it very approximately by considering the average price for music sold at this time. A typical set of six piano sonatas, for example, was 2 gulden 30 kreutzer in the 1780s, while a set of six string quartets could command about 4 gulden 30 kreutzer and single works—such as keyboard variations or arias— would fetch about 30 or 45 kreutzer. Thus at an average price of 2 gulden, the stock of French editions would have consisted of about five thousand copies.

Books, Atlases, and Maps

Books were not among the items Artaria published but were instead imported in significant numbers from Paris, London, Leipzig, and other major cities to be sold in Vienna. The list of books reported in Ledger 3 consists of eight pages under the heading "Opere" with a total count of 210 entries (see fig. 2.4).[27] Each title is given in a shortened form, with the name of the author, the number of copies held, the number of volumes for multipart works, the inventory valuation, and occasionally the format. The imprint is never specified, which means it is difficult to be sure of the edition held by the firm in cases where a title was published more than once.

The values assigned to the stock vary greatly, from only 1 livre for four copies of a book identified simply as the *Gründliche Anweisung*, to 500 livres for a single copy of Antoine Joseph Dezallier D'Argenville's treatise *La conchyliologie, ou Traité sur la nature des coquillages* (1757), a lavish work reflecting the penchant for studying shells among gentlemen amateurs of the period. In general, Artaria appears to have held only one copy of each book in stock, but a few items are represented in multiple copies: there were, for example, twenty-seven copies of Elizabeth Blackwell's *Herbarium Blackwellianum*, published in Nuremberg between 1750 and 1773,[28] and forty-four copies of an unidentified work by Metastasio in octavo format.[29] A few titles were entered in the list more than once and in different places: Joseph Smith Speer's *The West-India Pilot*, for example, appears four times.[30] This reinforces the notion that the inventory was compiled with direct reference to the shelves. In this scenario, newly acquired copies of Speer's book were added at convenient points, rather than matched with existing copies, thereby leading to multiple entries in the inventory. A few marginal annotations also suggest that the inventory was checked or audited after the details had been copied into the ledger.[31]

In its content, the stock encompasses a clearly defined range of topics principally associated with art, natural sciences, architecture, astronomy, and cartography. There is also a clear emphasis on titles prized as much for their artistic or visual qualities as for their literary or factual content, with many

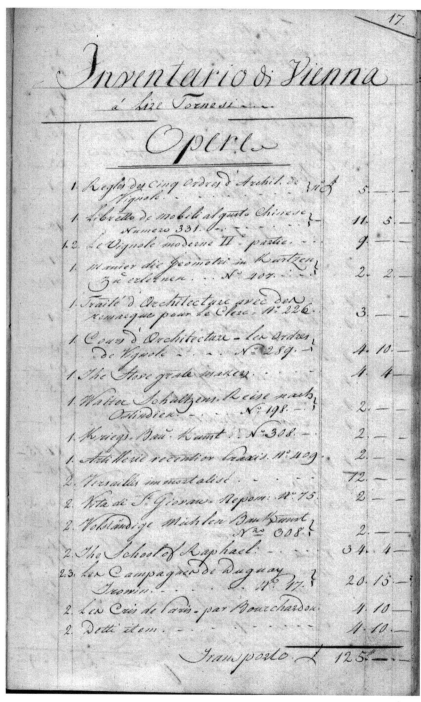

Figure 2.4. Artaria Inventory Ledger 3 (1784), 17. Books in stock. Reproduced by permission of the Wienbibliothek im Rathaus, Vienna, Austria.

items representing the high end of the market in terms of both artistic merit and monetary value.[32] Not surprisingly, books relating to art account for the largest proportion of the stock, with at least forty titles encompassing art history, dictionaries, studies of particular artists or periods, and books of prints. The "Oeuvre de Weirotter," for example, can be identified with a posthumous collected edition of the prints of the popular landscape etcher Franz Edmund Weirotter, published in 1775,[33] while an entry for a "Book of views by Piranesi, and other antique prints" underlines the importance of classical Italian prints in the firm's collection.[34] Didactic or reference works include such titles as Benjamin Ralph's *The School of Raphael; or, the Student's Guide to Expression in Historical Painting* (1759), Johann D. Preissler's *Gründlich-Verfasste Regüln* (1743), and Pierre Basan's *Dictionnaire des graveurs anciens et modernes* (1767).[35]

Another significant category, with about thirty entries, relates to natural sciences and natural history, covering such topics as birds, butterflies, zoology, and plants. Notable titles include Pierre Joseph Buc'hoz's *Collection de planches* (1782) and Thomas Pennant's *British Zoology* (1768–70).[36] At least twenty-one titles relate to architecture, complementing a significant theme covered in the firm's publication of prints, especially the *Sammlung von Aussichten der Residenzstadt Wien*. They include the *Règles des cinq ordres d'architecture* by Vignole—a French edition of a work first published in 1563—and Sébastien Le Clerc's *Traité d'architecture* (1714),[37] as well as William Thomas's *Original Designs in Architecture*, published in London in 1783.[38]

Atlases and books relating to travel and maritime navigation account for sixteen titles associated directly with the firm's burgeoning interest in cartography. The atlases include works published in the early eighteenth century by d'Anville and Gueudeville,[39] as well as more recent publications covering America, Great Britain, and Silesia. Also included here are two lavishly illustrated astronomical works: John Flamsteed's *Atlas coelestis*—the first comprehensive telescopic star catalog—published in London in 1729, and Andreas Cellarius's *Atlas coelestis; seu Harmonia macrocosmica* (1660–1708).[40] The remainder of the list encompasses religious works (notably bibles), interior design, history, military theory and famous military campaigns, literature, and theatre, with many titles that were highly collectible and prized for their iconographic content. Among the most lavish items was the *Cérémonies et coutumes religieuses de tous les peuples du monde*, an influential overview of all the known religions in the world richly illustrated with engravings by Bernard Picart.[41]

The firm employed two different numbering systems to identify the books in its possession. The first system appears to relate to the sequence in which the books were stored in the shop and may indicate that the shelves were numbered. The books are numbered consecutively from 1 to 33 in the left-hand column (although numbers 6, 8, 10, 20, 25, 26, 28, 29, 31, and 32 are not used), with between three and ten entries assigned to each number. In a few cases it is possible to say that works assigned to a particular number are related by subject. The number 16, for example, is assigned to six cartographical books (three atlases, two astronomical atlases, and a plan of Paris) on page 20, while a section headed "Works on Natural History" (Opere dell'Istoria naturale) follows on page 22. The second numbering system refers back to the firm's sale catalog issued in 1781, which was divided into sections by subject: numbers in the range 283 to 318, for example, relate to books on architectural topics.[42] A total of thirty-eight entries are numbered individually, not consecutively, in a range from 17 to 409, making it possible to identify most of these books precisely (see appendix 2.2). These thirty-eight titles represented only about 9 percent of the items advertised in the 1781 sale catalog. The remainder had presumably been sold in the intervening three years, suggesting a relatively high turnover of stock in this particular branch of the business and the fact that Artaria held only single copies of many items.

A few atlases are also listed in a separate inventory of Artaria's map collections, headed "Geografia" in Ledger 3 (page 33). They include an atlas of England, a portable atlas of Europe by Louis Brion de la Tour, a large atlas of Poland by Ricci Zanoni, and 295 copies of a children's map for instruction by Greppi.[43] The majority of the maps held by the firm derived from a single source: the Nuremberg map publisher Homanns Erben, the heirs of Johann Baptist Homann (1663–1724) who established the company in 1702. While Homann was the dominant map publisher in the eighteenth century, Artaria nevertheless supplemented its stock by acquiring maps published in England, France, Holland, and Germany in substantial numbers. Thus the inventory includes cumulative entries of "Various English, French, and German maps in 5 large boxes" and a collection of "English, French, Dutch, and French maps."[44]

Managing Demand

Understood in the broadest context, the eighteenth century witnessed a significant transformation in cultural dissemination, in which the market for cultural and luxury commodities expanded considerably and came increasingly under the control of professional dealers who did not directly contribute to the act of artistic creation. This intermediary role demanded a high level of discernment and entrepreneurial skill in selecting, commissioning, manufacturing, and selling products to reflect and influence taste among an increasingly literate and culturally active populace.[45] Viewed through the prism of Artaria's stock records for March 1784, the Viennese *Kunsthandlung* emerges as a particularly rich and diverse commercial proposition, reflecting the myriad interests of an active and engaged audience encompassing several levels of society. It was a space in which composers, artists, engravers, craftsmen, collectors, agents, and connoisseurs uniquely coincided, creating the potential for cross-fertilization across different forms of artistic endeavor and media, as well as social strata. The particular conditions that shaped the development of the *Kunsthandlung* were doubtless many and varied, associated very broadly with the opportunities (and limitations) presented not only by Vienna's particular demographic profile and urban geography but also by state encouragement of trade and artistic endeavor, notably after the creation of the Vereinigte Akademie der bildenden Künste in 1772. This helped create both the opportunity to develop multiple income streams associated with different media and the financial imperative to pool risks across various commodities, allowing Artaria to occupy a commercial space that supported the Enlightened Absolutist agenda to develop local artists and engravers.

Although Ledger 3 offers only a snapshot of Artaria's assets in March 1784, the stock levels documented by the firm are suggestive of the different volume of trade relating to each strand of activity, as the firm negotiated different levels of demand and varying income brackets. Initial print runs for music were relatively modest, at about 150 copies, but stocks were nonetheless maintained at an average of about 40 copies per edition. Prints were produced in larger numbers, with an average of 83 copies per item held in stock in March 1784 and initial runs of up to 1,000 copies for issues in the series of *Sammlung von Aussichten der Residenzstadt Wien.* This is in line with expectations that the print market was somewhat larger and more diverse than the market for printed music, with an audience encompassing not only various levels of the aristocracy but potentially also the emerging merchant, professional, and clerical classes. Despite the fact that the cultural market expanded considerably in the eighteenth century, it was nevertheless dominated by a relatively small cadre of very wealthy aristocratic patrons with sufficient disposable income to pursue interests in antiquarian prints and books that commanded high prices and were issued in limited numbers.[46] Artaria certainly catered to this market as well, cultivating close contacts with important collectors such as Charles-Joseph, Seventh Prince of Ligne (1735–1814), and Prince Albert Casimir August of Saxony, Duke of Teschen (1738–1822).[47] Ledger 3 demonstrates that the firm sold high-quality books and books of prints, keeping low levels of stock in most cases, so that by 1784 only thirty-eight of the titles advertised in the firm's 1781 book catalog were still available for sale.

The way stock is reported in Ledger 3 also reflects something of the exigency of managing a fluid situation, in which items were ordered, produced, stored, and sold over time. Thus we should not be surprised if methods of stock management changed as the firm refined its practices as the business expanded. This may account for the dual system of numbering books manifest in the ledger, reflecting the remnants of an older practice of identifying stock according to numbers assigned in the firm's 1781 sale catalog alongside a more flexible (or perhaps haphazard) system based on numbered locations in the shop or storeroom. Music, in contrast, was apparently not governed by a numeric system at the time the ledger was compiled in 1784. The firm's music sale catalogs were organized by genre rather than composer, and the entries within them were not numbered. Stock management, however, seemed to abide by a different system of organization in which an alphabetical sequence by composer was preferred, at least while the number of editions produced was relatively low. As the catalog of editions grew after 1784, however, plate numbers were introduced to exert greater control over the administration of the printing process, in which numbers acted as unique identifiers for tracking and accounting for music-engraved plates and printed copies, as well as providing a simple means of organizing the stock without the need for periodic rearrangement to make room for new editions in an alphabetic sequence.[48]

Prints were seemingly not subject to the same degree of control, perhaps because they took up less space generally but also because much of the stock was open for browsing in the shop: customers could select items according to interest or whim rather than peruse a catalog to select items to view and purchase. Unlike music, then, prints are reported in a fairly haphazard fashion in Ledger 3 with some regard for genre, as one might expect in a collection partly open for public consultation, but with no attempt to bring closer control over the stock. Perhaps for this reason, Artaria is not known to have issued a catalog dedicated to its stock of prints.

There were also areas of common currency among the main branches of the business: all were, for example, to a greater or lesser extent international in scope and outlook. Music was traded with foreign publishers in reciprocal agreements based on a system of trade discounts and bills of exchange; books were mostly imported from abroad for sale in Vienna, while prints and maps were similarly traded internationally. The firm commissioned Viennese and central European composers and engravers not only to cater to the local market (and to build capacity by nurturing local talent) but also to be able to offer distinctive products to trade with foreign dealers. Members of the firm also regularly attended the Frankfurt book fair not only to sell their own products but also to acquire works of art at auction, perhaps on behalf of customers in Vienna.[49] Thus even before the French Revolution, which had a major impact on the development of trade on a truly international level, Artaria's commercial interests and perspective extended beyond Vienna's city walls to embrace markets throughout Europe.

The relative values of each branch of the business are also indicative of the importance accorded to foreign trade (see table 2.2). Stocks of English, French, and Italian prints held in Vienna accounted for 21 percent of the business, while imported music held in Vienna amounted to 13 percent and books

Table 2.2. Summary of assets reported in Ledger 3

1784 Inventory	Value	%
Engravings (English, French, German)	40,597	21.0
Engravings and books in Mainz	29,995	15.5
Imported music in Vienna	25,209	13.0
Books in Vienna	16,343	8.4
Cash in Mainz	15,821	8.2
Music plates	14,325	7.4
Furniture in Mainz	9,017	4.7
Antique engravings and books	7,173	3.7
Furniture in Vienna	5,523	2.8
Cash	5,143	2.6
Maps	4,786	2.5
Engravings of Vienna (not Artaria imprint)	4,698	2.4
Music printed by Artaria	4,263	2.3
Small portraits	3,000	1.6
Strings for instruments	1,867	0.8
Merchandise left at Milan	1,565	0.8
Pastels	1,221	0.6
Frames	1,160	0.6
Printing paper	845	0.4
Portraits	848	0.4

held in Vienna accounted for 8.4 percent. Assets relating to Artaria's own pub-lications represent a fairly small proportion of the total valuation: the firm's stock of engraved music plates was valued at this time at just over 14,000 livres tournois, about 7 percent of the total capital. Stocks of unsold copies of the firm's editions accounted for less than 2.5 percent.

There are clear signs that the role of music in the *Kunsthandlung* changed over time as the market broadened. In other parts of Europe, by the 1780s printed music tended to be produced by specialist publishers, many with musical backgrounds. Firms such as Longman and Broderip in London, Leduc in Paris, and Breitkopf in Leipzig, for example, were exclusively dedicated to music. In 1784, there were signs of similar activity in Vienna, led by composers keen to gain financially from direct engagement with the market: thus both Franz Anton

Hoffmeister (1754–1812) and Leopold Kozeluch (1747–1818) started publishing their own music in that year and established music publishing businesses soon afterward.[50] The level of musical expertise individual members of the Artaria family brought to the business in the 1780s remains unknown, but music became an increasingly significant part of the firm's commercial identity during the first half of the nineteenth century, until it ceased producing new editions in the 1860s. Production values also changed over time. The firm at first sought to emphasize the visual dimension of the printed commodity, commonly presenting new editions with elaborate decorative title pages in the 1780s, some commissioned from notable engravers such as Johann Georg Mansfeld (1764–1817).[51] These decorative pages, however, gradually gave way to simpler designs as the firm's output grew, while page layouts and engraving styles became increasingly uniform. Thus music was initially presented as an elegant product to complement other visually appealing goods in the firm's premises but later evolved into something more utilitarian, intended for practitioners rather than commoditized as a luxury object in its own right.

Not enough is known about other similar businesses active in Vienna at the end of the eighteenth century to assess Artaria's achievement in comparative terms with any confidence, although some firms were apparently not as successful. The *Kunsthandlung* established by the Swiss dealer Christoph Torricella (1715–98) in the early 1770s, for example, ceased operating in 1785, leading him to auction his stock of engraved music plates. The reasons for Torricella's apparent failure are impossible to determine, although intense competition with Artaria around 1784 may have been a deciding factor, in addition to his advancing age.[52] Artaria at least seems to have been able to place the business on a secure financial footing by 1784. The total value of the business reported in Ledger 3 was 193,430 livres tournois, or approximately 89,000 gulden in Austro-Hungarian imperial currency, while profit was calculated as 18,694 livres, to be divided among the four partners in the business according to their shareholding.[53] This was clearly a significant valuation and compares favorably with the inventories of major wholesalers active in Vienna during the 1780s and 1790s, the majority of whom valued their businesses at less than 40,000 gulden with only five reporting assets of more than 100,000 gulden at the end of the eighteenth century.[54]

The Artaria firm therefore constituted a significant force in the cultural and economic landscape of late eighteenth-century Vienna, balancing a large volume of foreign imports to satisfy a market of culturally active and comparatively wealthy patrons with the stimulation of artistic creation in the city. In this respect, the printing press arguably operated in tandem with, or at least in a complementary fashion to, other cultural, economic, and political domains, reinforcing ideas of Enlightenment emancipation and artistic attainment across borders.

Appendix 2.1: Copies of Artaria
Editions Reported in Ledger 3

Plate number	Composer	Title	RISM number	Total copies reported in Ledger 3
14	Marianne von Auenbrugger and Antonio Salieri	Piano Sonata and *Ode*	A 2851	14
none	C. P. E. Bach	*Klopstocks Morgengesang am Schöpfungs Feste*	B 114	0
18	Luigi Boccherini	6 string quartets op. 32	B 3135	70
34	Luigi Boccherini	6 string quartets op. 33	B 3138	50
37	Luigi Boccherini	6 string trios op. 35	B 3089	150
40	Luigi Boccherini	3 string quintets op. 36	B 3179	0
52	Luigi Boccherini	Cello Concerto op. 34	B 3215	30
53	Basilius Bohdanowicz	12 polonaises for piano	B 3304	51
1	Paolo Bonaga	6 string trios op. 1, part 1	B 3442	13
2	Paolo Bonaga	6 string trios op. 1, part 2		
6	Georg Benda	Melodrama *Ariadne auf Naxos*	B 1870	11
none	Konrad Breunig	string quartets op. 7	n/k	0
3	Konrad Breunig	6 duets for violin and viola op. 7	B 4349	27
10	G. Antonio Capuzzi	6 string quartets op. 2	C 962	49
11	G. Antonio Capuzzi	6 string quartets op. 1	C 964	31
32	Muzio Clementi	3 piano sonatas op. 7	C 2779 and C 2780	47
36	Muzio Clementi	3 piano sonatas op. 9		15
7	Joseph Haydn	6 piano sonatas op. 30	H 3886	62

(continued)

Plate number	Composer	Title	RISM number	Total copies reported in Ledger 3
15	Joseph Haydn	6 divertimenti concertanti op. 31	H 3345	30
20	Joseph Haydn	12 Lieder, part 1	H 2617	49
24	Joseph Haydn	12 Lieder, part 2	H 2618	0
26	Joseph Haydn	6 string quartets op. 33	H 3414 H 3415	59
29	Joseph Haydn	Cantata *Ah come il core mi palpita*	H 2558	68
33	Joseph Haydn	6 *Sinfonie a grand orchestra* op. 35	H 3288	27
35	Joseph Haydn	Aria "Or vicina a te" from *L'incontro improviso*	H 2562	32
38	Joseph Haydn	Piano Concerto op. 37	H 3311	151
44	Joseph Haydn	*Raccolta di Menuetti Ballabili*	H 4011	65
48	Joseph Haydn	Symphony "Laudon" arranged for piano op. 36	H 4281	39
28	Franz Anton Hoffmeister	6 string quartets op. 7	H 5947	24
none	Michael Kerzelli	6 quartets op. 1	K 482	14
none	Michael Kerzelli	6 duos for 2 violins op. 2	K 483	0
4	Leopold Kozeluch	3 piano sonatas op. 1	K 1716	57
8	Leopold Kozeluch	3 piano sonatas op. 2	K 1719	61
14	Leopold Kozeluch	*Denis Klage*	K 1375	77
12	Leopold Kozeluch	3 piano trios op. 3	K 1469	78
16	Leopold Kozeluch	*La Chasse* for piano op. 5	K 1771	63
21	Leopold Kozeluch	3 piano trios op. 6	K 1478	45
23	Leopold Kozeluch	piano duet sonata op. 4	K 1641	35

(continued)

Plate number	Composer	Title	RISM number	Total copies reported in Ledger 3
31	Leopold Kozeluch	Cantata *Quanto e mai tormentosa*	K 1376	28
39	Leopold Kozeluch	Aria "Chloe siehst du nicht voll grauen?"	K 1380	32
none	Pietro A. D. B. Metastasio	36 canons	M 2460 and MM 2460	0
22	W. A. Mozart	6 violin sonatas op. 2	M 6678	54
25	W. A. Mozart	2 piano sonatas (4 hands)	M 6678	58
none	Franz Paul Rigler	12 *Oden und Lieder*	Lost	42
13	Franz Paul Rigler	2 piano sonatas op. 1/1	R 1691	239
23	Franz Paul Rigler	2 piano sonatas op. 1/2	R 1692	
19	Anton Stadler	musical table	SS 4281 I,57	52
10	J. F. X. Sterkel	12 pieces for piano op. 10	S 5997	9
51	J. F. X. Sterkel	6 piano trios op. 17	S 5918	37
none	J. F. X. Sterkel	10 pieces	Lost	34
13	Anton Ferdinand Titz	6 string quartets op. 1	T 779	48
9	Johann Vanhal	6 violin duets op. 28	V 571	42
49	Johann Vanhal	3 piano sonatas op. 29	V 673 and V 674	27
30	Johann Vanhal	2 piano trios and 1 piano quartet op. 30	V 410	49
50	Johann Vanhal	Piano Variations op. 31	V 729	65
5	Anton Zimmerman	3 violin sonatas op. 1	Z 222	33
17	Anton Zimmerman	Melodrama *Andromeda und Perseus*	Z 215	0
27	Anton Zimmerman	Piano Concerto op. 3	Z 219	29

Appendix 2.2: Books Listed in Ledger 3
Identified by 1781 Catalog Number.

1781 catalog number	Author and title
75	Bohuslav Balbín, *Das Leben des heiligen Johannis von Nepomuck, als eines Ertz-Martyrers über das Beicht-Sigill* (Augsburg: Pfeffel, 1729)
88	Jacques Saurin, *Discours historiques, critiques, théologiques, et moraux, sur les événemens les plus mémorables du vieux et du nouveau testament* (Amsterdam: Chez H. du Sauzet, 1720–39)
94	Pietro Santi Bartoli and Giovanni Pietro Bellori, *Admiranda romanarum antiquitatum ac veteris sculpturae vestigia anaglyphico opere elaborata, ex marmoreis exemplaribus quae Romanae adhuc extant, in capitolio, aedibus, hortisque virorum principum ad antiquam elegantiam* (Rome: Ioanne Iacobo de Rubeis, 1693)
95	Pietro Santi Bartoli, *Colonna Traiana eretta dal senato, e popolo Romano all'Imperatore Traiano Avgvsto nel svo foro in Roma: scolpita con l'historie della guerra dacica la prima e la seconda espeditione, e vittoria contro il re Decebalo* (Rome: de Rossi, 1673)
104	Angelo Fabroni, *Dissertation sur les statues appartenantes à la Fable de Niobé* (Florence: Moucke, 1779)
114	François Perrier, *Segmenta nobilium signorum e statuaru[m]* (Rome: de Poilly, 1638)
164	John Boydell and Thomas Jefferys, *Recueil des habillements de différentes nations, anciens et modernes, et en particulier des vieux ajustements anglois*, 4 vols. (London: Boydell and Jefferys, 1757)
166	Jacques Le Hay, *Recueil de cent estampes représentant differentes nations du Levant tirées sur les tableaux peints d'après nature [by Jean Baptiste van Mour] en 1707 et 1708 par les ordres de M. de Ferriol, ambassadeur du roi à la Porte. Et gravées en 1712 et 1713 par les soins de Mr Le Hay* (Paris: Sr. Le Hay; Sr. Duchange, 1714)
168	Gaetano Gherardo Zompini, *Le arti che vanno per via nella città di Venezia* (Venice: Zompini, 1753)
198	Wouter Schouten and Frans J. van der Heiden, *Ost-Indische Reyse: Worin erzehlt wird viel gedenckwürdiges, und ungemeine seltzame Sachen, bluhtige See- und Feld-schlachten, wieder die Portugisen und Makasser; Beslägerungen, Bestürmungen, und Eroberungen vieler fürnehmen Städte und Schlösser. Wie auch eine eigendliche Beschreibung der fürnehmsten Ost-Indischen Landschaften* (Amsterdam: Meurs, 1676)

(continued)

1781 catalog number	Author and title
205	Dezallier d'Argenville, *La conchyliologie ou Histoire naturelle des coquilles de mer, d'eau douce, terrestres et fossiles* (Paris: de Bure Aîné, first published in 1742)
240	*L'histoire naturelle éclaircie dans une de ses parties principales, l'ornithologie, qui traite des oiseaux de terre, de mer et de rivière tant de nos climats que des pays étrangers, ouvrage traduit du latin du "Synopsis avium" de Ray, augmenté d'un grand nombre de descriptions et de remarques historiques sur le caractère des oiseaux, leur industrie et leurs ruses* (Paris: Debure père, 1767)
246	Johann Michael Seligmann, *Sammlung verschiedener, ausländischer und seltener Vögel, worinnen ein jeder der selben nicht nur auf das genaueste beschrieben/sondern auch in einer richtigen und sauber illuminierten Abbildung vorgestellet wird,* 7 parts (Nuremberg: Johann Michael Fleischmann, 1770)
249	*Herbarium Blackwellianum emendatum et auctum, id est, Elisabethae Blackwell collectio stirpium: quae in pharmacopoliis ad medicum usum asseruantur, quarum descriptio et vires ex Anglico idiomate in Latinum conversae sistuntur figurae maximam partem ad naturale exemplar emendantur floris fructusque partium repraesentatio augentur et probatis botanicorum nominibus illustrentur. Cum praefatione Tit. Pl. D. D. Christophori Iacobi Trew* (Nuremberg: Typis Io. Iosephi Fleischmanni, 1750–73)
271	*Recueil des plantes du cabinet du roy* [title not identified further]
283	François Blondel, *Cours d'architecture enseigné dans l'académie royale d'architecture* (Paris: Chez l'auteur, 1671)
286	Sébastien Le Clerc, *Traité d'architecture avec des remarques et des observations* (Paris: P. Giffart, 1714)
288	Gabriel Louis Calabre Perau, *Description historique de l'hôtel royal des Invalides* (Paris: Guillaume Desprez, 1756)
290	Luigi Vanvitelli, *Dichiarazione dei disegni del Reale Palazzo di Caserta* (Naples: Regia Stamperia, 1756)
296	Pierre Contant d'Ivry, *Les oeuvres d'architecture de Pierre Contant d'Ivry,* part 1 (Paris: Chez Dumont [et al], 1769)
303	Domenico Rossi, *Studio d'architettura civile sopra gli ornamenti di porte e finestre tratti da alcune fabbriche insigni di Roma* (Rome: no pub., 1702)
304	Johannes-Jacobus de Rubeis, *Insignium romae templorum prospectus exteriores interioresque a celebrioribus architectis inventi* (Rome: no pub, 1644)

(continued)

1781 catalog number	Author and title
305	Robert Sayer, *Ruins of Athens, with Remains and Other Valuable Antiquities in Greece* (London: printed for Robert Sayer, 1759)
306	J. J. Sänger, *Vorstellung einiger modernen Gebäude: zum Pracht, zur Zierde und zur Bequemlichkeit eingerichtet* (Nuremberg: J. C. Weigel, 1722)
307	Sebastiano Serlio, *Il primo[-secondo] libro d'architettura, di m. Sabastiano Serlio, Bolognese* ([Venice]: [Per Cornelio de Nicolini da Sabbio a instantia de Marchio Sessa], 1551)
308	Leonhard Christoph Sturm, *Freundlicher Wett-Streit der Französischen, Holländischen und Teutschen Krieges-Bau-Kunst* (Augsburg: Jeremias Wolff, 1740)
309	Abraham Swan, *The British Architect: or, the Builders Treasury of Stair-Cases* (London: R. Sayer, 1740)
310	Jacques Barozzio de Vignole, *Livre nouveau ou Règles des cinq ordres d'architecture. Nouvellement revû, corrigé et augmenté par Monsieur B.*** architecte du roy. Avec plusieurs morceaux de Michel-Ange, Vitruve, Mansard, et autres célèbres architectes* (Paris: Ches Petit, 1767)
318	J. Wolf, *Das in Kupfer gestochene Schloss und Residenz des regierenden Fürsten Lobkowitz, Raudnitz an der Elbe, und des fürstlichen Hauses Ludwigsburg*, in Folio mit 40 Kupferblattern
321	Jean Bérain, *Oeuvres de J. Bérain contenant des ornements d'architecture et autres sujets* (Paris: no pub., 1711)
323	Johannes Gotfred Bradt, *Monumenta Fredensburgica jussu Friderici V. erecta* (Copenhagen: no pub., 1769)
325	François de Cuvilliés, *Morceaux de caprice à divers usages* (Paris: Chez l'auteur et chez Poilly, [1745?])
326	François de Cuvilliés, *Ornements*: "148 von Jungwirth und Lespilliez gestochenen Blättern"
327	François de Cuvilliés, *Morceaux de caprice à divers usages* (Paris: Chez l'auteur et chez Poilly, [1745?])
336	Pierre Ranson, *Oeuvres contenant un recueil de trophées, attributs, cartouches, vases, fleurs, ornements et plusieurs desseins agréables pour broder des fauteuils* (Paris: Esnauts et Rapilly, 1778)
339	Theodorus van Kessel, Adam van Vianen, Johan Smith, and Christiaen van Vianen, *Modelli artificiosi di vasi diversi d'argento et altre opere capriciozi: inventate et bozzate dal famozo Sr. Adamo di Viana, sendo la maggior parte da lui stesso battuti d'un pezzo d'argento: molto utili a tutti amatori dell'arte* (Utrecht: Christiano di Viana, [between 1646 and 1652?])

(continued)

1781 catalog number	Author and title
406	Ernst Friedrich Borgsdorff and Johann Andreas Pfeffel, *Neu-triumphirende fortification auff allerley situationen / defensivè und offensivè zu gebrauchen* (Vienna: Johann Georg Schlegel, 1703)
409	Michael Mieth, *Artilleriae recentior praxis, oder Neuere Geschutz-Beschreibung worinnen von allen vornehmsten Haupt-Puncten der Artillerie gründlich und ausführlich gehandelt, solches auch mit vielen Kupffer-Stücken erkläret wird* (Frankfurt: author, 1683)

Notes

I am grateful to Rudolf Rasch for his comments on an earlier draft of this chapter.

1. Johann Pezzl, *Beschreibung der Haupt- und Residenz-Stadt Wien* (Vienna: Armbruster, 1822), 315: "Die Kunsthandlungen verkaufen Kupferstiche, Zeichnungen, Landkarten, Musikalien, mathematische und optische Instrumente, Farbentusche, Zeichnungs-Materialien, Stich- und Strickmuster, Visitkarten, Unterhaltungsspiele, Bucher deren Haupteigenschaft die Kupfer ausmachen, auch Gemälde und Büsten."

2. Wienbibliothek im Rathaus, I.N. 178.881: Artaria Geschäftsinventar Nr. 3. The ledger consists of a leather-bound volume of sixty folios, paginated consecutively from fol. 2r to fol. 58v.

3. In subsequent ledgers, the firm switched to using Austrian imperial currency as the standard.

4. The inventories of the Mainz and Vienna shops are entered on fols. 2r–9r and fols. 10r–38v, respectively. For a transcription of the list of accounts drawn from the Vienna account book (fols. 25r–29r), see Rupert Ridgewell, "Mozart and the Artaria Publishing House: Studies in the Inventory Ledgers, 1784–1793" (PhD diss., Royal Holloway, University of London, 1999), appendix 5.i.

5. See "Music Printing in Mozart's Vienna: The Artaria Press," *Fontes Artis Musicae* 48, no. 3 (2001): 217–36; "Mozart's Publishing Plans with Artaria in 1787: New Archival Evidence," *Music and Letters* 83 (2002): 30–74; "Music Publishing and Economics," in *Music Publishing in Europe 1600–1900: Concepts and Issues, Bibliography*, ed. Rudolf Rasch (Berlin: Berliner Wissenschafts-Verlag, 2005), 80–103; "Artaria Plate Numbers and the Publication Process, 1778–87," in *Music and the Book Trade*, ed. R. Myers, M. Harris, and G. Mandelbrote (London: British Library and Oak Knoll, 2008), 145–78; "Mozart's Music on Sale in Vienna and Paris, 1780–1790," in *The Circulation of Music in Europe, 1600–1900: A Collection of Essays and Case Studies*, ed. Rudolf Rasch (Berlin: Berliner Wissenschafts-Verlag, 2008), 121–42.

6. *Wiener Zeitung*, July 28, 1770, 8: "Es wird den Kenner und Liebhabern hiemit kund gemacht, daß der Handelsmann Karl Artaria ein betrachtliches Assortiment von neuesten und allerfeinsten französischen und englischen Kupferstichen, wie auch von alleraresten Antiquen bekommen hat, und solche um einen ganz billigen Preiß hindann zu geben willens ist. Er logirt in der kleinen Dorothegasse im Tatenriederischen Hause zu ebner Erde."

7. Ledger 3, 27–32: "Stampe Francesi, ed Inglesi."

8. Ibid., 27: "In un gran Portafolio nel Magazino Stampe Francesi, ed Inglesi."

9. A representative entry reports "77 scenes of Rome by Piranesi" (77 Vedute di Roma del Piranesi), valued in sterling at 20 s each, making a total of £73.

10. The currency values here are taken directly from the ledger, where Artaria gives the original sterling price followed by the equivalent value in livres. The exchange rate applied here is approximately 23 livres to the pound, which is roughly consistent with the rate that prevailed at the time. See Rudolf Rasch, "The Internationalization of the Music Trade in the Eighteenth Century," in *Imprenta y edición musical en España (ss. XVIII–XX)*, ed. Begoña Lolo and José Carlos Gosálvez, Colección de Estudios 148 (Madrid: Universidad Autónoma, 2012), 35–64 (list of exchange rates in appendix 3).

11. Ledger 3, 38: "Stampe Vechie, ed Opere Antiche."

12. Ibid.: "Per diverse Opere, cioe Dissegni del Guercino, di Bartolozzi, Galleria Gerini, Opere del Mulinari, di Preste, &c.," "Stampe di Rembrand Orginali," and "Stampe che trovansi alla Biblioteca."

13. The contracts are transcribed in Günter Düriegl, "Die Wiener Veduten von Schütz, Ziegler und Janscha im Verlag Artaria," in *Der Verlag Artaria: Veduten und Wiener Alltagsszenen*, ed. Günter Düriegl and Reingard Witzmann (Vienna: Eigenverlag der Museen der Stadt Wien, 1981), 20–22.

14. These items are listed in a section containing eighteen entries headed "Prints of Vienna, not of our property" (Stampe di Vienna, non di nostro fondo), 56.

15. Ledger 3, 63–65: "Ritratti del nostro fondo." For a discussion of Artaria's output of prints, see Christoph Frank, "Das Wiener Unternehmen Artaria & Comp.," in *The European Print and Cultural Transfer in the 18th and 19th Centuries*, ed. Philippe Kaenel and Rolf Reichardt (Hildesheim, Germany: Olms, 2007), 609–45.

16. Ledger 3, 65: "Lasciat' à Milano."

17. Ibid., 67–70. There are eighty-four entries in total, including one for a "Vignette for the music catalogue," which was used in successive catalogs of the firm's music offerings published by Andreas Schmidt.

18. *Wienerisches Diarium*, no. 84 (October 19, 1776), 12.

19. Ibid., no. 64 (August 12, 1778), Nachtrag, 11–12; the same text was repeated in the next issue, no. 65 (August 15, 1778), Nachtrag, 17. It is also possible that Bonaga himself organized the publication and was responsible for determining the terms under which it was sold.

20. These entries are respectively headed "Musica di nostro fondo," 61–62, and "Rami di Musica in Stagno," 66–67. The inventory of engraving plates is reproduced and discussed in Ridgewell, "Artaria Plate Numbers and the Publication Process," 154–61.

21. Both editions were first advertised in the *Wiener Zeitung*, no. 68 (August 25, 1784), Anhang, 1949.

22. See, for example, Ridgewell, "Artaria Plate Numbers and the Publication Process," table 2, 174–78.

23. Ledger 3, 39–40: "Musica di Differenti Editori." This section begins with an entry for ten opera scores in handwritten copies with a total valuation of 168 livres.

24. Christian Schubart, *Etwas für Clavier und Gesang* (Winterthur: Heinrich Steiner, [1783]), RISM A/I, S 2249. The Birnbach concerto could be either opus 1 (B 2732) or opus 2 (B 2733); both were published without imprint. Christian Benjamin Uber, *Six divertissements pour le clavecin avec l'accompagnement d'une flûte, d'un violon, des deux cors de chasse et de la basse* (Leipzig: the author [Johann Gottlob Immanuel Breitkopf], 1783), RISM A/I, U 3; Johann Christoph Kaffka, *Musikalischer Beytrag für Liebhaber des deutschen Singspiels, beym Clavier, herausgegeben von Johann Christoph Kaffka. Erstes und zweytes Heft* (Breslau: Wilhelm Gottlieb Korn, 1783), RISM A/I, K 10; Heinrich Siegmund Oswald, *Lieder beym Clavier, mit einer begleitenden obligaten Violine dem Ernste und der guten Empfindung gewidmet ([1. und] Zweyter Teil)* (Breslau: Wilhelm Gottlieb Korn, 1782–83), RISM A/I, O 152 and O 153.

25. This was equivalent to 9,984 gulden at the exchange rate used in the ledger of about 2.18 livres per gulden.

26. See *Die Sortimentskataloge der Musikalienhandlung Artaria & Comp. in Wien: aus den Jahren 1779, 1780, 1782, 1785 und 1788*, ed. Otto Biba and Ingrid Fuchs (Tutzing, Germany: Hans Schneider, 2006), 99–100.

27. Ledger 3, 17–24: "Opere."

28. *Herbarium Blackwellianum emendatum et auctum, id est, Elisabethae Blackwell collectio stirpium: quae in pharmacopoliis ad medicum usum asseruantur, quarum descriptio et vires ex Anglico idiomate in Latinum conversae sistuntur figurae maximam partem ad naturale exemplar emendantur floris fructusque partium repraesentatione augentur et probatis botanicorum nominibus illustrentur. Cum praefatione Tit. Pl. D. D. Christophori Iacobi Trew* (Norimbergae, Germany: Typis Io. Iosephi Fleischmanni, 1750–73).

29. Ledger 3, 23: "Opera del Metastasio in 8vo."

30. Joseph Smith Speer, *The West-India Pilot: Containing Piloting Directions for . . . All . . . Parts of the West-Indies* (London: printed for the author, and sold by W. Griffen and W. Cook, 1766); also reissued in London by S. Hooper in 1771 with thirteen additional charts.

31. These annotations are limited to the words "troppo" in three places, "troppo f.12" against the entry for Brenner's *Galleria Imperiale*, and the comment "Erore solo £.30" for Piranesi's *Li Tempi Antichi* and *Campi Merzio*.

32. For discussion of the visual qualities of books, see Megan L. Benton, "The Book as Art," in *A Companion to the History of the Book*, ed. Simon Eliot and Jonathan Rose (Oxford: Blackwell, 2007), 493–507.

33. *Œuvre de F. E. Weirotter, peintre allemand, mort à Vienne en 1771* (Paris: Chez Basan and Poignant, 1775).

34. Ledger 3, 18: "Libro di Vedute dal Piranesi, ed altro Stampe Antiche."

35. Benjamin Ralph, *The School of Raphael; or, the Student's Guide to Expression in Historical Painting* (London: Boydell, 1759); Johann D. Preissler, *Die Durch Theorie Erfundene Practic: Oder Gründlich-Verfasste Regüln Deren Man Sich Als Einer Anleitung Zu Berühmter Künstlere Zeichen-Wercken Bastens Bedienen Kan* (Nürnberg: Bey ihme zu finden, 1743); Pierre François Basan, *Dictionnaire des graveurs anciens et modernes depuis l'origine de la gravure; avec une notice des principales estampes qu'ils ont gravées. Suivi des catalogues des oeuvres de Jacques Jordans, & de Corneille Visscher. Nouvelle édition* (Paris: author, 1767).

36. Pierre Joseph Buc'hoz, *Collection de planches, représentant au naturel ce qui se trouve de plus intéressant et de plus curieux parmi les animaux, les végétaux, et les minéraux, pour servir à l'intelligence de l'Histoire générale des trois règnes de la nature* (Paris: author and Durand, 1782); Thomas Pennant, *British Zoology* (London: printed for Benjamin White, 1768–70).

37. Sébastien Le Clerc, *Traité d'architecture avec des remarques et des observations* (Paris: P. Giffart, 1714); *Livre nouveau ou regles des cinq ordres d'architecture, par Jacques Barozzio de Vignole. Nouvellement revû, corrigé et augmenté par Monsieur B.*** Architecte du Roy. Avec plusieurs morceaux de Michel-Ange, Vitruve, Mansard, et autres célebres architectes* (Paris: Chereau, 1767).

38. William Thomas, *Original Designs in Architecture . . . Consisting of Twenty-Seven Copper-Plates, in Folio; Which Contain Plans, Elevations, Sections, Ceilings and Chimney Pieces, for Villas and . . . to Which Are Prefixed a Suitable Introduction and a Description, Explaining the . . . Designs* (London: printed for the author, 1783).

39. J. B. B. d'Anville, *Atlas Général* (Paris: author, 1737–80); Nicolas Gueudeville, *Atlas historique, ou nouvelle introduction à l'histoire, à la chronologie & à la géographie ancienne & moderne* (Amsterdam: Chez Zacharie Chatelain, 1735).

40. John Flamsteed, *Atlas coelestis* (London: Margaret Flamsteed and James Hodgson, 1729); Andreas Cellarius, *Atlas coelestis; seu Harmonia macrocosmica*, engraved by Pieter Schenk and Gerard Valk (Amsterdam: [publisher not known], 1660–1708).

41. Bernard Picart, *Cérémonies et coutumes religieuses de tous les peuples du monde; representées par des figures dessinées de la main de Bernard Picard, avec une explication historique, & quelques dissertations curieuses* (Amsterdam: J. F. Bernard, 1723).

42. For a description of this catalog, see Frank, "Das Wiener Unternehmen Artaria & Comp." The catalog was first advertised in the *Wiener Zeitung*, no. 57 (July 18, 1781), Anhang, unnumbered p. 4, and carries the title "Verzeichniß aller in unserer Handlung vorfindigen Kunstwerken, bestehend in Gallerien, und andern Sammlungen, Bibeln, und geistlichen Sachen, Statuen, Antiquitäten, Basrelief, Portraits, Nationalfiguren, Kaufrüfe, Moden, malerischen Reisen, Aussichten, und Landschaften, Naturgeschichten in alle 3 Reiche abgetheilt, Architekturwerke, Ornamenten, Haus- und aller Arten Verzierungen, geographische Ablässe, Karten, und Kriegspläne, geometrische, und perspektivische Werke, Grundregeln der Zierung durch alle Klassen &c. Dann ein Blatt, worauf die allerneuesten, und erst angekommenen Musikalien angemerkt. Werden beyde ohnentgeldlich abgefolgt."

43. Ledger 3, 33: "295 Carte Giochi Instrutivi dal Greppi."

44. Ibid.: "Diverse Carte Inglesi, Francesi, e Tedesche in 5 gran Cartoni" and "Carte Inglese, Olandese, e Francesi."

45. See J. Brewer, "The Most Polite Age and the Most Vicious Attitudes towards Culture as a Commodity, 1660–1800," in *The Consumption of Culture 1600–1800*, ed. A. Bermingham and J. Brewer (London: Routledge, 1995), 341–61.

46. For a discussion of the demographic associated with the music market in England during the same period, see Robert D. Hume, "The Value of Money in Eighteenth-Century England: Incomes, Prices, Buying Power—and Some Problems in Cultural Economics," *Huntington Library Quarterly* 77, no. 4 (2014): 373–416.

47. For more information about Artaria's dealings with Ligne and others, see Frank, "Das Wiener Unternehmen Artaria & Comp."

48. See Ridgewell, "Artaria Plate Numbers and the Publication Process."

49. The Getty Provenance Index Database, accessed January 4, 2016, http:// piprod.getty.edu/starweb/pi/servlet.starweb, lists Artaria as the buyer at Frankfurt on twelve occasions before 1800 of works by such artists as Ferdinand Bol (1616–80), Justus Juncker (1703–67), and Johann Wolfgang Rorschach (1664–1730). According to Rudolf Rieger, Artaria was the only dealer in graphic arts represented at the Frankfurt fair consistently from the late 1770s onward. See Rudolf Rieger, "Graphikhandel im 18. Jahrhundert: Die Firma Artaria und Johann Gottlieb Prestel," in *Brücke zwischen den Völkern—Zur Geschichte der Frankfurter Messe. Band II: Beiträge zur Geschichte der Frankfurter Messe*, ed. Patricia Stahl (Frankfurt am Main: Historisches Museum, 1991), 203–7.

50. Music copying was, however, undertaken by specialist shops in Vienna at this time.

51. Notable examples of decorative title pages are found in Artaria's editions of Haydn's piano sonatas op. 30 (plate number 7), Haydn's six divertimenti op. 31 (plate number 15), Zimmermann's *Andromeda und Perseus* (plate number 17), Mozart's six violin sonatas op. 2 (plate number 22), Hoffmeister's six string quartets op. 7 (plate number 28), Sterkel's six piano trios op. 17 (plate number 51), and Mozart's "Haydn" string quartets (plate number 59).

52. See Alexander Weinmann, *Kataloge Anton Huberty, Wien, und Christoph Torricella*, Beiträge zur Geschichte des Alt-Wiener Musikverlages, Reihe 2, Folge 7 (Vienna: Universal Edition, 1962), 89–91.

53. The total value of the business is reported in the balance account in Ledger 3, 76–77, under the headings "Ristretto dell'Inventario qui retro" and "Ristretto delli Debiti qui retro."

54. P. G. M. Dickson has produced a list of the most significant wholesalers based on their submissions to the *Merkantil- und Wechselgericht* (Mercantile and Exchange Court), the government body responsible for enacting commercial legislation in Vienna. See P. G. M. Dickson, *Finance and Government under Maria Theresia, 1740–1780* (Oxford: Clarendon, 1987), 326.

Part Two

Edifying Readers

Chapter Three

Morality and the "Fair-Sexing" of Telemann's Faithful Music Master

Steven Zohn

It was a blustery Thursday afternoon in early February 1729 as the Hamburg music lover Rudolph Burmeister finished his cup of coffee, bookmarked his place in a journal article about the advantages of educating women, and got up from his table at the coffeehouse. He walked a few blocks toward the city's center, crossed the Trostbrücke spanning the Nikolaifleet channel of the Alster River, then hurried past city hall and into the stock exchange, where a proprietor at the music stall greeted him warmly. "It just arrived," the man said with a wink, handing Burmeister a freshly printed bifolium of music. It was the latest lesson from the Faithful Music Master: four densely engraved pages of music containing the second movement of a cello sonata, an aria recently sung to great applause at Hamburg's Gänsemarkt opera house, a passepied from a suite for violin or oboe with continuo, an *Air* for trumpet and continuo, a *Marche* and *Retraite* for harpsichord, and a demonstration of unusual chord progressions. It had been two weeks since the previous lesson, and Burmeister was eager to learn how the sonata and suite would continue and to discover what new works lay in store for him. He rushed home to play through the music on his violin and clavichord; later, he would compare notes with his three brothers, all of whom were equally eager pupils of the Faithful Music Master.

Something like this imaginary vignette must have played out during the 1720s in many German coffeehouses and bookshops, where periodicals of all kinds were eagerly consumed by an educated public hungry for news, advice, and enlightenment on a variety of topics.[1] Burmeister and his brothers were in fact loyal patrons of Hamburg's leading musician, Georg Philipp Telemann, whose latest publishing venture was Germany's first journal of music. *Der getreue Music-Meister*, or the Faithful Music Master, was issued biweekly by the composer between November 1728 and November 1729 in twenty-five issues called "Lection" (lesson), for a total of one hundred pages of music.[2] As indicated on the title page (and in Telemann's informative preface; see appendix 3.1), the journal promised something for everyone—a compendium of scorings, styles, and genres delivered in an accessible format that instructed through exemplary models and entertained with wit and humor:

> The Faithful Music-Master, who proposes to present all types of musical pieces for singers and instrumentalists, suited for various voices and almost all instruments in use and which consist of moral, operatic, and other arias, trios, duets, solos, etc., sonatas, overtures, etc., as well as fugues, counterpoints, canons, etc., therefore most everything that may occur in music according to the Italian, French, English, Polish, etc., serious, lively, and amusing styles, little by little in a lesson every fourteen days through Telemann.[3]

Lacking much in the way of specifically musical models for his journal, Telemann would have drawn inspiration most directly from literary serials such as the moral weeklies and monthly miscellanies that appeared in London from the 1690s and in Hamburg, Leipzig, and Zurich from the early 1720s. These periodicals aimed to educate and edify a literate and mostly urban readership of aristocrats, civil servants, professionals, merchants, master craftsmen, and their families—the same middle- and upper-class target audience for Telemann's musical publications, a few of which he explicitly identified as "moral."[4] The ideal moral citizen (and, of course, consumer of moral literature and music) is embodied in the fictional character Sophroniscus, whose family life is the subject of the weekly *Der Biedermann* (The Man of Probity; Leipzig, 1727–28), edited by Leipzig University professor Johann Christoph Gottsched. Sophroniscus, a well-educated, humane, happy, and virtuous nobleman, leads a life that demonstrates the moral imperatives of self-sufficiency, self-improvement, and moderation. He is cosmopolitan in outlook, nondogmatic in his religiosity, and an active and devoted father who takes the education of his children seriously.[5] It was the Sophroniscuses of the world that the Faithful Music Master aimed to enlighten and improve by exposing them to "most everything that may occur in music."

Perhaps because of its hybrid nature—a serial music publication that took its cue primarily from literary predecessors—modern commentators have largely overlooked *Der getreue Music-Meister*. In particular, the nature of its relationship to moral journals has remained unexamined.[6] In this chapter, I consider the ways *Der getreue Music-Meister* reflected and furthered the ideals of English and

German moral journals, many of which aimed not only to instruct and entertain but also to promote the education of women for the benefit of society at large. I argue that, like its immediate forerunners in Hamburg and Leipzig, *Der getreue Music-Meister* contributed to the interrelated projects of enlightening women and constructing a German cultural identity through the purification and refinement of the native language, in this case both literary and musical.

The First Part, in Which We Meet the Faithful Music Master and His Periodical Relatives

Telemann's claim in the opening paragraph of his preface that this was the first journal "with real music to appear in Germany" may be a tacit acknowledgment of earlier French and English examples. For instance, between 1695 and 1732 the Ballard firm in Paris issued monthly or seasonal *recueils* and *meslanges* of motets, airs, and dances by assorted French and Italian composers.[7] During the first quarter of the eighteenth century, the London firm of John Walsh and John Hare published its *Monthly Mask of Vocal Music*, each issue with four or five pages containing theatrical and other songs in English and eventually in Italian as well. Walsh and Hare's publishing rivals Daniel Wright and Richard Meares issued their own song periodicals during this period (sometimes borrowing the title *Monthly Mask*), as did John Cluer and Bezaleel Creake (*The Monthly Apollo*).[8] Perhaps closer to Telemann's journal in spirit, if not in actual content, were literary periodicals such as Paris's *Le Mercure galant* (1672–74 and 1677–1724; from 1724 as *Le Mercure de France*) and London's *The Gentleman's Journal; or, the Monthly Miscellany* (1692–94), which offered songs alongside news, history, philosophy, poetry, questions and answers, book notices, and other items of interest to a general readership. More contemporary with *Der getreue Music-Meister* was *The Universal Mercury* (London, 1726), balancing news, speeches, poems, odes, and death and marriage notices with songs, though only the words to the latter were printed. Earlier, *The Muses Mercury; or, the Monthly Miscellany* (London, 1707–8) had promised "Poems, Prologues, Songs, Sonnets, Translations, and other Curious Pieces" on its title page, likewise including just the texts to songs and secular cantatas.[9]

The extent to which Telemann was aware of these and similar publications is unknown, but he no doubt kept his eye on the English market for printed music. Twelve of his publications, including *Der getreue Music-Meister*, were available for purchase at the London shop of bookseller Cornelius Crownfield in 1728.[10] As corresponding agent to the Eisenach court between 1725 and 1730, Telemann gathered news from London and claimed to write to his contact there in English.[11] Only a few years after *Der getreue Music-Meister*, he adopted the use of pewter engraving plates in apparent emulation of Walsh and Hare, and his practice of selling some of his printed collections by advance subscription, including the journal, likely also derived from the model of English books and music.[12] Telemann was especially shrewd in this respect, for he consistently broke up multimovement compositions—and occasionally even single movements—between issues, thereby providing a strong incentive for consumers to subscribe to the journal rather than purchase issues individually.

The same strategy was pursued by three later German journals of music: the *Musikalisches Allerley von verschiedenen Tonkünstlern*, published by Friedrich Wilhelm Birnstiel in Berlin between 1760 and 1763; the *Musikalisches Mancherley*, published by Georg Ludwig Winter in Berlin between 1762 and 1763; and the *Musikalisches Vielerley*, edited by Carl Philipp Emanuel Bach and published by Michael Christian Bock in Hamburg in 1770. These publications followed in the footsteps of multiauthor song and keyboard anthologies such as Friedrich Wilhelm Marpurg's *Berlinische Oden und Lieder* (Berlin, 1756 and 1759) and *Raccolta delle più nuove composizioni di clavicembalo* (Berlin, 1756–57), but their more diverse contents broken into weekly or biweekly issues, each a bifolium in length, suggests that their ultimate inspiration may have been *Der getreue Music-Meister*.[13] In fact, Birnstiel's brief preface to the *Musikalisches Allerley* reads very much like Telemann's title page:

> These pages will continue to appear every Saturday and are devoted to collecting and gradually revealing the newest musical efforts of good composers in vocal and instrumental works, pieces for keyboard, violin, flute, etc., smaller and larger compositions, odes, arias, etc., polonaises, minuets, marches, etc., duets, trios, fugues, and sinfonias, etc., characteristic pieces and sonatas in the German, Italian, and French styles. I recommend them for the gracious approval of connoisseurs and amateurs and personally vouch for them, especially as the collection will be assembled through selection and scrutiny, without any composition being admitted indiscriminately.[14]

Whatever inspiration Telemann may have drawn from early French and English music periodicals and literary journals, he was surely also thinking of London's moral weeklies and their German imitators when, in the first paragraph of his preface, he invoked "so-called monthly journals, or those that appear piecemeal at various times." Moral weeklies typically alternated or combined essay and epistolary formats, with the editors supplying most of the essays and at least some of the letters signed by readers. By far the most influential among them were London's the *Tatler*, the *Spectator*, and the *Guardian*, all appearing between 1709 and 1714. Although Johann Mattheson soon published *Der Vernünfftler* (Hamburg, 1713–14), which included translated excerpts of the *Tatler* and the *Spectator*, no fully original German-language moral weeklies appeared until 1721.[15] So our Faithful Music Master arrived on the scene toward the beginning of a German publishing phenomenon that by the middle decades of the century had given rise to dozens of moral journals.

Telemann's principal German models for *Der getreue Music-Meister* would no doubt have been the three most widely read moral journals: *Die Discourse der Mahlern* (The Discourse of Painters; Zurich, 1721–23), *Die vernünfftigen Tadlerinnen* (The Sensible Female Scolds; Leipzig, 1725–26), and above all the locally produced *Der Patriot* (The Patriot; Hamburg, 1724–26), which was highly praised, widely circulated, and reissued in book format in 1728–29, just as the Faithful Music Master commenced his lessons.[16] The principal editors of *Der Patriot*—Michael Richey, Barthold Heinrich Brockes, and Christian Friedrich Weichmann—all had close professional ties to Telemann; and the publisher of the journal, Johann Christoph Kißner, also sold Telemann's printed annual cycle of church cantatas, *Harmonischer Gottes-Dienst* (including some libretti by Richey), in 1725–26. Thus visitors to Kißner's bookshop in 1726 could pick up issues of *Der Patriot* along with cantatas by Telemann.[17] The composer may also have been spurred on by two periodicals written by his Hamburg colleague Mattheson: the learned journal *Critica Musica* (Hamburg, 1722–25) and the more popular *Der Musicalische Patriot* (Hamburg, 1728), which appeared in the months preceding *Der getreue Music-Meister*.[18] In *Der Musicalische Patriot*, Mattheson claimed that music—and opera in particular—uplifted bourgeois life, instructed audiences in virtue, and elevated society as a whole.[19]

Mattheson's view with respect to opera was directly opposed by Gottsched, who began his extended anti-opera campaign in the December 20, 1728, issue of *Der Biedermann*. But opera's moral force was soon affirmed by Johann Georg Hamann, editor of the journal *Die Matrone* (The Matron; Hamburg, 1728–30) and, like Richey and Brockes of *Der Patriot*, the author of several librettos set by Telemann. In the August 25, 1729, issue of his journal, Hamann claimed that opera, like spoken comedy and tragedy, should offer a moral lesson. He also proposed that the greater pleasure delivered by opera made its didactic message more digestible, citing the example of Telemann's 1727 opera *Sancio, oder die siegende Grossmuth*, TVWV 21:20, to a libretto by Johann Ulrich König.[20] Perhaps, then, it is no coincidence that the Faithful Music Master's own moral lessons included numerous excerpts from his recent operas, including three arias from *Sancio*, the first appearing just a few weeks before Gottsched's diatribe in *Der Biedermann*.

A closer reading of Telemann's preface reveals further connections between the journal and its periodical models. Those whom the Faithful Music Master "aims to benefit and entertain" in the first paragraph are evidently the amateurs, or "Music-Liebhaber," addressed in the fifth. We find formulations similar to "benefit and entertain" in *Memoirs for the Ingenious; or, the Universal Mercury* (London, 1694), which aimed at "a Familiar Style" while choosing "such Subjects as may not only be Pleasant, but the Knowledge of them really

Profitable to the Vulgar"; and in the promise of the *Monthly Miscellany; or, Memoirs for the Curious* (London, 1707–9) to "please the Ingenious and instruct the meaner Capacities."[21] The *Universal Mercury* claimed in its first issue, worth quoting here at some length, that it would attract a broad audience by instructing without pedantry and entertaining through variety:

> To *divert* and to *instruct* are the Ends every new Writer promises the Publick to pursue; but the great Difficulty lies in the Manner of doing it: Our Minds are generally unapt to be taught, especially by any one who assumes a magisterial Air; and on the other Hand, we soon consider those Works as trifling and impertinent, which are only calculated to please our Imaginations, without conveying proper Instructions. As the Authors of the *Universal Mercury* therefore are satisfied, that the Generality of Mankind are soon weary of any one Thing, however amiable or useful in it self; they design to entertain their Readers with Variety, and to be as unconfin'd in their Subjects as in their Title. The *Learned*, in the Course of this Work, will meet with *Philosophical Transactions, Memoirs of Literature, Physical Controversies*, and *Lists of Books*, printed both at Home and Abroad; the *Gay Part* of the Town shall have *News* from the *Court*, the *Park*, the *Masquerade*, the *Opera*, and the *Play-Houses*; the *Mechanick* may often find useful Discoveries in his way; nor shall the *Tradesman* have reason to complain that his Interest is forgot. . . . The *Ladies*, to whom we shall always shew a particular Regard, will not only have the Benefit of that part of our Work which is calculated for the *Gay*, but may ever and anon expect an *Instructive Novel*, and to be entertained with such *Poems* and *Songs* as were never published, or those which are only handed about by the *Curious*.[22]

To be sure, both a pedagogical light touch and a diversity of offerings are central to the Faithful Music Master's approach. Telemann well knew how to make his readers' "instruction agreeable and their Diversion useful," to borrow Joseph Addison's phrase from the *Spectator*, and moreover, how to entice them to swallow "the black Potion of *Instruction*, by promising the Sugar-Plumb of *Delight*," as James Ralph put it in 1728.[23] One wonders whether Telemann's plan, announced in the fourth paragraph of his preface, to print analyses of his own pieces that "would show all sorts of advantages that might profitably be applied in practice" was ultimately aborted because it threatened to introduce too strong an authorial voice or an off-putting "magisterial Air" (as the *Universal Mercury* would have it). Variety could also serve to demystify music's more arcane aspects. If a canon were placed beside a frothy *galanterie*, as the Faithful Music Master often did, then the former might be rendered a bit less intimidating. Literary historian J. Paul Hunter detects a similar desire in John Dunton's *Athenianism* (London, 1710) "to surprise readers with novel ideas, subjects, structures, attitudes, and styles—to mix the ordinary and familiar with the strange and surprising so as to domesticate the puzzling and complex."[24]

Besides its potential commercial advantages, the continuation (or interruption) of longer works across multiple issues of *Der getreue Music-Meister* may have helped satisfy readers' desire for diverting variety through formal idiosyncrasy and digression.[25] In the first issues, interruptions of multimovement works were consistently signaled by phrases such as "Das übrige folget künftig" (the remainder to follow in the future), "Der Rest künftig" (the rest to come), or "Nächstens mehr" (more shortly).[26] But such indications appeared only sporadically during the rest of the journal's run, often leaving readers in suspense as to when and how—or even if—sonatas and suites would continue.[27] In one important aspect, the Faithful Music Master limited his repertory, for he presented no sacred vocal works—a stricture entirely in keeping with the emphasis in moral journals on the secular.[28] The same was true of the *Musikalisches Allerley* and *Musikalisches Mancherley*, though C. P. E. Bach did include two chorale preludes and two sacred odes in his *Musikalisches Vielerley*.

It was in the name of variety—and, one suspects, self-preservation—that Telemann announced, in the third paragraph of his preface, that he "will not be opposed if others wish to make some contribution to filling [the journal's pages] up, whereby the names of the authors will be added, should they make them known." Although only two works penned by others appeared in the journal's first eight issues, the Faithful Music Master eventually provided works by a number of eminent German musicians, including Johann Sebastian Bach, Ernst Gottlieb Baron, Johann Georg Pisendel, Sylvius Leopold Weiss, and Jan Dismas Zelenka. For some of these composers, the journal represented a unique opportunity to see their music in print. Similar appeals to readers for letters, poems, and other publishable content became a conventional feature of moral journals, as was the offer to suppress authors' names upon request.[29] Such contributions, whether written under real readers' names or editorial pseudonyms, provided at least the appearance that the journal's audience had a hand in constructing its text. The Faithful Music Master identified all of his contributors, who thereby added their own moral voices to a broadened conversation about musical styles and genres. But these were professional musicians, not the amateurs referred to in the journal's preface. Similarly, Birnstiel and C. P. E. Bach consistently identified contributors to the *Musikalisches Allerley* and *Musikalisches Vielerley*, the latter publication even including musicians' professional affiliations. But Winter did so only occasionally in the *Musikalisches Mancherley*, and then only in the cases of Johann Friedrich Agricola, C. P. E. Bach, Carl Friedrich Christian Fasch, and Johann Philipp Kirnberger. Were the other contributors loath to reveal their identities?

The Second Part, in Which the Faithful
Music Master Benefits and Entertains His Readers

Amateurs did in fact have an opportunity to interact with the Faithful Music Master's text, and not merely by reading, practicing, or performing the music. In asking readers to act as musical authors or sleuths, the contrapuntal exercises and canons helped close the gap between composer and consumer, teacher and pupil, in a moral-instructional manner. For example, one issue follows the continuation of a Telemann opera aria with a chromatic fugue subject accompanied by five "solutions," that is, different versions of the *comes* that are to follow the *dux* at an interval of time determined by the reader. For most of the solutions, the counterpoint is invertible. Later, the Faithful Music Master provided a realization of the second solution, resulting in a perpetual canon.[30] A further demonstration of counterpoint, this time primarily intended for readers' edification, is provided by the "Etliche *Contrapunctische* Veränderungen des ersten Tacts der Telemannischen *Sonatin*en" (several contrapuntal variations on the first measure of the Telemann sonatina), the reference being to Telemann's *Sei suonatine per violino e cembalo* (Frankfurt, 1718).[31] The original publication featured a beautifully engraved pastoral frontispiece in which printed music placed beside a Roman pitcher and examined by cherubs turns out to be the theme of the first sonatina with various contrapuntal permutations—an Arcadian episode as a teachable moment for those looking closely enough. As illustrated more clearly in the Faithful Music Master's reprinting (fig. 3.1), the sonatina theme is first given a countersubject (a variant of the bass accompaniment), is shown to be invertible at the twelfth, then is melodically inverted against the countersubject, and finally is played against itself in retrograde—all of which is heady stuff for an unassuming *galant* theme, the take-away message being the compatibility of the natural and learned styles.[32]

Elsewhere, the Faithful Music Master presents his readers with three subjects and invites them to compose fugues (fig. 3.2).[33] This is not only the journal's most rigorous compositional exercise—one to which only well-trained amateurs or professionals would be equal—but also serves to illustrate different fugal styles such as the stile antico of the first subject, the more modern, dance-like idiom of the second, and the sober chromaticism of the third. Perhaps of equal importance and apparently unnoticed by previous commentators, the fugue subjects collectively function as a souvenir of a specific event: the auditions held in July 1727 for the vacant organist position at Hamburg's St. Jacobikirche, an occasion that would have been attended by only a handful of musicians and city council members. As part of the audition process, Telemann presented each organ applicant with four chorale melodies on which to improvise preludes and four subjects—three reprinted in *Der getreue Music-Meister*—

Figure 3.1. "Etliche Contrapunctische Veränderungen des ersten Tacts der Telemannischen Sonatinen." *Der getreue Music-Meister* (Hamburg: Telemann, 1728), Lection 2.

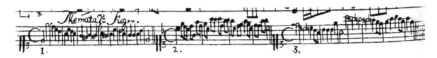

Figure 3.2. "Themata zu Fugen." *Der getreue Music-Meister* (Hamburg: Telemann, 1729), Lection 21.

on which to improvise fugues.[34] Some of the journal's Hamburg readers may have been able to connect these subjects with the Jacobikirche auditions, and I suspect that many more would have made the general association of a set of fugal subjects with organ trials, perhaps even fancying themselves as imaginary applicants as they attempted to work out an exposition or two at home.

Earlier in the journal, beneath the continuations of a lute suite by Ernst Gottlieb Baron and the well-known bassoon sonata by Telemann (TWV 41:f1), is an instance of "the black Potion of *Instruction*" combined with "the Sugar-Plumb of Delight": an excerpt from a comic scene belonging to Telemann's otherwise lost opera *Die verkehrte Welt*, TVWV 21:23 (Hamburg, 1728), in which various contrapuntal techniques and tempo-related styles are announced by the text and illustrated by the music (fig. 3.3):[35]

Diß ist ein Contrapunct in Augmentatione.
Der: alla Duodecima; Der: alla Decima;
und dieser all'Ottava.
So klingt der cancricante;
diß ist Relatio harmonica;
und diß Adagio, Presto, Andante.

[This is a counterpoint in augmentation.
This, at the twelfth; this, at the tenth;
and this, at the octave.
The crab canon sounds like this;
this is relatio harmonica;
and this [is] Adagio, Presto, Andante.]

Included are an augmentation canon in invertible counterpoint; invertible counterpoint at the twelfth, tenth, and octave; a crab canon; "relatio harmonica," or invertible counterpoint producing only consonances; an adagio cantabile; an alla breve fugue with the typical "Presto" marking; and an andante with ostinato accompaniment. Although this fragmentary scene illuminates several aspects of the composer's art, it simultaneously pokes fun at the dry manner in which counterpoint was often taught. As David Yearsley has suggested, the inclusion of a crab canon—commonly considered one of the most mysterious creatures in the contrapuntal realm but which is actually far more compositionally straightforward than it initially appears—adds to the humorous effect for those in the know.[36] The union of satire with pedagogy embodied in this scene is entirely characteristic of moral journals.[37] It resurfaces in *Der getreue Music-Meister* with the "Intrada, nebst burlesquer Suite," TWV 40:108, a violin duet with grotesque dances portraying characters or scenes from Jonathan Swift's *Gulliver's Travels*, which had recently appeared in German translation in Hamburg.[38] Once again, counterpoint is called into humorous and instructive service, as the brief "Lilliputsche Chaconne" (notated in sixty-fourth and one-hundred-twenty-eighth notes) is loosely canonic throughout.

Four more canons by J. S. Bach, Zelenka, the Dresden kapellmeister Johann Christoph Schmidt, and a "Mr Dirnslot" scattered throughout the Faithful Music Master's lessons require his reader-pupils to translate shorthand notation into a composition or, as in the case of Bach's "Hudemann" puzzle canon, BWV 1074, to "solve" enigmatic notation.[39] These works seem especially likely to have been commissioned from the authors, given their comparatively esoteric nature. Telemann himself contributed the Sonata in B-Flat Major for viola or viola da gamba and continuo (or for various duet combinations), TWV 41:B3, which is strictly canonic throughout its four movements. Together with the examples discussed above, these canons form a body of contrapuntal exercises and exemplars that, although modest in size, is apparently without parallel in other eighteenth-century music periodicals. Yet it is noteworthy that C. P. E. Bach posed a similar compositional challenge to purchasers of his *Musikalisches Vielerley* when he printed a palindromic minuet in enigmatic notation, Wq 116/5, before providing the written-out solution in a later issue (fig. 3.4).[40] In the solution, the second four-measure phrase of the original notation is read back-to-front after the first, then the first four-measure phrase is read back-to-front after the second. No such musical puzzles had appeared in the *Musicalisches Allerley* or *Musicalisches Mancherley*, raising the possibility that Bach was directly inspired by his father's puzzle canon and the other contrapuntal "lessons" in his godfather's journal.

In an insightful study of Telemann's relationship to musical tradition, Keith Chapin has argued that the scene from *Die verkehrte Welt*, together with "einige plötzliche Eintritte in entfernete Accords" (several sudden modulations to

Figure 3.3. "Scene aus der Oper: Die verkehrte Welt." *Der getreue Music-Meister* (Hamburg: Telemann, 1729), Lections 13–14.

distant keys), is the composer's way of poking fun at the learned style and that the Faithful Music Master's placement of these and other contrapuntal curiosities at the ends of substantial works, at the bottoms of pages, and often in a reduced font indicates his relegation of them to a secondary status at best. Chapin further views the fugal exercises and canons as excluding much of the journal's readership, who would have lacked the training to complete, realize, or fully appreciate them.[41] Yet I argue that, on the contrary, the Faithful Music Master's effort to instruct his readers in the art of fugue, canon, invertible counterpoint, and modulation was an inclusive act, and placing the canons and their compact kin anywhere but at the bottoms of pages would probably have wreaked havoc with the layout of individual issues. If the composition of fugues to given subjects assumes the kind of training associated with professional musicians, I suspect that many, if not most, of the journal's reader-pupils would have been up to the challenge of realizing the enigmatic notation of BWV 1074, coordinating a fugal subject with its answers, and apprehending the mechanics of invertible counterpoint.

Be that as it may, even those with little training may have benefited from such music. A letter from the Patriotische Gesellschaft of "Christianstadt" to *Der Patriot* reported that the learned essays in that journal were frequently read

Figure 3.4. C. P. E. Bach, enigmatic notation and solution for the Menuet in C Major, Wq 116/5. *Musikalisches Vielerley* (Hamburg: Michael Christian Bock, 1770), nos. 5 and 12. Reprinted Basel: Mark A. Meadow, 1983.

with profit by the unlearned: "The pages of *Der Patriot*, in addition to their exceptional pleasantness and clear expression, are to be preferred to other learned writings in that they also frequently fall into the hands of unlearned and similar people who in fact read them primarily out of curiosity, leading to increased insight and better application of their intellect without their knowledge or intention."[42] But we should not assume that the Faithful Music Master's readers were predominantly amateurs: the organist, composer, and writer Johann Gottfried Walther apparently owned a copy of the journal; members of the Dresden Hofkapelle owned at least two copies; and Telemann thought it appropriate to inquire whether the Auric court wished to purchase a subscription.[43] Clearly, the Faithful Music Master's lessons appealed to a broad spectrum of musical interests and abilities.

But why include a series of sudden modulations that do not produce even a fragmentary composition (fig. 3.5)?[44] An answer is suggested by a little-studied manuscript by C. P. E. Bach containing various sketches, canons, and exercises in modulation. This compilation, titled *Miscellanea Musica*, Wq 121, was apparently prepared after Bach's death by his principal copyist, Johann Heinrich Michel, from assorted loose leaves of paper.[45] Although much of this material may have been intended for pedagogical purposes, it is also possible, even likely, that some of it was destined to serve as raw material for Bach's own compositions. Of particular interest to us are the quick enharmonic modulations to remotely related keys and multiple examples of chord progressions between more closely related keys (fig. 3.6). Such exercises suggest that the similar progressions provided by the Faithful Music Master are to be understood not merely as exotic curiosities for musical *Liebhaber* but also (and perhaps more importantly) as a rare glimpse into the compositional workshop, where inspiration might take the form of a few chords jotted down on a stray scrap of paper.

Besides offering consumers an opportunity to interact with and help construct the text of *Der getreue Music-Meister* (with a few chuckles thrown in for good measure), the "canons [and] counterpoints," as they are referred to in the journal's index, represented an important vista within the Faithful Music Master's broadly conceived moral-instructional landscape. Perhaps Telemann was thinking in geographical terms similar to those of Johann Beer, whose *Bellum musicum* of 1701 illustrated the musical terrain of an allegorical war waged by Queen Compositio and her daughter Harmonia against musical bunglers such as beer fiddlers, village schoolmasters, and organists. As reproduced in figure 3.7, the upper-left-hand corner of Beer's map ("Nova et Accurata Totius Regni Musici Descriptio"; New and Completely Accurate Representation of the Musical Realm) shows the "Regio Contrapuncti Duplicis" (Region of Double Counterpoint), where the towns of "alla Octava" and "alla Duodecima" are comfortably nestled between forested glades harboring fugues, suspensions, and canons (the "Sylva fugarum," "Sylva Sycopationum," and "Sylva Canonica," respectively). Beer's peace treaty condemns counterpoint for not fighting against the bunglers and adding "little interest to harmony," for which indiscretions it must live in the desert with canons and suspensions. But the treaty also warns that "if one sees no counterpoint in the land, one can be sure that bad times are coming and the bunglers will prevail."[46] Thus, as Stephen Rose has observed, the map not only equates contrapuntal procedures with mysterious, dark forests but further "suggests that counterpoint is a necessary buffer zone between figural music and the bunglers, and a way to distinguish a competent composer from a Frenchified dandy."[47]

For the Faithful Music Master, occasional visits to the contrapuntal region served to thin the canopy of these dark forests for his reader-pupils. Further confirmation that the land of counterpoint offered fertile, moral-instructional ground for musical *Liebhaber* comes in a tongue-in-cheek report of "moral news from the musical realm" in the journal *Der Musicalische Patriot* (Brunswick, 1741–42), edited by Johann Jakob Henke. Here we learn that in the city of

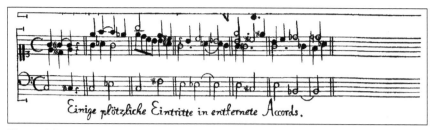

Figure 3.5. "Einige plötzliche Eintritte in entfernete Accords." *Der getreue Music-Meister* (Hamburg: Telemann, 1729), Lection 6.

Figure 3.6. C. P. E. Bach, *Miscellanea Musica,* Wq 121, page 22 (B-Bc, 5895).

Figure 3.7. Johann Beer, "Nova et Accurata Totius Regni Musici Descriptio," detail. From *Bellum musicum oder musicalischer Krieg* (no pl.: no pub., 1701). Reproduced by permission of Peter Lang.

Contrapunctopolis, "an ingenious artist has invented a machine that easily and unfailingly discovers errors in all fugues submitted to it by the investigator and from one canon makes many hundreds more, at the same time giving the most artistic and delicate performance one might behold. A rare thing."[48] Although Henke takes a satirical stab at the eighteenth-century fascination with automatons and musical machines, as well as at the mechanical nature of contrapuntal instruction, he apparently regards the moral status of fugues and canons as self-evident.

The Third Part: "Fair-Sexing" the Faithful Music Master

The second paragraph of Telemann's preface describes Hamburg, or perhaps Germany as a whole, as "a place where music appears to have its fatherland, as it were; where the highest and most reputable persons consider the art of music worthy of their attention; [and] where various noble families count virtuosos of both sexes among themselves." This expression of civic or national pride and recognition of the musical contributions of women echoes the chief aspirations of *Der Patriot* and *Die vernünfftigen Tadlerinnen*, namely, the elevation of the German language and the education of women in part to encourage a more natural mode of writing and speaking in the native tongue. Several of the Faithful Music Master's lessons more tangibly advance these causes, suggesting a philosophical kinship between the music journal and its periodical forerunners.

Devoting attention to women and their concerns as a way of building a female audience—what Jonathan Swift, in a derisive reference to the *Spectator*, called "fair-sexing it"—had long been an important focus of moral journals.[49] As Kathryn Shevelow notes, editors of English periodicals published between 1691 and 1713—men such as Joseph Addison, Daniel Defoe, John Dunton, Peter Motteux, and Richard Steele—extended

> numerous invitations to women to read, to write for, and to correspond with, the periodical; they declared the "equality" of women to men; they crusaded with varying degrees of intensity for improvements in women's education, coupling them with sometimes more vigorous crusades for improvements in women's behavior; they proclaimed their intention to use their periodicals to defend and serve women; and they variously represented women, as readers, as writers, as correspondents, and as illustrative figures, in their periodical texts.[50]

This self-consciously progressive and enlightened project to improve the social and educational standing of women had its limits, however, for it affirmed the normative association of femininity with domesticity and sought to define precisely what women should learn.[51] Of course, the project also had commercial motivations, insofar as it cast women "as the victims of social prejudice and neglect, and transformed their protest of their neglect into a merchandizing scheme for the periodicals themselves, constituted as remedies for social ills."[52]

The ruse behind *Die vernünfftigen Tadlerinnen* was that the three male editors or "sensible female scolds"—Gottsched, Hamann, and Johann Friedrich May—wrote under exclusively female pseudonyms, giving the impression that the journal was written for women by women.[53] These men, members of Leipzig's Deutschübende poetische Gesellschaft (later the Deutsche Gesellschaft), wished to cultivate the kind of common sense or "natural reason" that, in their view, women exemplified. As Katherine R. Goodman has observed of their attitude, "'Woman' embodied the average citizen who could address readers in a language which all citizens understood. . . . *Die vernünfftigen Tadlerinnen* constructed ideal female voices to serve as enlightened examples of what actual women might become, with the ultimate goal of elevating German national culture and challenging the intellectual hegemony of the French and the English."[54] The journal's project constituted a major salvo in the gender war fought over women's participation in German intellectual life, a war in which Gottsched was one of the principal combatants.[55] Hamann subsequently impersonated a forty-six-year-old widow from Upper Saxony as editor of *Die Matrone*, which began publication only months before *Der getreue Music-Meister*. In his first issue, Hamann acknowledged the influence of *Die vernünfftigen Tadlerinnen* and *Die Discourse der Mahlern* and indeed continued to promote the purity of the German language.[56]

The principal editors of *Der Patriot* were founders and members of Hamburg's Patriotische Gesellschaft (successor to the Teutschübende Gesellschaft), a society concerned with cultivating the German language and freeing it from foreign influence, in particular from the common practice of peppering texts with French, Italian, English, and Latin loan words (a priority shared with Gottsched and *Die vernünfftigen Tadlerinnen*). *Der Patriot* promoted clear thinking together with an unadorned, natural style of writing: "ein Teutscher ist gelehrt, wenn er sein Teutsch versteht" (a German is learned when he understands his own German), as the journal declared in its second issue.[57] The editors made a conscious effort to write consistently in such a way that even a craftsman and a farmer could benefit from the journal.[58]

Along with promoting the German "vermischter Geschmack" (mixed taste), a hybrid musical language amalgamating the French, Italian, English, and Polish idioms that native writers claimed was greater than the sum of its parts (a superior, if not quite pure, mode of expression), *Der getreue Music-Meister* reflects the emphasis on clarity of verbal expression in *Der Patriot* and *Die vernünfftigen Tadlerinnen*.[59] As early as its fifth issue, there is a shift from Gothic script (*Frakturschrift*) for German vocal texts to the Latin font previously reserved for foreign languages. One might interpret this move as a gesture toward the journal's non-German readership, small as it may have been, or as an acknowledgment that Gothic script did not print especially well.[60] But its effect was to place German on at least a visual par with French, English, and Italian while removing a sense of linguistic insularity. Perhaps not coincidentally, the first German vocal work to use the Latin font is the strophic minuetaria "Das Frauenzimmer," TVWV 25:37, in which music becomes a metaphor for perceived differences between the sexes (fig. 3.8):[61]

Das Frauenzimmer
verstimmt sich immer
nach Lust und Wind.
Drum Schade vor die Männer,
die keine rechte Kenner
vom Stimmen sind.

Die meisten Männer
sind schlechte Kenner
von Melodie.
Drum Schade vor die Frauen,
die ihnen sich vertrauen
zur Harmonie.

[Women always
Put themselves out of tune
Through air and wind.
So it's a shame for men,
Who aren't proper connoisseurs
Of tuning.

Most men
Are poor connoisseurs
Of melody.
So it's a shame for women
That they place their trust
In harmony.]

The author of these brief and unflattering verses—including a comparison of the female body to a musical instrument and a play on "stimmen/Stimmen," referring both to tuning and the overly active voices of women—was none other than Michael Richey, Telemann's colleague at Hamburg's Johanneum school and, as we have seen, the principal editor of *Der Patriot*.[62] The two had originally collaborated on "Das Frauenzimmer" in April 1724, when it was the sixth of seven arias heard during the otherwise lost Hamburg wedding serenata *Ihr zaubernden Töne! entzücket, berücket die Herzen*, TVWV 11:6.[63]

Figure 3.8. "Das Frauenzimmer," TVWV 25:37. *Der getreue Music-Meister* (Hamburg: Telemann, 1729), Lection 5.

If "Das Frauenzimmer" fails to emphasize the intellectual pursuits and achievements of women, two other works in the journal are more successful in this respect. The only cantata in *Der getreue Music-Meister*—and the first secular cantata published by Telemann—is *Ich kann lachen, weinen, schertzen*, TVWV 20:15, a setting of a libretto that had appeared a year earlier in Christiane Mariane von Ziegler's *Versuch in gebundener Schreib-Art* (Essay in the Poetic Mode; fig. 3.9).[64] Ziegler (1695–1760), a student and protégée of Gottsched, went on to publish two more volumes of her own poetry in addition to one of letters between 1729 and 1739; she won the Deutsche Gesellschaft's prize for poetry in 1732 and 1734 and was crowned imperial poet laureate by the philosophical faculty of the University of Wittenberg in 1733.[65] Whereas J. S. Bach had set nine of her sacred cantata libretti in 1725 (BWV 103, 108, 87, 128, 183, 74, 68, 175, and 176), Telemann's cantata is the earliest known setting of her secular poetry and the first setting of any of her texts to appear in print.

Why Telemann turned to Ziegler's poetry remains unclear, but there may have been long-standing personal connections between the two. She was the daughter of the former Leipzig merchant and bürgermeister Franz Conrad Romanus (1671–1746), who in 1701 helped launch Telemann's professional career as a composer by "coaxing" the young university student to write a sacred vocal work for the Leipzig Thomaskirche every two weeks and then supporting his appointment as organist and music director of the Neue Kirche in 1704.[66] Thus Telemann may have known her from the time she was a small

Figure 3.9. *Ich kann lachen, weinen, schertzen*, TVWV 20:15, mm. 1–13. *Der getreue Music-Meister* (Hamburg: Telemann, 1729), Lection 19.

child. Three decades later, she was listed among the advance subscribers to Telemann's *Musique de table* of 1733 ("Mad.^me de Ziegler. Leipzig."), which was probably heard during the musical salons she hosted in her Leipzig home and garden. These salons included performances of music Ziegler sometimes obtained from out-of-town kapellmeister, and in the 1729 poem "Zu einer Garten-Musik," she hears a beautiful overture and mentions Telemann, Bach, and Handel as possible composers.[67]

Although none of Ziegler's correspondence with musicians appears to survive, her published volume of letters, the *Moralische und vermischte Send-Schreiben, an einige Ihrer vertrauten und guten Freunde gestellet* (Moral and Miscellaneous Epistles to Several of Her Acquantainces and Good Friends), includes one to an unidentified kapellmeister who could well be Telemann. The undated, and possibly fictitious, letter was written in response to a package of music the musician sent to Ziegler, who expresses her pleasure with the two trios, overture-suite, and two concertos, though she would have preferred the latter works to be "zärtlicher und schmeichelhaffter, und nicht so ernsthafft" (more tender and flattering, and not so serious).[68] Regarding the trios, Ziegler supposes that they were originally for oboes but have been adapted for her to play on flute, then requests of her correspondent that "the next time you send me a company of musical peoples [*Noten-Völckern*], you mustn't bother yourself with translating, as I am of the firm opinion that a piece losing its proper instruments through arrangement will forfeit the greatest part of its pleasantness."[69] The "musical peoples" could refer to two Telemann overture-suites characterizing various foreign peoples or perhaps to the trio-suite portraying historical and mythological women in *Der getreue Music-Meister*, discussed below.[70] In this respect, it may be more than coincidental that Ziegler signs the letter "Dero getreue Freundin" (Your faithful friend), one of only two signoffs in the volume that use "getreue."[71] Elsewhere in the letter, Ziegler reveals her musical aesthetics to be closely aligned with Telemann's:

> I have come to believe that playing an adagio requires a greater artist than playing an allegro, since the former strikes me as much more lovely and charming. I know many who display great dexterity in their playing and are therefore widely considered to be virtuosos. But as far as grace and embellishments are concerned, one must look for them among the rests. Most art surely consists more of elegance than velocity; therefore, those who only have eyes and ears for leaping notes often prefer to make more out of a brief minuet or polonaise than a concerto or overture-suite and turn *galanterie* compositions into the kind of artificial and heavily scored pieces that cause us the greatest difficulty in learning them, very much against all reason. But to each his own.[72]

Telemann's similar distaste of virtuosity for its own sake is well-known from his recollection of first encountering concertos early in his career.[73] And Ziegler's apparent preference for minuets, polonaises, and other *galanterien* over "artificial and heavily scored pieces" not only places her in good company among *Liebhaber* of the time but recalls Telemann's dedicatory poem to his recently published minuet collection, the *Sept fois sept et un menuet* (Seven Times Seven and One Menuet; Hamburg, 1728), TWV 34:1–50, in which we read:

> Und ist dir ein Concert von vielen Stimmen wehrt,
> so darf die Menuet sich darum nicht verstecken.
> Zudem diß kleine Ding ist so geringe nicht.
> Denn wißt, daß man dabey gar viel erwägen müsse:
> Gesang und Harmonie, Erfindung und Gewicht,
> Und was es mehr bedarf, sind keine taube Nüsse.

> [And if you value a concerto with many parts,
> The menuet needn't suffer by comparison.
> Moreover, this little thing is not so modest.
> For know that one must give much consideration to it:
> Melody and harmony, invention and weightiness,
> And what it doesn't need are empty heads.]

Regardless of whether Ziegler's correspondent was Telemann (or was intended to remind her readers of the composer), it redounded to the Faithful Music Master's moral credentials that she was a frequent contributor to *Die vernünfftigen Tadlerinnen*, writing under as many as ten male pseudonyms.[74] Her contributions to this journal argued that women were men's equals, spoke more eloquently than men, should receive better educational opportunities than was generally the case, and ought to be allowed to write poetry without the involvement of male editors. The fact that Ziegler played the recorder and flute—instruments seldom associated with German women—further reflects her advocacy of women's rights to operate in realms normally dominated by men.[75] The libretto Telemann chose for *Der getreue Music-Meister* is not typical of Ziegler's secular cantatas, in which women are often "chaste objects of male desire" in an imagined pastoral setting.[76] Instead, the two arias and recitative promote a moral message of maintaining equanimity in the face of hardship, the first aria proudly proclaiming:

Ich kan[n] lachen, weinen, schertzen,
Alles ist mir einerley.
Mein gesetzter Sinn kan sagen,
Vor den allergrösten Plagen
Hab ich weder Furcht noch Scheu.[77]

[I can laugh, cry, joke;
It's all the same to me.
My composed mind can say:
I have neither fear nor dread
Of the greatest troubles.]

If the first volume of Ziegler's *Versuch in gebundener Schreib-Art* was intended as a provocation—a collection of predominantly *galant*, secular poetry rather than the sacred poetry more usually associated with women; frequent sexual and erotic references; and publication under the author's real name, unusual for women at the time—then the Faithful Music Master's inclusion of one of its texts may be considered provocative as well and perhaps even a rejoinder to the severe criticism Ziegler endured in the aftermath of the volume's appearance during 1728–29.[78] At the same time, the moral theme of *Ich kann lachen, weinen, schertzen* was itself uncontroversial.

There is, finally, an additional connection between *Der getreue Music-Meister* and *Die vernünfftigen Tadlerinnen*. Gottsched and his editor colleagues appear to have selected their pastoral pseudonyms of Calliste (Gottsched), Phyllis (May), Iris (Hamann), and Clio (Lucas Geiger) from the *Nutzbares, galantes und curiöses Frauenzimmer-Lexicon* (Useful, Gallant, and Curious Women's Dictionary), a wide-ranging collection of practical information on French court gallantry, orthodox religion, household tips, and female figures from history and mythology.[79] The dictionary was recommended by *Die vernünfftigen Tadlerinnen*, and earlier by *Die Discourse der Mahlern* and *Der Patriot*, as belonging to a proper *Frauenzimmer-Bibliothek* (lady's library).[80] Yet in their invocation of Arcadian female characters, the editors of *Die vernünfftigen Tadlerinnen* failed to pay homage to the adventurers, heroines, scholars, rulers, and religious heretics also found in the *Frauenzimmer-Lexicon*. For Goodman, this omission reflects the journal's view that, despite the innate equality of the sexes, women's "(divinely) assigned social role is different"; that women ought to be better educated but not on a par with men and certainly not to the extent that they might wish to assume societal roles outside the traditional ones of housekeeper, wife, and mother.[81]

The exemplary women absent from *Die vernünfftigen Tadlerinnen* are supplied by the Faithful Music Master in a characteristic trio-suite (TWV 42:C1) that includes five movements bearing their names.[82] That Telemann also used the *Frauenzimmer-Lexicon* as a source for these names, and in doing so tacitly endorsed the aims of both the dictionary and *Die vernünfftigen Tadlerinnen* with respect to female education, is suggested by the presence in the *Lexicon* of entries corresponding to the suite's movement titles: Clælia, a courageous Roman maiden who escaped from the Etruscan king Lars Porsenna; Corinna, a Greek poet; Dido, queen of Carthage; Lucretia, the martyred wife of the Roman nobleman Tarquinius Collatinus; and Xantippe, the sharp-tongued wife of Socrates.[83] The suite is scored for two recorders, flutes, or violins and continuo, with the option of doubling the treble parts in concerto grosso fashion. Following the prelude ("Introduzzione a tre"), a curious hybrid of French overture and da capo form, are rude syncopations for Xantippe, an elegiac sarabande for Lucretia, a jolly rigaudon for Corinna, and rushing triplets for Cl[a]elia (fig. 3.10). Dido receives a movement expressing both sadness and desperation in "Triste" solos alternating with "Disperato" tuttis.

Telemann's modest portrait gallery of admirable historical and mythological women not only conflates the literary and the musical, as does the Gulliver Suite (with which it overlaps in *Der getreue Music-Meister*), but also invokes the visual, as if to insist that these women deserve their own spots on the wall. In fact, such aural portraits may be likened in function to the painted and engraved portraits that were ubiquitous in eighteenth-century daily life and which, as art historian Louise Lippincott observes, not only "recorded history, heroes, virtue, and friendship" but also "taught morality, enforced loyalty, and represented tradition." Because judging the quality of portraits involved primarily attentiveness to detail and a measure of common sense rather than extensive knowledge of history, literature, and aesthetics, portraiture, as Lippincott notes, "was considered an appropriate aesthetic interest for women, not only as sitters but also as painters and patrons."[84] Like visual and literary portraits, those in the suite encourage women readers to imagine themselves as the titled personages: every "female" at eighteen, Edward Mangin observed decades later, "sees her picture" in a novel's "charming and sorrowful heroine."[85] The Faithful Music Master's heroines, flawed though they may be, hint at what modern women might achieve while making a not-so-veiled reference to the educational project of *Die vernünfftigen Tadlerinnen*.[86]

Figure 3.10. "Clelia," mm. 1–9. Trio in C Major, TWV 42:C1. *Der getreue Music-Meister* (Hamburg: Telemann, 1729), Lection 16.

Reading *Der getreue Music-Meister* as a moral journal promoting the refinement and elevation of German culture and elucidating the role educated women might play in achieving that goal reveals its course of instruction as progressive and ethically minded. As a published poet who associated closely with Hamburg's leading literary figures, a self-proclaimed autodidact impelled to educate others, and a successful entrepreneur who was sensitive to his customers' needs, Telemann designed *Der getreue Music-Meister* to be as much an instrument for moral improvement as its literary counterparts.[87] No other eighteenth-century journal of music, it seems fair to say, offered consumers such an engaging mixture of entertainment and enlightenment. Like the spectators, tattlers, and patriots of his day, the Faithful Music Master could edify readers sitting in armchairs at home or around tables at popular coffeehouses. One didn't have to be positioned at a keyboard or behind a music stand to profit from his lessons.

Appendix 3.1: *Der getreue Music-Meister*, Preface

Geneigte Leser!

[1] Es würde das gegenwärtige Werk, von dessen Inhalte der Titul bereits hinlängliche Nachricht ertheilet, ohne Vor-Rede geblieben seyn, wann ich nicht den Raum dieses leren Blates mit etlichen schwarzen Buchstaben zu schmücken gedächte. Bey solcher Gelegenheit könnte ich meinen Lesern dessen Wehrt schmeichlerisch anpreisen; allein, wie ich mich dadurch einer unordentlichen Selbst-Liebe schuldig machte, also würde ich selbiges vieleicht auch in Verdacht bringen, als ob es dergleichen Aufputzes bedürfte. Demnach sage ich nur, daß es ein musicalisches Journal sey, und, meines Wissens, das erste, so, vermittelst wirklicher Music, in Teutschland, zum Vorschein kommt. Haben sonst die so genannten monatliche, oder solche, Schriften, die zu gewissen Zeiten Stückweise herauskommen, vielfältig ihre Liebhaber gefunden, so solte ich glauben, es werde auch diese nicht gar verworfen werden, da sie, mit jenen, den Zweck hat, zu nutzen und zu belustigen.

[2] Man könnte mir indeß etwan einwerfen, daß es von einer einzelnen Person nicht wenig gewagt sey, dergleichen Werk zu unternehmen, worin so vielerley Sachen vorgetragen werden sollen. Es ist wahr, und habe ich mich desswegen lange bedacht, ehe ein fester Schluß gefasset worden; ich sehe auch im Voraus, daß manche

Gentle Reader!

[1] The present work, the contents of which are already adequately described by the title, would have remained without a preface had I not thought to decorate the space of this empty page with a few black letters. With such an opportunity, I could have flatteringly extolled its worth to my readers. However, since I would thereby have been guilty of an inappropriate self-love, I would perhaps have cast suspicion on myself as requiring such finery. Accordingly, I shall only say that it is a musical journal and, to my knowledge, the first with real music to appear in Germany. If the so-called monthly journals, or those that appear piecemeal at various times, have found their many enthusiasts, then I expect that this one will not be rejected by those whom it aims to benefit and entertain.

[2] One could surely make the point, however, that it is quite daring for a single person to undertake a work in which such varied things are to be presented. This is true, and I have thought about it at length before coming to a firm conclusion. I foresee that many lessons may be accompanied with a certain amount of

Lection mit etwas Schweiß begleitet seyn dürfte, ob ich mich schon einiger massen darauf verlassen könnte, daß mich die Noten bisher fast so bald gesuchet, als ich mich nach ihnen umgesehen. Aber, weil der Mensch der Arbeit wegen, und um dem Nächsten zu dienen, lebet, so habe ich mich endlich diese Hinderniß nicht anfechten lassen, zumal, da ich darauf gerechnet, ich würde zur muntern Fortsetzung dieser Sätze auch dadurch angefrischet werden, weil ich mich an einem Orte befinde, wo die Music gleichsam ihr Vaterland zu haben scheinet, wo die höchsten und ansehnlichsten Personen die Ton-Kunst ihrer Aufmerksamkeit würdigen, wo verschiedene vornehme Familien Virtuosen und Virtuosinnen unter den ihrigen zehlen, wo so mancher geschickter Lehrling der Music die Hoffnung machet, daß sie hier beständig wohnen werde, und wo endlich der Schau-Platz so viele bündige Gedancken auswärtiger Componisten durch die auserlesensten Stimmen dem Gehöre mittheilet.

perspiration, though to some degree I have been able to depend on the fact that so far the notes have sought me almost as soon as I have looked for them. However, because man lives for work and in order to serve others, I have in the end not let this obstacle hinder me, especially as I have reckoned that I would thus be inspired to the lively continuation of these pieces, for I find myself in a place where music appears to have its fatherland, as it were; where the highest and most reputable persons consider the art of music worthy of their attention; where various noble families count virtuosos of both sexes among themselves; where so many skillful students of music hope to live permanently; and where, finally, so many terse thoughts of foreign musicians are heard on the stage, performed by the most select voices.

[3] Damit aber diese Blätter desto mehr Veränderung haben mögen, so lasse ich mir nicht entgegen seyn, wenn auch andere, zu deren Anfüllung, einigen Beytrag thun wollen, da man denn die Namen der HHrn. Verfasser, wo Sie solche kund machen, hinzufügen wird, sich aber auch zugleich ausbedinget, daß Sie das Einzuschickende Post-frey machen wollen.

[3] In order that these pages may have all the more variety, I will not be opposed if others wish to make some contribution to filling them up, whereby the names of the authors will be added, should they make them known, but on the condition that the contributions are sent with sufficient postage.

[4] Sollte dieser Music-Meister mit einer gütigen Aufnahme beehret, mithin dessen Lectionen fortgesetzet werden, so dürfte ich, wenn es meine Geschäffte zulassen, von Zeit zu Zeit über jedes Stück desselben eine Untersuchung drucken lassen, so sich aber nur auf meine eigenen Stücke beziehen würde, und wodurch ich allerhand Vorteile zeigen könnte, die in der Practic mit Nutzen anzuwenden wären.

[4] Should this Music-Master meet with a warm reception, so that its lessons continue, I may, when my duties permit, print a discussion of each piece from time to time (but only concerning my own pieces), in which I would show all sorts of advantages that might profitably be applied in practice.

[5] Weiter habe ich nichts mehr vorzutragen, als daß ich von den Music-Liebhabern mir eine gewogene Meinung, so wohl über diese, als meine übrige, Arbeit erbitte, der ich verharre

[5] I have nothing further to express, except to request a favorably disposed opinion of me from musical amateurs, as much for this as my other work, to whom I remain

Deroselben
ergebenst- und dienst-schuldigster
Telemann.

Your
most humble and obedient
Telemann.

Notes

I am grateful to Ann Le Bar for helpful comments on an earlier version of this chapter.

1. The appeal of the periodical in London, which in many respects set the tone for continental publications, is neatly summed up by Shawn Lisa Maurer, *Proposing Men: Dialectics of Gender and Class in the Eighteenth-Century English Periodical* (Stanford: Stanford University Press, 1998), 12: "The periodical offered its readers an invaluable means of orienting themselves within the dizzying abundance of a rapidly changing world both by making that world familiar to them and by telling them what and how to think about it." Compare the description of Hamburg's coffeehouses during the period 1727–29 in Thomas Lediard, *The German Spy; or, Familiar Letters from a Gentleman on His Travels thro' Germany to His Friend in England*, 2nd ed. (London: T. Cooper, 1740), 95: "I visited, the next Morning, the most noted Coffee-house, kept by an *Italian*, called *Galli*, where there was a handsom[e] Appearance of fashionable Company; but I found their Meeting there was only to play at Billiards, or Tables, read the

News, or spend an Hour in Conversation, without the least Sign of any Business being transacted; And, I am told, it is the same in other Coffee-houses."

2. Although it is not known whether the Burmeisters subscribed to *Der getreue Music-Meister* (no list of subscribers was printed), they can be connected to at least three other Telemann publications issued by the composer in Hamburg: Rudolph and Hieronymus were the dedicatees of the *Continuation des sonates méthodiques* (1732); Rudolph, Hieronymus, Johann Wilhelm, and Henricus appear in the list of advance subscribers to the *Musique de table* (1733); and Rudolph, Hieronymus, and Johann Wilhelm were the dedicatees of the *XII Solos à violon ou traversière* (1734).

3. Telemann, *Der getreue Music-Meister* (Hamburg: Telemann, 1728–29), title page: "Der getreue / Music-Meister, / welcher / so wol für Sänger als Instrumentalisten / allerhand Gattungen musicalischer Stücke, / so auf verschiedene Stimmen und fast alle gebräuchliche Instrumente / gerichtet sind, / und / moralische, Opern- und andere Arien, / dessgleichen / TRII, DUETTI, SOLI etc. / SONATen, OUVERTUREn, etc. / wie auch / FUGEN, CONTRAPUNCTe, CANONES, etc. enthalten, / mithin / das mehreste, was nur in der Music vorkommen mag, / nach Italiänischer, Französischer, Englischer, Polnischer, etc. / so ernsthaft- als lebhaft- und lustiger Ahrt, / nach und nach alle 14. Tage / in einer LECTION / vorzutragen gedenket, / durch / Telemann." All translations in this chapter are my own.

4. For example, the two sets of *VI moralische Cantaten* (Hamburg, 1735 and 1736), TVWV 20:23–28 and 20:29–34. For commentary on and critical editions of these works, see Steven Zohn, ed., *Georg Philipp Telemann: Kammerkantaten*, Georg Philipp Telemann: Musikalishe Werke, vol. 44 (Kassel: Bärenreiter, 2011). An impression of the audience for Telemann's publications can be gained from the lists of advance subscribers printed in his *Musique de table* (Hamburg, 1733) and *Nouveaux quatuors en six suites* (Paris, 1738). See Steven Zohn, *Music for a Mixed Taste: Style, Genre, and Meaning in Telemann's Instrumental Works* (New York: Oxford University Press, 2008), 359–66.

5. See John Van Cleve, "Family Values and Dysfunctional Families: Home Life in the Moral Weeklies and Comedies of Bach's Leipzig," in *Bach's Changing World: Voices in the Community*, ed. Carol K. Baron (Rochester, NY: University of Rochester Press, 2006), 94–96.

6. For an overview of the music in *Der getreue Music-Meister*, see Zohn, *Music for a Mixed Taste*, 400–410. The journal's production and dissemination are discussed throughout chapter 7. A list of the journal's contents is provided in Martin Ruhnke, ed., *Georg Philipp Telemann: Thematisch-Systematisches Verzeichnis seiner Werke*, vol. 1 (Kassel: Bärenreiter, 1984), 242–46. *Der getreue Music-Meister* and several other serial music publications by Telemann are listed alongside Hamburg literary periodicals in Holger Böning and Emmy Moepps, *Hamburg: Kommentierte Bibliographie der Zeitungen, Zeitschriften, Intelligenzblätter, Kalender und Almanache sowie biographische Hinweise zu Herausgebern, Verlegern und Druckern periodischer Schriften: Von den Anfängen bis 1765* (Stuttgart-Bad Cannstatt: Frommann-Holzboog, 1996), esp. cols. 364–67 (*Der getreue Music-Meister*). Böning and Moepps (col. 424) quote a newspaper advertisement for

Telemann's serially issued collection of songs with pedagogical commentary, the *Singe- Spiel- und General-Bass-Übungen* (Hamburg: Telemann, 1733–34), that refers to the publication as a "Journal," making explicit the connection between literary and music periodicals. Holger Böning, *Der Musiker und Komponist Johann Mattheson als Hamburger Publizist: Studie zu den Anfängen der Moralischen Wochenschriften und der deutschen Musikpublizistik* (Bremen: Edition Lumière, 2011), 408–17, draws a suggestive parallel between Telemann's serial publication of the *Harmonischer Gottesdienst* (Hamburg, 1725–26) and *Auszug derjenigen musicalischen und auf die gewönlichen Evangelien gerichteten Arien* (Hamburg, 1727) and the weekly publication of sermon drafts in Hamburg.

7. These included the *Recueil d'airs sérieux et à boire de différents auteurs* (monthly from 1695 to 1724) and the *Meslanges de musique latine, françoise et italienne . . . Suite du recüeil de differents Auteurs* (seasonally from 1725 to 1732).

8. The Walsh-Hare *Monthly Mask* appeared in the years 1702–11, 1717–27, and 1737–38. Concerning this and other song periodicals in London, see Olive Baldwin and Thelma Wilson, "'Revived by the Publisher of the Former Masks': The Firm of John Walsh and the *Monthly Mask*, 1717–27 and 1737–38," *Royal Musical Association Research Chronicle* 42, no. 1 (2009): 1–44.

9. One might also link *Der getreue Music-Meister* with the private *Klavierbüchlein* tradition, represented most famously by several manuscript notebooks compiled by the Bach family in Köthen and Leipzig for instructional and recreational purposes. See, among recent writings on these notebooks, Yael Sela, "Anna Magdalena Bach's *Büchlein* (1725) as a Domestic Music Miscellany," *Understanding Bach* 5 (2010): 87–97, http://www.bachnetwork.co.uk/understanding-bach/ub5/; David Yearsley, "Death Everyday: The Anna Magdalena Bach Book of 1725 and the Art of Dying," *Eighteenth-Century Music* 2, no. 2 (2005): 231–49.

10. A 1728 catalog of Telemann's publications listing Crownfield as his London agent is reproduced in Georg Philipp Telemann, *Briefwechsel*, ed. Hans Grosse and Hans Rudolf Jung (Leipzig: VEB Verlag für Musik, 1972), 124–25, and transcribed in Ruhnke, *Thematisch-Systematisches Verzeichnis*, 231–32.

11. The composer's 1725 letters to the Eisenach court mentioning his London correspondence are transcribed in Telemann, *Briefwechsel*, 81 and 83. No English-language writings by him are known.

12. Zohn, *Music for a Mixed Taste*, 347–48, 367–68.

13. As might be expected, the emphasis in these journals is on keyboard music (sonatas and single movements, many bearing characteristic titles) and German songs and odes. Most of the works in the two Berlin publications are by local composers (esp. Johann Friedrich Agricola, C. P. E. Bach, Carl Fasch, Carl Heinrich Graun, and Johann Philipp Kirnberger); the *Musicalisches Vielerley* also contains music by Berliners but is dominated by Bach and his brother Johann Christoph Friedrich. In all three publications, instrumental chamber music is far less common than in *Der getreue Music-Meister* (which included music for recorder, chalumeau, viola pomposa, viola da gamba, horn, and lute, none of which instruments appear in the later journals), and there is an almost complete lack of the kind of pedagogical material provided by the Faithful Music Master.

14. Friedrich Wilhelm Birnstiel, *Musikalisches Allerley von verschiedenen Tonkünstlern* (Berlin: Birnstiel, 1760), preface: "Nachricht. Diese Blätter werden alle Sonnabende fortgesetzt, und sind dazu bestimmt, die neuesten musikalischen Versuche guter Tonmeister in Sing- und Spielsachen, Clavier- Violin- und Flötenstücken, etc. kleinern und größern Aufsätzen, Oden, Arien, etc. Polonoisen, Menuetten, Märchen, etc. Duetten, Trios, Fugen und Synfonien, etc. charakterisierten Stücken und Sonaten, im deutschen, italienischen, und französischen Geschmack, zu sammeln, und nach und nach zum Vorschein zu bringen. Ich empfehle sie dem gütigen Beyfalle der Kenner und Liebhaber, und verspreche mir selbigen um desto eher, weil die Sammlung mit Wahl und Prüfung unternommen, und nicht jeder Aufsatz ohne Unterscheid in selbige aufgenommen werden wird."

15. However, as Böning points out (*Der Musiker und Komponist Johann Mattheson als Hamburger Publizist*, 188–93), elements of later moral weeklies are already present in Johann Frisch's *Erbauliche Ruh-stunden / Das ist: Merkwürdige und nachdenkliche Unterredungen* (Hamburg: Henrich Heuß, 1676–80).

16. On the circulation of *Der Patriot*, which reached five thousand copies (with an actual readership estimated between eleven thousand and sixty thousand), see Herbert Rowland, "The Journal *Der Patriot* and the Constitution of a Bourgeois Literary Public Sphere," in *Patriotism, Cosmopolitanism, and National Culture: Public Culture in Hamburg 1700–1933*, ed. Peter Uwe Hohendahl (Amsterdam: Rodopi, 2003), 68. The influence of *Der Patriot* extended to Britain, for Thomas Lediard (*The German Spy*, x–xi) noted that his travelogue of Germany had borrowed allegories and fables from the journal, "a weekly Paper publish'd in *Hamburg*, in Imitation of our incomparable *Spectators*, and which is allow'd, by all good Judges, to come up the nearest to the Spirit of those great Originals, of any Thing that has been publish'd of that Nature." Other German moral journals from this period, published mainly in Leipzig and Hamburg, are likely to have been known to Telemann; for example, *Der Leipziger Spectateur* (Frankfurt, Hamburg, and Leipzig, 1723), *Der Leipziger Patriot* (Leipzig, 1724), *Der rechtschaffene Rahtgeber* (Hamburg, 1724), *Der Patriotische Medicus* (Hamburg, 1724–27), *Leipziger Socrates* (Leipzig, 1727–28), *Der allgemeine und alles-verbessernde Patriot* (Hamburg, 1727–28), *Die Matrone* (Hamburg, 1728–30; discussed below), and *Der Sachsen Spiegel* (Leipzig, 1728). For lists of German-language moral weeklies and similar periodicals published before 1730, see Wolfgang Martens, *Die Botschaft der Tugend: Die Aufklärung im Spiegel der deutschen Moralische Wochenschriften* (Stuttgart: J. B. Metzler, 1971), 544–45, 548–49; Böning and Moepps, *Hamburg: Kommentierte Bibliographie*.

17. Kißner was also the publisher of Telemann's *Auszug derjenigen musicalischen und auf die gewönlichen Evangelien gerichteten Arien* in 1727.

18. For recent studies of Mattheson's journals, including *Der Vernünfftler*, *Critica Musica*, and *Der Patriot*, see Böning, *Der Musiker und Komponist Johann Mattheson als Hamburger Publizist*, chapters 4, 6–7; Martin Krieger, "*Vernünfftler* und *Patriot*: Johann Mattheson und das Netzwerk der Hamburger Patrioten," in *Johann Mattheson als Vermittler und Initiator: Wissenstransfer und die Etablierung neuer Diskurse in der ersten Hälfte des 18. Jahrhunderts*, ed. Wolfgang Hirschmann and

Bernhard Jahn (Hildesheim, Germany: Olms, 2010), 61–74; Dirk Hempel, "*Der Vernünfftler:* Johann Mattheson und der britisch-deutsche Kulturtransfer in der Frühaufklärung," in Hirschmann and Jahn, eds., *Johann Mattheson als Vermittler und Initiator,* 99–113. Telemann assisted Mattheson in lining up advance subscribers to the second part of *Critica Musica* in 1724. See Telemann, *Briefwechsel,* 216.

19. Böning, *Der Musiker und Komponist Johann Mattheson als Hamburger Publizist,* 371–77; David Yearsley, "The Musical Patriots of the Hamburg Opera: Mattheson, Keiser, and *Masaniello furioso,*" in Hohendahl, ed., *Patriotism, Cosmopolitanism, and National Culture,* 34–35.

20. Gloria Flaherty, *Opera in the Development of German Critical Thought* (Princeton: Princeton University Press, 1978), 94–95, 102–4. As we shall see below, the notion that pleasure and entertainment make instruction more palatable was common in moral journals.

21. *Memoirs for the Ingenious; or, the Universal Mercury* 1, no. 1 (January 1694): "The Preface," [v]; *Monthly Miscellany; or, Memoirs for the Curious* 1, no. 1 (January 1707): "The Preface," [ii]. In 1734, Telemann himself used the identical formulation in a note following the last work in his serially published "journal" *Singe- Spiel- und General-Bass-Übungen:* "We hereby bring these exercises to a close and hope that the desired goal of benefiting and entertaining has been attained" (Hiermit beschliessen wir diese [Ü]bungen, u[nd] wünschen, dass der abgezielte [Z]weck, nützen u[nd] zu belustigen, erlanget seȳn möge).

22. *Universal Mercury* 1, no. 1 (January 1726): 1–2 (italics original). This passage from the preface to Edward Bysshe's *The Art of English Poetry* (London: R. Knaplock, E. Castle, and B. Tooke, 1702), referencing a collection of quotations, captures the desire for pleasure and variety embodied by moral journals and *Der getreue Music-Meister:* "The Melange of so many different Subjects, and such a Variety of Thoughts upon them (which, if I am not deceiv'd, give an agreeable Goût to the whole) may not satisfie you so well as a Composition perfect in its kind on one intire Subject; but possibly it may divert and amuse you better, for here is no thread of Story, nor connexion of one Part with another, to keep the Mind intent, and constrain you to any length of Reading"; quoted in Darryl P. Domingo, "Unbending the Mind: Or, Commercialized Leisure and the Rhetoric of Eighteenth-Century Diversion," *Eighteenth-Century Studies* 45, no. 2 (2012): 207.

23. *Spectator* 1, no. 10 (March 12, 1711): 1 (italics original); James Ralph, *The Touch-Stone; or, Historical, Critical, Political, Moral, Philosophical and Theological Essays upon the Reigning Diversions of the Town* (London: Printed and sold by the booksellers of London and Westminster, 1728), 130; quoted in Domingo, "Unbending the Mind," 224.

24. J. Paul Hunter, *Before Novels: The Cultural Contexts of Eighteenth-Century English Fiction* (New York: W. W. Norton, 1990), 298.

25. Domingo ("Unbending the Mind," 211) finds English authors satisfying this desire through "luxuriant, illogical, and mixed metaphors; typographical blanks and lacunae; interpolated tales; burlesque erudition; and the devices of digressive wit." Hunter (*Before Novels,* 47) also notes the discursive quality of

eighteenth-century novels, which often incorporate "stories-within" the main narrative.

26. Lection 1, pp. 1, 4; Lection 3, p. 10.

27. For example, no verbal cues indicate continuations of the duet for pairs of recorders, flutes, or violas da gamba, TWV 40:107 (Lections 3–5), and the suite for violin, oboe, or flute and continuo, TWV 41:g4 (Lections 3–7). One could easily guess that a sonata would eventually run to three or four movements in a fast-slow-fast or slow-fast-slow-fast sequence, but the number and character of suite movements were more unpredictable.

28. The preface to *Memoirs for the Ingenious; or, the Universal Mercury* 1, no. 1 (January 1694): sig. A2, noted that "for *Theology*, we leave it wholly to *Divines*, except such Parts of it as may fall in our way with *History*, *Chronology*, or *Genealogies*."

29. On this phenomenon, see Kathryn Shevelow, *Women and Print Culture: The Construction of Femininity in the Early Periodical* (London: Routledge, 1989), 37–47. The editors of *The Muses Mercury; or, the Monthly Miscellany* 1, no. 1 (January 1707): "Introduction," [vii], announced that "any person that is pleas'd to send us a Poem, or any Thing else for our *Mercury*, is desir'd to Forbid us Printing his Name to it, if he is not willing to have us make use of it; Otherwise we shall take it for granted that he will not be displeas'd if we do it." *Tatler* 1, no. 7 (April 23–26, 1709): 1, called upon its readers to render assistance just a few weeks after commencing publication: "If any Gentleman or Lady sends to *Isaac Bickerstaff[e]* Esq; at Mr. *Morphew's* near *Stationers-Hall*, by the Penny-Post paid, the Grief or Joy of their Soul, what they think fit of the Matter shall be related in Colours as much to their Advantage, as those in which *Gervase* has drawn the Agreeable *Chloe*." *Der Patriot*, too, encouraged readers to submit letters and later recognized the best ones with prizes. See Rowland, "The Journal *Der Patriot*," 55.

30. Lection 8, p. 30; Lection 10, p. 39.

31. Lection 2, p. 8.

32. In figure 3.1, the measures numbered 1–4 on the left are paired with the corresponding numbered measures on the right. Concerning the *Sei suonatine* and its frontispiece, including a reproduction of the engraving, see Zohn, *Music for a Mixed Taste*, 278–81. See also the discussion of the contrapuntal variations in David Yearsley, *Bach and the Meanings of Counterpoint* (Cambridge: Cambridge University Press, 2002), 124–25.

33. Lection 21, p. 82.

34. The fugue subjects and chorale melodies given to the Jacobikirche applicants are reprinted in Heinrich Miesner, *Philipp Emanuel Bach in Hamburg: Beiträge zu seiner Biographie und zur Musikgeschichte seiner Zeit* (Heide, Germany: Emil Sund, 1929), 124. Miesner's transcription of the fourth subject (third in *Der getreue Music-Meister*) departs from the published version in several respects. For the chorale melodies and fugue subjects connected with organ auditions held by Telemann in 1759, see Georg Philipp Telemann, *Der Tag des Gerichts: Ein Singgedicht in vier Betrachtungen von Christian Wilhelm Alers; Ino: Kantate von Karl Wilhelm Ramler*, ed. Max Schneider, Denkmäler deutscher Tonkunst, vol. 28 (Graz: Akademische Druck- und Verlagsanstalt, 1958), xliv. Concerning

organ auditions in eighteenth-century Hamburg more generally, see Arnfried Edler, *Der nordelbische Organist: Studien zu Sozialstatus, Funktion und kompositorischer Produktion eines Musikerberufes von der Reformation bis zum 20. Jahrhundert* (Kassel: Bärenreiter, 1982), 193–200; Jürgen Neubacher, "Der Hamburger St. Petri-Organist Johann Ernst Bernhard Pfeiffer (1703–1774) und die Organistenproben unter Mattheson (1725) und Telemann (1735)," in *"Critica musica": Studien zum 17. und 18. Jahrhundert: Festschrift Hans Joachim Marx zum 65. Geburtstag,* ed. Nicole Ristow, Wolfgang Sandberger, and Dorothea Schröder (Stuttgart: J. B. Metzler, 2001), 222, 226; Steven Zohn, "Naïve Questions and Laughable Answers: An Eighteenth-Century Job Interview," in *Coll'astuzia, col giudizio: Essays in Honor of Neal Zaslaw,* ed. Cliff Eisen (Ann Arbor, MI: Steglein, 2009), 62–92.

35. Lection 13, pp. 51–52; Lection 14, p. 55. The scene is transcribed in Yearsley, *Bach and the Meanings of Counterpoint,* 149.

36. Yearsley, *Bach and the Meanings of Counterpoint,* 148–55.

37. For example, in the *Spectator* 1, no. 10 (March 12, 1711): 1, Addison promised that he would "endeavour to enliven Morality with Wit, and to temper Wit with Morality." Rowland ("The Journal *Der Patriot*," 67) observes that satire is one of the "principal modes of expression" in *Der Patriot,* in which "one encounters numerous comical ideas and considerable whimsy, such as the magic instruments that crop up here and there," even though "the authors are so concerned they will be misunderstood that they directly interpret the vast majority of their satiric dreams, allegories, and the like."

38. Lection 8, pp. 29, 32; Lection 9, p. 36; Lection 10, p. 40; Lection 11, p. 44. Jonathan Swift, *Des Capitains Lemuel Gulliver Reisen in unterschiedliche entfernte und unbekandte Länder,* trans. Christoph Gottlieb Wend, 3 vols. (Hamburg: Thomas von Wierungs Erben, 1727–28). Although early moral weeklies were generally critical of novels, Swift's was one of the few to meet with editorial approval: only months before the Faithful Music Master printed his duet, *Der Biedermann* ("Drey und sechzigstes Blatt" [July 19, 1728]: 49) included the *Reisen Gullivers* on a short list of pleasant and instructive novels. For a discussion of the duet with reference to Swift's novel, see Zohn, *Music for a Mixed Taste,* 329–31.

39. Lection 4, p. 16 (Zelenka, ZWV 179); Lection 15, p. 60 (Schmidt); Lection 17, p. 68 (Bach); Lection 19, p. 75 (Dirnslot).

40. No. 5, p. 20; no. 12, p. 48 ("Erste Menuet").

41. Keith Chapin, "Counterpoint: From the Bees or for the Birds? Telemann and Early Eighteenth-Century Quarrels with Tradition," *Music and Letters* 92, no. 3 (2011): 404–7. Although six of ten contrapuntal items appear in small print, such reduced notation is not otherwise confined to the "Lilliputsche Chaconne" and the alternative continuo part for the "Napolitana" ("Bass zur Hautbois d'Amour"; Lection 10, p. 40), as Chapin claims (405). Small print is also used for the last five measures of the "Giga" concluding Telemann's "Ouverture à la Polonoise" (or "Ouverture burlesque") for keyboard, TWV 32:2 (Lection 22, p. 88); the ritornellos framing "Ich folge dir bis zur Welt ende" from the opera *Die Last-tragende Liebe, oder Emma und Eginhard,* TVWV

21:25 (Lection 23, p. 90); and the last ten measures of the "Vivace" from the "Sonata di chiesa à diversi stromenti," TWV 41:g5 (Lection 23, p. 92). Although Chapin is correct that the aria from *Die verkehrte Welt* is unusual in requiring a page turn and being split up between two issues of the journal, it is not quite true that elsewhere "Telemann respected the integrity of discrete movements and arias" (405). There are six additional examples of arias or instrumental movements continued across issues: "Süsse Worte! wehrte Zeilen!" from the opera *Sancio, oder die siegende Grossmuth*, TVWV 21:20 (Lections 7–8); "Più del fiume dà diletto" from the opera *Aesopus bei Hofe*, TVWV 21:26 (Lections 10–11); the opening movement of the trio suite, TWV 42:C1 (Lections 11–12); the second movement of the Sonata in F Minor for bassoon and continuo, TWV 41:f1 (Lections 12–13); the pastoral aria "Säume nicht, geliebte Schöne," TVWV 25:38 (Lections 21–22); and "Ich folge dir bis zur Welt ende" (Lections 23–24).

42. *Der Patriot*, no. 69 (April 26, 1725): "die Patriotischen Blätter, ausser ihrer besonderen Annehmlichkeit und deutlichen Ausdrückung, vor andern gelehrten Schrifften auch diesen Vorzug haben, daß sie zugleich häuffig in ungelehrter und solcher Leute Hände gerahten, welche zwar selbige mehrentheils aus Neugierde lesen, gleichwohl aber dabey unvermerckt und ohne ihre Absicht zu mehrerer Einsicht und besserem Gebrauche ihres Verstandes gelencket werden." The journal printed two earlier letters from the Patriotische Gesellschaft of Christianstadt (no. 57, February 1, 1725; no. 59, February 15, 1725). In his commentary to the modern edition of *Der Patriot*, Wolfgang Martens describes the first letter as a "presumably authentic submission" but also suggests that Christianstadt is a fictitious location rather than the present-day Polish city of Krzystkowice. See Martens, ed., *Der Patriot*, vol. 4 (Berlin: Walter de Gruyter, 1984), 212, 214, 217. If the three Christianstadt letters were entirely fabricated by the editors of *Der Patriot*, then the above quotation can be read as an aspirational view of the journal's readership.

43. For Walther's reference to *Der getreue Music-Meister*, see his letter to Heinrich Bokemeyer of March 8, 1735, in Johann Gottfried Walther, *Briefe*, ed. Klaus Beckmann and Hans-Joachim Schulze (Leipzig: VEB Deutscher Verlag für Musik, 1987), 186. Telemann's letter to the Auric court is transcribed in Telemann, *Briefwechsel*, 123. A second copy of the journal at the Sächsische Landesbibliothek–Staats- und Universitätsbibliothek Dresden (D-Dlb, Mus. 2392-B-1) surfaced as recently as 2011. See "Leere Fächer füllen sich," Hofmusik Dresden, July 15, 2011, http://hofmusik.slub-dresden.de/news/details/single/leere-faecher-fuellen-sich/.

44. Lection 6, p. 24.

45. This scenario is suggested by David Yearsley, "C. P. E. Bach and the Living Traditions of Learned Counterpoint," in *C. P. E. Bach Studies*, ed. Annette Richards (Cambridge: Cambridge University Press, 2006), 192. The *Miscellanea Musica* is held at the library of the Koninklijk Conservatorium in Brussels (B-Bc, 5895). For an inventory of its contents, see Ulrich Leisinger and Peter Wollny, eds., *Die Bach-Quellen der Bibliotheken in Brüssel: Katalog* (Hildesheim: Olms, 1997), 352–55.

46. Johann Beer, *Bellum musicum* (n.p., 1701), sig. E1r and E2r. Modern edition in Johann Beer, *Sämtliche Werke*, vol. 12, no. 1, ed. Ferdinand van Ingen and Hans-Gert Roloff (Bern: Peter Lang, 2005), 435–36: "Der gedoppelte Contrapunct sich von den Stümpern nicht zum fechten begrauchen lassen / Er auch der Harmonie nicht allzu grosses Interesse bringet / als soll derselbe nebst denen Canonibus und Syncopationibus in der Terra deserta wohnen. . . . Wann man in dem Land keinen Contrapunct sehe / solle man nur sicher gläuben / daß böse Zeiten kommen / und die Stümper überhand nehmen werden."

47. Stephen Rose, *The Musician in Literature in the Age of Bach* (Cambridge: Cambridge University Press, 2011), 176.

48. *Der Musicalische Patriot*, no. 15 (December 21, 1741): 119: "Moralische Neuigkeiten aus dem Reiche der Music. Contrapunctopolis. Hier hat ein geschickter Künstler eine Machine erfunden, vermittelst welcher man zu allen aufgegebenen Fugen gar leicht ohne allem Fehler den Verfolger finden, und aus einem Canone viele hundert andere machen und zugleich die allerkünstlichste und niedlichste Ausführung für sich sehen kann. Ein rar Stück." On Henke's journal, see Böning, *Der Musiker und Komponist Johann Mattheson als Hamburger Publizist*, 435–39.

49. Jonathan Swift, *Journal to Stella: Letters to Esther Johnson and Rebecca Dingley, 1710–1713*, ed. Abigail Williams (Cambridge: Cambridge University Press, 2013), 384 (letter 40, February 8, 1712): "I will not meddle with the Spectator, let him fair-sex it to the world's end."

50. Shevelow, *Women and Print Culture*, 3–4.

51. For a survey of German attitudes toward women's education at this time, see Peter Petschauer, "Eighteenth-Century German Opinions about Education for Women," *Central European History* 19, no. 3 (1986): 262–92.

52. Shevelow, *Women and Print Culture*, 53.

53. For a general study of the journal, see Susanne Niefanger, *Schreibstrategien in moralischen Wochenschriften: Formalstilistische, pragmatische und rhetorische Untersuchungen am Beispiel von Gottscheds "Vernünfftigen Tadlerinnen"* (Tübingen: Niemeyer, 1997).

54. Katherine R. Goodman, *Amazons and Apprentices: Women and the German Parnassus in the Early Enlightenment* (Rochester, NY: Camden House, 1999), 72, 93.

55. Katharine R. Goodman, "From Salon to *Kaffeekranz*: Gender Wars and the *Coffee Cantata* in Bach's Leipzig," in Baron, ed., *Bach's Changing World*, 190–200.

56. See Böning and Moepps, *Hamburg: Kommentierte Bibliographie*, cols. 354–64; Holger Böning, *Welteroberung durch ein neues Publikum: Die deutsche Presse unter der Weg zur Aufklärung: Hamburg und Altona als Beispiel* (Bremen: Edition Lumière, 2002), 259–61. During the eighteenth century, it was not unusual for English-speaking male writers to publish as women for one reason or another. For example, Benjamin Franklin began his literary career in the 1720s by writing essays for the *New-England Courant* as the young widow Silence Dogood, who advocated women's education. See Susan Staves, "'The Abuse of Title Pages': Men Writing as Women," in *A Concise Companion to the Restoration and Eighteenth Century*, ed. Cynthia Wall (Malden, MA: Blackwell, 2005), 164–66.

57. *Der Patriot*, no. 2 (January 13, 1724); quoted in Martens, *Die Botschaft der Tugend*, 410.

58. *Der Patriot*, no. 36 (September 7, 1724).

59. On Telemann's relationship to and promotion of the "vermischter Geschmack," see Zohn, *Music for a Mixed Taste*, 3–5.

60. In the preface to his so-called biblical sonatas, Johann Kuhnau observed that "Im übrigen sind die anfänglich in Italiänischer Sprache unter die Noten gesetzten Worte behalten worden / theils weil die teutsche Schrifft im Kupffer-Stiche nicht gar wohl gerathen will" (It remains to be said that the Italian words originally inserted beneath the music have been retained partly because German letters do not come out too well in engraving). Kuhnau, *Musicalische Vorstellung Einiger Biblischer Historien, In 6. Sonaten / Auff dem Claviere zu Spielen / Allen Liebhabern zum Vergnügen versuchet von Johann Kuhnauen* (Leipzig: Kuhnau, 1700), [vii].

61. Lection 5, p. 18.

62. Imagery similar to Richey's is found decades later in a song text from Johann Friedrich Wilhelm Wenkel's *Clavierstücke für Frauenzimmer* (Berlin, 1771). The song is reprinted and discussed in Matthew Head, *Sovereign Feminine: Music and Gender in Eighteenth-Century Germany* (Berkeley: University of California Press, 2013), 52–53.

63. The serenata's text was reprinted after Richey's death as "Das Concert des Ehestandes / in einem Singgedichte / bey dem / Coldorf- und Tönnieschen / Vermählungsfeste / in Hamburg / 1724. den 18 April / nach Telemannischer Aufführung," in Michel Richey, *Deutsche Gedichte*, vol. 2 (Hamburg: Johann Georg Fritsch, 1764), 133–40.

64. Lection 19, pp. 74–75; Lection 20, pp. 78–79; Christiane Mariane von Ziegler, *Versuch in gebundener Schreib-Art* (Leipzig: Johann Friedrich Brauns sel. Erben, 1728), 212.

65. On Ziegler's life and career, see Mark A. Peters, *A Woman's Voice in Baroque Music: Mariane von Ziegler and J. S. Bach* (Aldershot: Ashgate, 2008), chapter 1; Goodman, *Amazons and Apprentices*, chapters 4–6.

66. Telemann recounts his contact with Romanus in his 1718 and 1740 autobiographies: "Lebens-Lauff mein Georg Philipp Telemanns; Entworffen In Frankfurth am Mayn d.10.[–14.] Sept. A. 1718," in Johann Mattheson, *Grosse General-Baß-Schule. Oder: Der exemplarischen Organisten-Probe* (Hamburg: Johann Christoph Kißner, 1731; repr. Hildesheim: Georg Olms Verlag, 1968), 173; Johann Mattheson, *Grundlage einer Ehren-Pforte* (Hamburg: Mattheson, 1740; repr. Kassel: Bärenreiter, 1969), 359.

67. The poem appeared in Ziegler's *Versuch in gebundener Schreib-Art, anderer und letzter Theil* (Leipzig: Johann Friedrich Brauns sel. Erben, 1729), 297. Cited in Peters, *A Woman's Voice in Baroque Music*, 21.

68. Christiana Mariane von Ziegler, *Moralische und vermischte Send-Schreiben, an einige Ihrer vertrauten und guten Freunde gestellet* (Leipzig: Johann Friedrich Brauns sel. Erben, 1731), 393. The possibility that Telemann was the letter's addressee is also raised by Mark A. Peters, "Christiana Mariana von Ziegler's

Sacred Cantata Texts and Their Settings by Johann Sebastian Bach" (PhD diss., University of Pittsburgh, Pittsburgh, PA, 2003), 101–2.

69. Ziegler, *Moralische und vermischte Send-Schreiben*, 392: "Ich will Sie indessen ersuchen, daß, wenn Sie mir eine Compagnie von Noten-Völckern wiederum einschicken solten, Sie sich nicht mit der Ubersetzung bemühen dürfften, weil ich der sichern Meynung bin, daß einem Stücke, welches von seinen eigenthümlichen Instrumente in die Versetzung verfällt, der gröste Theil der Annehmlichkeit benommen werde."

70. The overture-suites are TWV 55:G4 (including movements titled "Les Allemands anciens," "Les Allemands modernes," "Les Suédois," and "Les Danois") and 55:B5 ("Les Turcs," "Les Suisses," "Les Moscovites," and "Les Portugais"). For discussions of these works, see Zohn, *Music for a Mixed Taste*, 75–80.

71. The other instance is "Dero unveränderte getreue Freundin" (Your unchanging, faithful friend). *Moralische und vermischte Send-Schreiben*, 340. Among the other eighteen signoffs in the volume, many of which appear multiple times, there is also one instance of "treue" (64).

72. Ziegler, *Moralische und vermischte Send-Schreiben*, 393: "Es bedüncket mich, daß adagio einen grössern Künstler zu spielen, als allegro, erfordere, wiedenn das erstere mir weit lieblicher und entzückender vorkömmt. Ich kenne viele die bey ihren Spielen eine grosse Fertigkeit bezeigen, und deswegen von manchen vor Virtuosen gehalten werden, wenn man aber nach Anmuth und Manieren fraget, so muß man selbige unter den Pausen mit suchen. Die meiste Kunst bestehet wohl in der Zierlichkeit mehr, als in der Geschwindigkeit, daher diejenigen; so nur auf die springenden Noten sehen und hören, offt aus einer flüchtigen Menuet oder Polognese mehr als aus einen Concert oder Ouvertüre machen, und die Galanterie-Compositiones denenjenigen künstlich und schwer gesetzten Stücken, die uns in Erlernung selbiger die gröste Mühe machen, vielmahls wider alle Billigkeit vorziehen. Doch einem jeden nach seinen Geschmack."

73. Mattheson, *Grosse General-Baß-Schule*, 176.

74. Goodman, *Amazons and Apprentices*, 68.

75. In a letter to one of her female friends (*Moralische und vermischte Send-Schreiben*, 406–9), Ziegler explained that she favored wind instruments over the more usual lute and keyboard (both of which she played as well) because of the honor such novelty could win her and because many French women played the flute. Ziegler was also praised as a singer, as noted in Goodman, "From Salon to *Kaffeekranz*," 211.

76. Goodman, *Amazons and Apprentices*, 141.

77. Ziegler, *Versuch in gebundener Schreib-Art*, 211.

78. On the nature of this criticism and the steps Ziegler took to address it, see Goodman, *Amazons and Apprentices*, 146–52.

79. Gottlieb Siegmund Corvinus, *Nutzbares, galantes und curiöses Frauenzimmer-Lexicon* (Leipzig: Johann Friedrich Gleditsch und Sohn, 1715). See Regina Nörtemann, "Schwache Werkzeuge als öffentliche Richterinnen: Zur fiktiven weiblichen Herausgeber- und Verfasserschaft in Moralischen Wochenschriften

des 18. Jahrhunderts," *Archiv für Kulturgeschichte* 72, no. 2 (1990): 389. Letters published in *Der Patriot*, many of which appear to have been written by the editors, were often signed with pastoral or humorous (male) pseudonyms such as Philotheus, Jephilandro, J. H. Sanfftmuht, Curiosus Neographus, Mimus, Sincerinus, Philander, Theophilus, Euphemius von Allermann, and Caspar Volatilius. Rowland, "The Journal *Der Patriot*," 55.

80. Goodman, *Amazons and Apprentices*, 83–84.

81. Ibid., 85.

82. Lection 11, p. 41; Lection 12, p. 47; Lection 13, p. 52; Lection 14, p. 56; Lection 15, p. 60; Lection 16, p. 64; Lection 17, p. 68.

83. Corvinus, *Frauenzimmer-Lexicon*, cols. 359, 372, 415–16, 1175, 2149–50. Among the five women, only Dido, Lucretia, and Xantippe have entries in two other popular literary reference works of the time: Johann Christoph Männling's *Poetisches Lexicon darinnen die schönsten Realia und auserlesensten Phrases aus denen berühmtesten Poeten Schlesiens so dann eine vollständige Historia Mythologica derer heydnischen Götter und Göttinnen* . . . (Frankfurt an der Oder: Schrey, 1700), 106, 241, 457; and Johann Georg Hamann's *Poetisches Lexicon oder nützlicher und brauchbarer Vorrath von allerhand poetischen Redens-Arten, Beywörtern, Beschreibungen, scharffsinnigen Gedancken und Ausdrücken; nebst einer kurtzen Erklärung der mythologischen Nahmen, aus den besten und neuesten deutschen Dichtern zusammen getragen* . . . (Leipzig: Groß, 1737), 343, 622, 912. Männling's dictionary was revised as *Deutsch-Poetisches Lexicon, der auserlesensten Phrasiologi, aus denen vornehmsten Poëten* . . . *und andern hellen Sternen Schlesiens* . . . *nebst der Historia Mythologica, der heydnischen Götter und Göttinen* . . . (Frankfurt an der Oder: Schrey, 1715), and Hamann's dictionary, first published in 1725, saw further editions in 1751 and 1765.

84. Louise Lippincott, "Expanding on Portraiture: The Market, the Public, and the Hierarchy of Genres in Eighteenth-Century Britain," in *The Consumption of Culture 1600–1800: Image, Object, Text*, ed. Ann Bermingham and John Brewer (London: Routledge, 1995), 81–82.

85. Edward Mangin, *An Essay on Light Reading* (London: Carpenter, 1805), 14; quoted in Peter H. Pawlowicz, "Reading Women: Text and Image in Eighteenth-Century England," in Bermingham and Brewer, eds., *Consumption of Culture*, 49.

86. Although perhaps intended to appeal especially to women readers of *Der getreue Music-Meister*, the suite does not readily fall into the category of music "for the fair sex," in the sense of later published works aimed at an exclusively female clientele. On this repertory, see Head, *Sovereign Feminine*, chapter 2.

87. A partial list of Telemann's published poetry is given in Steven Zohn, "Telemann, Georg Philipp," §4: "Hamburg," *Grove Music Online*, accessed July 15, 2014, www.oxfordmusiconline.com. On Telemann's status as an autodidact and its implications for his public image, see Zohn, *Music for a Mixed Taste*, 380–81; Steven Zohn, "Images of Telemann: Narratives of Reception in the Composer's Anecdote, 1750–1830," *Journal of Musicology* 21, no. 4 (2005): 479–85.

Chapter Four

Eighteenth-Century Mediations of Music Theory

Meter, Tempo, and Affect in Print

Roger Mathew Grant

If the Enlightenment is understood as an event in the history of mediation—as Clifford Siskin, William Warner, and others have productively suggested—then printed music made a considerable contribution to that event.[1] The pages of music scores formed an important part of both public and private life in the eighteenth century, and new forms of publication allowed consumers increased access to them. This century saw the growth of music engraving, the invention of lithography, and a huge increase in the sheer number and variety of music printers and publishers.[2] These developments took place within a rapidly evolving world of print culture more generally, as the proliferation of journals changed the quotidian relationships between print materials and their consumers while also affording new opportunities to advertise commercial print goods. Scholarship on book history and on music printing and publishing has begun to draw attention to the important role printed artifacts played in the history of thought and in everyday life.[3]

Still, not all of the Enlightenment's printed objects were either books or scores; some were a bit of both. Put another way, a huge quantity of printed music is often ignored or forgotten in discussions of eighteenth-century book history: the musical examples included in books about music. Apart from simply falling between the typical scholarly divisions, musical examples present interesting challenges to the history of mediation. Hidden from direct view within the pages of words that enclose them, they are nodes of connection between media that allow us to ask questions about the uses and conceptualizations of print material. They are integrated into the text that surrounds them—and most often dependent upon it for complete comprehensibility—but they cannot be read in the same way as that text, and they do not have the same function.[4]

One particular type of example, focused on meter and affect, dramatizes the disparity between media that are mixed on the page. Eighteenth-century books on music often contained lengthy taxonomies of meter in the form of omnibus musical examples. These taxonomies were intended to demonstrate the uses and varieties of meters and were also meant to build and reaffirm the sensibilities that allowed musicians to gauge the correct tempi and affects for pieces of music. The notion that musicians should be able to determine the right or "just" tempo, the *tempo giusto*, from the meter signature, note values, and character of a piece of music was alive and well in the eighteenth century, though the method of communicating this knowledge in written form was fraught with difficulty. Print dissemination had made it abundantly clear to Europeans that there was no way to control the wide remit of music. As Sarah Adams has demonstrated, the eighteenth century was a crucial turning point in the international dissemination of printed music, with well-developed networks of distribution allowing for exchanges of musical material that traversed the furthest reaches of continental Europe, Scandinavia, and beyond.[5] As composers and theorists acknowledged that music notation might circulate in new and unexpected ways, they also came to the concomitant realization that there was no way to ensure that their music would always fall into the hands of a musician who was able to determine the just tempo from the notation alone. Taxonomies of meter were one attempt to solve this problem, though the object of their focus was the single thing they could never successfully communicate. Lacking any objective time unit for tempo measurement (Maelzel's mechanical metronome was first patented and distributed in 1815), taxonomies of meter would ultimately fail in their efforts to capture musical time. But in the period during which they were produced, they did important if imprecise work for meter, tempo, and the related sciences of feeling and affect to which these concepts were bound.

Taxonomies of meter are forgotten aspects of both book history and affect theory, and as such they constitute a significantly understudied facet of Enlightenment mediation. They are also important sources for the history of music as a commodity. The many different forms they took chronicle shifting attitudes about the communicative abilities of didactic prose and musical examples, as well as changing relationships between the circulation of knowledge about music and its consumption. These taxonomies tell the story of an aspirational but finally unhappy relationship among print commodities, performance, and the passions. Bringing these curious fragments of printed music into the foreground, a tale of the missed connections between affect and consumer print culture emerges in rich detail.

Two Taxonomies

Charles Antoine Vion's *La musique pratique et theorique* (1742) is an unassuming little book with the modest goal of introducing its readers to the basic elements of musical practice and literacy, not unlike many of the early modern *musica practica* treatises that served as its models.[6] But open its pages to the chapter on meter and one finds a surprising outpouring of examples. This chapter is easily the most eye-catching for the wealth of printed music lavished on the explanation of meter; it occupies roughly an eighth of the entire book, using seventy musical examples to make its point.

Vion calls this chapter a "Modele des differens Degrés de Mouvement, pour toutes sortes de Mesures": not simply a collection of information on meter but a "*modele*," or tool, for discerning the relationship between the different meter signatures and the tempo and feeling appropriate to each of them. To accomplish this task, he pairs explanatory prose with excerpts from the music of his day. He follows each of the seventeen meter signatures described with a short collage of incipits bearing identifying labels. These are drawn from works as celebrated as Lully's operas and as obscure as exercises from the older theorist Michel L'Affilard. The prose and examples are meant to be used in cross-reference with each other such that tempo and affect are properties that emerge from a synthetic understanding of the words and the printed music collected under the heading of each meter signature.

To understand how Vion's tool for tempo might have worked, consider the difference he draws between the meters C ($\frac{4}{4}$) and 2 ($\frac{2}{2}$). "The measure of four is beat *slowly*," we are told. It is often employed "for the recitatives of motets, cantatas, and of opera," though it might also be used for allemandes, sonatas, and adagios.[7] These prefatory words introduce us to a stately meter, not to be rushed, which is associated with a particular set of generic contexts. The examples that follow, reproduced as figure 4.1, are intended to reinforce and further nuance this point through the sonic properties they encode. They include a recitative from Nicolas Bernier's "Motet du tres St. Sacrement" from his opus 2 collection (the first example), the first words sung by Angélique in the first act of Lully's *Roland* (the second example), and the opening of Campra's motet "Florete prata" (the sixth example).[8] We get some idea of this meter signature from the prose and examples presented here and a still better idea of it when we contrast this information with that provided for the next meter signature, 2 (fig. 4.2): "The measure of two 2 is ordinarily fast: one employs it in the overtures of opera, marches, ballets, branles, bourées, etc."[9] The corresponding example set for 2 includes pieces that are easily contrasted with those in the C collection. It begins, for instance, with the opening of the prologue from Lully's *Roland* (the first example, marked OUVERTURE); it also includes the first sung music in that same opera (the second example) and a gavotte from Act II, Scene 5 (the fifth example). Vion takes care to include a march (the fourth example, from André Cardinal Destouches's opera *Issé*), a branle (the sixth example, which is from Jacques-Martin Hotteterre's opus 2, fourth suite), and a ballet (the seventh and final example, Joseph Bodin de Boismortier's opus 52, the third ballet).

Contemplating this ensemble of words and notation together, we can begin to gauge the differences in tempo and affect Vion meant to communicate about these two meters. The reserved qualities and moderate tempo of C stand in contrast to the lively dances and energy of the lighter signature 2, and the music Vion has assembled affords an opportunity to call to mind these qualities in a more effective and immediate way than prose while also lending the discourse the authority of established musical practice. Vion's examples allow us to glimpse how the *tempo giusto* system might have functioned and the role of books like his in its codification and reinforcement.

Not all example sets were as well organized and coordinated as Vion's. Johann Philipp Kirnberger's *Die Kunst des reinen Satzes in der Musik* (1771–79) contains one of the century's most extensive discussions of tempo, meter, and rhythm, accompanied by multifarious musical examples. But Kirnberger's opening set of excerpts worked rather differently than those in Vion's volume. After explaining the nature of *tempo giusto* and the way meters and note values work together to indicate it, Kirnberger asks his readers to contemplate a lengthy, unlabeled assemblage of incipits, reproduced as figure 4.3.

Stretching across five pages in the treatise, this unwieldy composite example is difficult to overlook. It stands between the introductory words on tempo and meter and the specific explanations of each meter signature contained in subsequent sections. Like the examples in Vion's volume, this collection stages interactions between and among the meters, though Kirnberger features only four (C, $\frac{3}{4}$, $\frac{6}{8}$, and $\frac{3}{8}$) in this elaborate display. On closer scrutiny it becomes apparent that this example is meant to draw on previous experience—perhaps even tacit knowledge—to allow a range of affective qualities to emerge from the notated elements on the page. The Allemande from J. S. Bach's Sixth Partita (the fourth excerpt in C) is, for instance, intended to be slower than the animated Corrente from the same piece (the last excerpt in $\frac{3}{8}$). Even though both of these excerpts of music contain many short note values, the syncopated character and the generic expectations of the Corrente work in tandem with the $\frac{3}{8}$ meter signature to bring its speed up past the reserved quality of the Allemande's C meter signature. Kirnberger also varies qualities within the

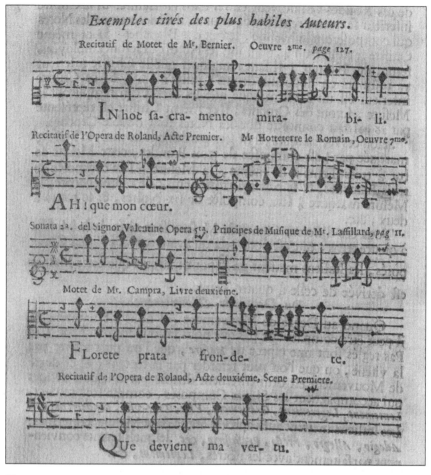

Figure 4.1. Examples for meter signature C in Charles Antoine Vion, *La musique pratique et theorique* (Paris: Jean-Baptiste-Christophe Ballard, 1742), 22. Courtesy of the Irving S. Gilmore Music Library, Yale University, New Haven, CT.

categories of meter he has set out: the third excerpt in $\frac{6}{8}$, from François Couperin's "La Diligente," is meant to be felt in two, with triple subdivisions of each beat. The preceding example in that same meter, however, features mid-measure cadences, showing that its $\frac{6}{8}$ meter is really composed of two smaller units of $\frac{3}{8}$ combined within each measure.[10] As Kirnberger explains, "Each of these excerpts distinguishes itself from the others through a characteristic motion that is felt primarily through the differences found in tempo and meter and—for those in which the same tempo and meter is found—the differences in note values in which the melody is composed."[11] The space created

Figure 4.2. Examples for meter signature 2 in Charles Antoine Vion, *La musique pratique et theorique* (Paris: Jean-Baptiste-Christophe Ballard, 1742), 23. Courtesy of the Irving S. Gilmore Music Library, Yale University, New Haven, CT.

for their comparison in the printed music of this example takes up a majority of the pages devoted to tempo in Kirnberger's text, and it is followed by the more detailed treatments of each of the twenty-four meter signatures his book describes. Though it might have been possible for readers to refer back to this collage of incipits after having read and absorbed the doctrine that follows, none of the examples contained within it is ever explained or even mentioned in the rest of Kirnberger's text. Kirnberger expected his readers to have a certain amount of experience and knowledge on the connection between tempo and notation.

For their lengthy sets of examples to work, both Vion and Kirnberger relied upon the basic conceptual structure of mimetic transference as a central component of aesthetic experience. In this view, art mediated the world for its beholders, and the effect of art depended on its ability to imitate nature and the naturally expressive. Although music had never done an excellent job of reproducing nature's beautiful objects (apart, perhaps, from waterfalls and birdcalls), it could nevertheless invoke the passions by means of imitating

Figure 4.3. Johann Philipp Kirnberger, *Die Kunst des reinen Satzes in der Musik* (Berlin and Königsberg: G. J. Decker and G. L. Hartung, 1776), 2:107–11.

Figure 4.3.—*(continued)*

Figure 4.3.—*(concluded)*

sounds tied to their natural expression. The doubling of the passion repre-sented in the pathway of signification from nature, through art, to our senses wrapped affect theory up with aesthetics.[12]

Kirnberger's investment in classical mimesis is explicit in the prose he uses to introduce his composite example. Indeed, the example itself seems to be the outgrowth of an aesthetic directive on the affective capacities of meter that finally exceeds the ability of his explanatory words and finds its most complete form in the five pages of printed music that follow:

> The composer must never forget that every melody should be a natural and true representation or depiction of a mood or feeling, insofar as these can be depicted by a succession of tones. The term *Gemüthsbewegung*, which we Ger-mans give to passions or affections, already points to their analogy with *Bewe-gung* [tempo]. In fact, every passion and every feeling—in its internal effect as in the terms through which it is made manifest—has its faster or slower, fiercer or calmer *Bewegung*, and the composer must accurately capture this according to the type of feeling he has to express. . . .
>
> But *Bewegung* in music is not simply confined to the various degrees of slowness and speed. For just as there are some passions in which "impressions flow forth in regular manner like a gentle stream; others in which they surge ahead faster with a moderate gurgling but without delay; others in which the sequence of impressions resembles a wild river swollen by heavy rain that rushes violently away, carrying with it everything that happens to be in its path; and still others in which the mind is like a wild sea in its impressions, hammering the shore powerfully, then retreating and crashing again with new force"; so can the *Bewegung* of a melody be severe or tender, skipping or steady, fervid or languid, even when the degree of speed or slowness is the same, depending on the type of note values out of which the melody is com-posed. Consider the following examples.[13]

Not only does this passage lay bare Kirnberger's commitment to classical mimetic ideals, it also demonstrates his adaptation of this doctrine to the intri-cate workings of the *tempo giusto* system in great detail. Speed and slowness were not enough to communicate the passions. Instead, the passions—like the *tempo giusto*—were emergent properties created out of particular combinations of meter, note values, and characteristic composition. With correct application, the performer not only arrived at the just tempo but could also achieve the transmission of just feeling. Music could thereby fulfil the mimetic imperative of the era's principal aesthetic theory.

On the one hand, Kirnberger's abstract directives about music reach out-side themselves to a world of practice through the example set, in an attempt to make concrete the points set forth in prose. But on the other, the text also interlinks with documents on aesthetics, folding itself into the contemporary conversation on mimesis. The second paragraph quoted above contains a quotation Kirnberger borrowed from the aesthetic encyclopedia compiled by his collaborator Johann Georg Sulzer, the *Allgemeine Theorie der schönen Künste*. Sulzer writes at the head of the quoted article, "The correct expression of the sentiments or passions in all of their special tintings is the most important—if not the only—merit of a perfect musical composition."[14] Sulzer, Kirnberger, and their circle contributed discourse to a body of theory that was increasingly interested in music as the arch imitator of the passions. Earlier in the century, for example, the Abbé Dubos had related music's affective capabilities to the mimetic capacity of the visual arts: "Just as the painter imitates the features and colors of nature, so the musician imitates the tones, accents, sighs, inflections of the voice, and indeed all of those sounds with which nature exudes the sentiments and passions."[15] Charles Batteux extended that comparison, suggesting that musical experience could act as "a sort of canvas that is meant to carry, sustain, conduct, and connect the various passions."[16] For James Beattie, the "end of all genuine music is to introduce into the human mind certain affections, or susceptibilities of affection." There is, he continued "[an] analogy, if not similitude, between certain musical sounds, and mental affections."[17] Music in this tradition was a conduit of affective relays, and meter—as Kirnberger and many others were keen to explain—was one of its chief devices.[18]

In this sense, the books of music theory that provided elaborate sets of examples to explain the affects and tempi of meter signatures were doing the work of mediating between the world of aesthetic theory and the world of performance. The musical examples in these books occupied an interstitial space, translating the domain of sound for the intellectual environment that called upon it to do so much. They supplemented aesthetic theory with a technology of music symbols, supplying the best-known format of demonstration available to books in printed letters. Without its examples, this body of theory would have been reduced to sets of unsubstantiated proclamations or perhaps collections of citations to music its readership might have already known.

But a closer look at some of these example sets raises questions about whether they really could have escaped the problem of foreknowledge—whether the material and intellectual conditions within which their technology operated could ever have skirted the issue of previous experience. The authors of these didactic examples were not only trying to elucidate a point of aesthetic theory, they were also wrestling with a problem of tempo notation through the very medium that had created it. Unlike other types of examples, these amalgamated the symbols of notation to demonstrate a musical parameter that had no proper place in inscription. So, by contrast with examples related to harmony, for instance, in which the marks on the page that make up a vertical sonority directly signify a particular combination of precise pitches, these examples do not show the markings for the objects of their study (tempo and affect). Instead, they show the marks of the other parameters more tradition-ally notated (pitch, rhythm, meter, register, and so forth) and leave the tempo and affect as judgments to be distilled therefrom. Even if they did not require the reader to know the pieces within the example (which is itself debatable), they needed to be read within a certain tradition of notational interpretation that demanded a great deal of training. Because tempo—and certainly affect—were not qualities that had found definitive expressions through music nota-tion, these examples could only come close to their ultimate goal without ever mediating tempo successfully.

The Limits of Print

Examples in treatises, because they provide many different types of informa-tion at once, are telling markers of these books' imagined consumers. Not only can we learn what general sorts of music were sold and enjoyed alongside them vis-à-vis their intertextual references, we can also assess the worlds of musical knowledge and experience within which they were indended to circulate. This becomes acutely apparent in examples concerning meter, tempo, and affect specifically because the object of these examples was impossible to capture within the book. Examples and prose squirm past this akwardness in myriad revealing ways. They also have something to tell us about an eighteenth-cen-tury awareness of the changing patterns in which music was consumed and distributed.

Toward the close of his influential *Gradus ad parnassum* (1725), Johann Joseph Fux includes a section on the variety of fugue subjects. As part of this demonstration, he provides an example in which he reproduces a single duet in three notational contexts, shown in figure 4.4. The first version of this canon, in the long notes of the *stile antico*, is kept at a fairly lively tempo with its ¢, *alla breve* meter signature. By contrast, the same duet in C requires shorter note values and the Italian term Presto to bring it up to speed with the origi-nal. Diminuting the note values further in the third example, Fux reins in the tempo with the marking Adagio. Ideally, all three versions sound at roughly the same speed, though the notational differences imply subtle shadings of affect. Here, Fux draws on the eighteenth-century belief that shorter note values indi-cate faster tempi, though meter signatures and tempo terms can alter their implied speed. His example relies on his trained readers' ability to understand the equivalences and interpret the meter signatures, note values, and paratexts in conjunction with each other. Because the example—like the others in his treatise—aims at verisimilitude but cannot sound for its readers, their knowl-edge of the emergent property of tempo must do this extra work.

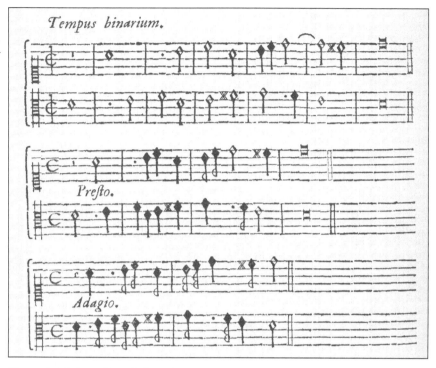

Figure 4.4. Johann Joseph Fux, *Gradus ad parnassum* (Vienna: Johann Peter van Ghelen, 1725). In *Monuments of Music and Music Literature in Facsimile*, series 2, vol. 24 (New York: Broude Brothers, 1966), 238. Reproduced by permission of Broude Brothers.

What for Fux seems obvious is for Kirnberger, writing in the middle of the century, slightly less straightforward. Further into his treatment of meter, in an effort to distinguish between $\frac{6}{8}$ and $\frac{6}{16}$, he interrupts the course of his discussion with an unprepared rhetorical question: "To whom is this Bach Fugue unknown?" Below it, he reproduces an incipit of the Fugue in F Major in $\frac{6}{16}$ (BWV 880) from the second book of *Das wohltemperierte Klavier*, along with a version of the same theme written in $\frac{6}{8}$ (fig. 4.5). He continues: "If one translates this theme into $\frac{6}{8}$, the tempo is instantly no longer the same, the pace is quite labored, the pitches—particularly the passing tones—are delivered with too heavy a weight; in short, the expression of the entire piece is worse, and it is not at all the one that Bach gave to it."[19] Within a single paragraph, Kirnberger mixes presumed knowledge and instruction, words and music notation—all in a somewhat anxious mood. Although he assumes that the consumers of his text have heard and can call to mind performances of the Fugue in F Major (their own or someone else's), he is nevertheless concerned to preseve the

Figure 4.5. Johann Philipp Kirnberger, *Die Kunst des reinen Satzes in der Musik* (Berlin and Königsberg: G. J. Decker and G. L. Hartung, 1776), 2:119.

workings of the tradition of notation that will support its performance in the future. His impassioned attention to the function of meter signatures and note values in indicating the just tempo and affect of the piece simultaneously plays on insider knowledge (we are meant somehow to see that the expression and pace are "instantly no longer the same" from the example) and a fear that this knowledge is no longer generally held.

When Heinrich Christoph Koch, writing later in the century, aimed to draw a comparison of $\frac{2}{2}$ and $\frac{2}{4}$, his words were less anxious and much more resigned. He begins by asserting that slower phrases should be set in $\frac{2}{2}$ and faster phrases in $\frac{2}{4}$ and explains: "Were this accepted as a rule, then the following phrase [A] when set in $\frac{2}{2}$ would always be performed with a slower tempo, and when as in the following [B] it is set in $\frac{2}{4}$, it would by contrast always be performed more quickly" (fig. 4.6; meter signatures are not included in the examples).[20] Koch does not sustain this conditional hopefulness for long, however. The differentiaton between $\frac{2}{2}$ and $\frac{2}{4}$ seems, he tells us, "more coincidence than intent, because the use of these two metric types for the purpose of the speed of the tempo is totally arbitrarily supposed."[21] Koch's pair of examples shares much with Kirnberger's: the intertwining of prose and printed music, the focus on melody, the effort to draw out the differences between two closely related meter signatures. But Koch seems less certain of his audience in many ways. He does not rely on the consumers of his book to reproduce a typical peformance of Bach from memory for the purpose of indicating a just tempo; nor does he assume that his readership or the consumers of print music in general can be counted upon to act in any uniform way when interpreting the marks of music notation.

Koch's detectable frustration in this passage is not simply an indication of a conservative attitude about meter; instead, it reveals a growing awareness of the circulation and dissemination of notated musical objects, musical practices, and discourses on music. The idea that meter signatures indicated tempi and affects and that theorists could demonstrate these correlations with a writing technology that refused to make them explicit could only have survived in a

ein engeres Verhältniß gebracht würden. Wäre dieses als Regel angenommen, so müßte alsdenn nothwendig folgender Saz, wenn er in den Zwey‑zweyteltact eingekleidet wäre, z. E.

jederzeit in einer langsamen Bewegung, in folgen‑der Einkleidung in den Zweyvierteltact hingegen

Figure 4.6. The first phrase is set in $\frac{2}{2}$, and then the same phrase is set in $\frac{2}{4}$. From Heinrich Christoph Koch, *Versuch einer Anleitung zur Composition* (Leipzig: Adam Friedrich Böhme, 1787), 2:292.

world in which music and print were consumed (or thought to have been consumed) within a fairly bounded sphere of shared musical experiences. Koch knew—and his colleagues were begninng to understand—that this was no longer the case.[22] As such, the examples they left us are records of a brief window during which print commodities attempted to remediate a problem of print and to capture feeling and knowhow on a page that resisted them.

When the German-trained theorist A. F. C. Kollmann published his 1796 *Essay on Musical Harmony* in London, he included in its preface a nervous caveat concerning his exclusion of certain musical examples:

I have nothing particular to observe in this place, than that I hope, my not having introduced in this Essay any examples from the compositions of authors now residing in this country, will not be construed into a total unac-quaintance with their works, or a want of due regard for them; as I have done it merely for the purpose of not appearing partial to some, and prejudiced against others.[23]

Instead of excerpts from compositions, Kollmann opted for newly composed, generic musical examples in his discussion of tempo and meter.[24] His treatise, like those before it, takes great care to outline the different work of meter signatures, note values, and characteristic gestures in the determination of tempo and affect. Still, Kollmann reports, "hardly two in ten will take one and the same movement in an equal degree of quickness. This being still a great imperfection in the signature of musical movements."[25] Kollmann's is one of many eighteenth-century treatises to mention the possibility of a chronometric designation for tempo—a mechanical form of mediation to subsitute for the untranslatability of explication and exemplification in theoretical treatises.[26] But there was something for Kollmann that wouldn't allow for this level of abstraction in musical feeling, and it seemed as though no chronometer would be able to deliver with nuance what trained musicians could intuit from notation. For Kollmann, "The only guide to the true movement of a composition hiterto is an acquaintance with the manner and intention of the author."[27] At the close of the eighteenth century it seemed as though no mediation was sucessful enough to accomplish the task of communicating tempo and affect. The consumers of one's book might not have the necessary familiarity with any repertoire—Kollmann was particularly attuned to this situation—and the mathematical precision of the chronometer was as yet unsuitable for the work of expression. Only direct access to the composer would do.

The dream of unfettered tempo communication was nothing other than the utopic opposite of the period's frustrations with the existing forms of mediation. For better or worse, Maelzel's metronome would ultimately fulfill the goal of quantifying musical tempo, finally wresting it completely away from meter signatures and note values. But just before this occurred—just before this decisive mediator for tempo took its place in musical practice—there was a pointed awareness concerning the geographies of music's consumption and the patterns of music's circulation. An anonymous contributor to the Leipzig *Allgemeine musikalische Zeitung* in 1813 was more than ready to embrace any device that would quantify tempo. "The advantages of such an instrument have always been obvious," he extolled.

> To cite only one example: I heard Mozart's Overture to *Don Giovanni* rehearsed by the master himself with the former Guardasonischen Gesellschaft in Prague; I then also heard it, among other places, in Paris, Vienna and Berlin. In Paris the Adagio was taken but an inconsiderable amount slower, in Vienna, faster by a huge margin, and in Berlin, almost twice as fast as Mozart. In all three locations the Allegro was more or less faster than his.[28]

Regardless of whether his report was true, this early nineteenth-century critic was able to marshal authority on the basis of having heard "the master himself"—Kollmann's ideal method. It was clear that Mozart's printed overture was no longer an adequate form of mediation for its tempo and that some other device was needed. Crucially, though, the musical dissemination at issue in this report did not take place across vast distances or through unknown languages; Mozart's music was not even translated correctly in the music capitals of Europe. What work, then, could printed commodities have hoped to do to combat this problem of notation? By the early nineteenth century, as if in accordance with the insurmountable problems of print mediation, music theory texts no longer contained examples attempting to relate meter, tempo, and affect.

The Affects in Print

Antoine-Nicholas de Condorcet's posthumously published *Esquisse d'un tableau historique des progrès de l'esprit humain* (1795) espoused a view of human progress grounded in rationality, attaining its apex in the eighteenth century and ever advancing toward enlightenment. Writing at the century's end, he observed a momentous shift in the production of knowledge that had occurred with the advent of print. The printing press, in his narrative, had afforded new access to information to anyone with the ability to read, connecting individuals across the learned world with each other and with knowledge they could leverage to the advantage of all humanity. His enthusiasm for print spills over into a litany of the types of texts that could be used to these ends:

> Elementary books, dictionaries, works in which one assembles a multitude of facts, observations, and experiences with all their details and in which all of the proofs are developed and all of the doubts discussed; valuable collections that contain all that has been observed, written, and thought in one particular branch of the sciences, or the results of a year's work of all the scholars of a single country; tables and charts of every sort, some of which offer to the eyes that which the mind can only grasp with difficult work, others that will indicate the fact, observation, number, formula or object that one has need of knowing, while still others—in convenient form and methodical order—finally present the materials from which genius draws new truths: all these means of securing, facilitating, and accelerating the march of the human spirit are due to the advantages of printing.[29]

Although they are not explicitly named in his ebullient catalog, we can see music theory texts standing beside Condorcet's reference works, dictionaries, and instruction books, for they carry on the task he was so convinced would lead to the betterment of civilization. Of course, these books were transformed by as much as they helped to transform the mediation of knowledge.

The advent of widely disseminated, printed music dramatically changed the way exemplification in theory treatises functioned, as Cristle Collins Judd has shown with respect to sixteenth-century music theory.[30] These changed artifacts were then incorporated into an ongoing process in which the technology of print became both the subject and the medium of knowledge.

Condorcet's celebration of print, for all its beautiful hopefulness, encapsulates a curious Enlightenment tension: the printed book had compiled and codified, extracted and distilled knowledge, but it had also aimed for comprehensiveness, encompassing "all proofs" and discussing "all doubts," aggregating "a multitude of facts" for dissemination to all peoples. Music theory, too, had to face the gauntlet of abstraction and ubiquity. Its examples on meter were meant to function as normative descriptions for the system of *tempo giusto* so the medium of printed music could do its work. In this sense they were supposed to epitomize those relationships and tabulate them through exemplification. But these texts were also supposed to account for everything and go everywhere, to take care of every possibility and translate for every situation. These examples faced the impossible dual imperatives of quintessence and universality.

In an age in which music was praised for the mimetic transmission of affect, music theory was valued for facilitating and documenting that exchange. It used the tools of print—with all their inherent contradictions—to mediate between the commodity of printed music and its consumers. But as Condorcet was more than ready to admit, print was not an especially friendly host to the affects. In fact, it was the printed letter that had allowed humanity to escape "the tyrannical empire . . . exercised over the passions." Print, Condorcet explains, made possible "a more certain and durable power over reason where all the advantage is for truth, since what art loses in the power of seduction it gains in the power of enlightenment."[31] And so in his view, the Enlightenment mediation of knowledge was designed to tame the unbridled power of the passions—it was intended to corral and contain the mimetic transference of affect. This goal encapsulated twin period impulses: on the one hand, enlightened knowledge aimed to investigate the content of sensory impressions and our affective responses to them; on the other, it sought out ways of stabilizing this drastic knowledge with the epistemological rigor of rational taxonomy.[32]

Nowhere could this be more apparent than in music theory texts, the documents that had hoped to explain the musical transmission of affect; this was, as Sulzer told us, "the most important—if not the only—merit of a perfect musical composition."[33] But before the contradictions of these historical circumstances were fully unfolded—before the widespread adoption of Maelzel's metronome as the ultimate device for communicating tempo—documents of music theory rehearsed this drama of missed connections on their pages in the aspirational, mediating work of their musical examples.

Notes

1. Clifford Siskin and William Warner, eds., *This Is Enlightenment* (Chicago: University of Chicago Press, 2010).
2. Anik Devriès-Lesure, "Technological Aspects," in *Music Publishing in Europe, 1600–1900: Concepts and Issues, Bibliography*, ed. Rudolf Rasch (Berlin: Berliner Wissenschafts-Verlag, 2005), 64–89; Axel Beer, "Composers and Publishers: Germany 1700–1830," in Rasch, ed., *Music Publishing in Europe, 1600–1900*, 159–81; Bianca Maria Antolini, "Publishers and Buyers," in Rasch, ed., *Music Publishing in Europe, 1600–1900*, 209–40. See also Stanley Boorman, Eleanor Selfridge-Field, and Donald W. Krummel, "Printing and Publishing of Music," in *Oxford Music Online*, accessed May 5, 2014, www.oxfordmusiconline.org.
3. See, for example, the essays collected in *Music and the Cultures of Print*, ed. Kate van Orden (New York: Garland, 2000), particularly Roger Chartier, "Afterword: Music in Print," 325–41. More generally, see Chartier, *The Order of Books*, trans. Lydia G. Cochrane (Stanford: Stanford University Press, 1994).
4. The methodological framework I have in mind follows the impulse set forth—for much earlier music and music theory—in Cristle Collins Judd, *Reading Renaissance Music Theory: Hearing with the Eyes* (Cambridge: Cambridge University Press, 2000).
5. "This period can also be regarded as a turning point in the history of music publishing, a time during which music printing techniques improved due to the extensive use of engraving, music began to be circulated more frequently in printed rather than manuscript form, a large number of publishers went into business, and the public indicated increasing interest and demand." Sarah Adams, "International Dissemination of Printed Music during the Second Half of the Eighteenth Century," in *The Dissemination of Music: Studies in the History of Music Publishing*, ed. Hans Lenneberg (Lausanne, Switzerland: Gordon and Breach, 1994), 22.
6. Charles Antoine Vion, *La musique pratique et theorique* (Paris: Jean-Baptiste-Christophe Ballard, 1742), 21–32. I have preserved the original orthography and spelling of titles and quotations. All translations are my own.
7. "La Mesure à quatre se bat *Lentement*. . . . On n'employe d'ordinaire cette Mesure que pour les Récitatifs de Motets, de Cantates, d'Opera. Elle convient encore aux Pieces de Musiques Instrumentales, comme aux Allemandes, aux Sonates, aux Adagio, &c." Ibid., 21–22 (italics original).
8. The fifth example provides a curious twist: although Vion indicates that the meter C is suitable for Adagios, this excerpt is the incipit of the Allegro from Robert Valentine's Flute Sonata op. 5, no. 2 (which follows on that sonata's opening Adagio). Selections such as this complicate the idea of easy translatability for which these taxonomies of *tempo giusto* might, at first blush, provide hope.
9. "La mesure à deux 2 est pour l'ordinaire vive: on l'employe dans les Ouvertures d'Opera, les Marches, les Ballets, les Branles, les Bourées, &c." Vion, *La musique pratique et theorique*, 22.

10. This difference—between a "tripled" (*triplirt*) version of $\frac{6}{8}$ and a "compounded" (*zusammengesetzt*) measure of two smaller $\frac{3}{8}$ measures—is taken up in Nicole Schwindt-Gross, "Einfache, zusammengesetzte und doppelt notierte Takte: Ein Aspekt der Takttheorie im 18. Jahrhundert," *Musiktheorie* 4, no. 3 (1989): 203–22; Markus Waldura, "Marpurg, Koch, und die Neubegründung des Taktbegriffs," *Musikforschung* 53, no. 3 (2000): 237–53; Helmut Breidenstein, *Mozarts Tempo-System* (Tutzing: Hans Schneider, 2011), 75–78; and more generally in Claudia Maurer Zenck, *Vom Takt* (Vienna: Böhlau, 2001); Danuta Mirka, *Metric Manipulations in Haydn and Mozart* (Oxford: Oxford University Press, 2009); Roger Mathew Grant, *Beating Time and Measuring Music in the Early Modern Era* (Oxford: Oxford University Press, 2014).

11. "Jedes dieser beyspiele unterscheidet sich von den übrigen durch eine charakterisirte Bewegung, die erstlich durch die Verschiedenheit des Tempo und der Taktart, und bey denen die von einerley Tempo und Taktart sind, durch die Verschiedenheit der Notengattungen, aus denen die Melodie zusammengesetzt ist, fühlbar wird." Johann Philipp Kirnberger, *Die Kunst des reinen Satzes in der Musik*, vol. 2 (Berlin and Königsberg: G. J. Decker and G. L. Hartung, 1776), 111.

12. This composite system is characterized not only in Foucault's description of a classical age of representation but also in what Jacques Rancière called the "representative" regime and what M. H. Abrams identified as a kind of mimetic pragmaticism in early modern aesthetic theories. Michel Foucault, *The Order of Things* (New York: Pantheon Books, 1970; reprint edition New York: Vintage, 1973); Michel Foucault, *The Archaeology of Knowledge*, trans. A. M. Sheridan Smith (New York: Pantheon Books, 1972); Jacques Rancière, *The Politics of Aesthetics: The Distribution of the Sensible*, trans. and with an introduction by Gabriel Rockhill (London: Continuum, 2004); Jacques Rancière, *The Politics of Literature* (Cambridge: Polity, 2011); M. H. Abrams, *The Mirror and the Lamp: Romantic Theory and the Critical Tradition* (Oxford: Oxford University Press, 1953).

13. "Der Componist muß nie vergessen, daß jeder Gesang eine natürliche und getreue Abbildung oder Schilderung einer Gemüthslage oder Empfindung seyn soll, in so fern sie sich durch eine Folge von Tönen kann schildern lassen. Der Name Gemüthsbewegung, den wir Deutschen den Leidenschaften oder Affekten geben, zeiget schon die Aehnlichkeit derselben mit der Bewegung an. In der That hat jede Leidenschaft und jede Empfindung, so wol in ihrer innerlichen Würkung, als in der Rede, wodurch sie sich äußert, ihre geschwindere oder langsamere, heftigere oder gelassenere Bewegung, und diese muß auch der Componist, nach der Art der Empfindung, die er auszudrücken hat, richtig treffen. . . . Aber die Bewegung in der Musik ist nicht blos auf die verschiedenen Grade des Langsamen und Geschwinden eigenschränkt. Denn so wie es Leidenschaften giebt, in **denen die Vorstellungen, wie ein sanfter Bach einförmig fortfließen; andere, wo sie schneller, mit einem mäßigen Geräusch, aber ohne Aufhaltung fortströhmen; einige, in denen die Folge der Vorstellungen den durch starken Regen aufgeschwollenen wilden Bächen gleicht, die ungestüm daher rauschen, und alles mit sich fortreißen, was**

ihnen im Wege steht; und wieder andere, bey denen das Gemüth in seinen Vorstellungen der wilden See gleicht, die ist gewaltig gegen das Ufer anschlägt, denn zurücke tritt, mit neuer Kraft wieder anzuprellen, so kann auch die Bewegung in der Melodie bey dem nemlichen Grad der Geschwindigkeit oder Langsamkeit heftig oder sanft, hüpfend oder gleichförmig, feurig oder matt seyn, nachdem die Art der Notengattungen, aus denen die Melodie zusammengesetzt ist, gewählet wird. Man sehe folgende Beyspiele." Kirnberger, *Die Kunst des reinen Satzes in der Musik*, 2:106–7. Kirnberger's bold type indicates a quotation, though in truth he is paraphrasing Sulzer, who writes: "Es giebt Leidenschaften, in denen die Vorstellungen, wie ein sanfter Bach, einförmig fortfließen; bey andern ströhmen sie schneller, mit einem mäßigen Geräusche und hüpfend, aber ohne Aufhaltung; in einigen gleicht die Folge der Vorstellungen den durch starken Regen aufgeschwollenen wilden Bächen, die ungestüm daher rauschen, und alles mit sich fortreißen, was ihnen im Wege steht. Bisweilen gleicht das Gemüth in seinen Vorstellungen der wilden See, die ist gewaltig gegen das Ufer anschlägt, denn zurüke tritt, um mit neuer Kraft wieder anzuprellen." Johann Georg Sulzer, "Ausdruk in der Musik," in *Allgemeine Theorie der Schönen Künste*, ed. Johann Georg Sulzer with assistance from Johann Philipp Kirnberger and Johann Abraham Peter Schultz, vol. 1, 2nd ed. (Leipzig: Weidmannschen Buchhandlung, 1792), 272.

14. "Der richtige Ausdruk der Empfindungen und Leidenschaften in allen ihren besondern Schattirungen ist das vornehmste, wo nicht gar das einzige Verdienst eines vollkommenen Tonstükes." Sulzer, "Ausdruk in der Musik," 271.

15. "Ainsi que le Peintre imite les traits & les couleurs de la nature, de même le Musicien imite les tons, les accens, les soûpirs, les inflexions de voix, enfin tous ces sons à l'aide desquels la nature même exprime ses sentiments & ses passions. Tous ces sons, comme nous l'avons déjà exposé, ont une force merveilleuse pour nous émouvoir, parce qu'ils sont les signes des passions instituez par la nature dont ils ont reçû leur énergie." Abbé Dubos, *Reflexions critiques sur la poësie et sur la peinture*, vol. 1 (Paris: Jean Mariette, 1719), 634–35.

16. "dans la Musique & la Danse, l'action ne sera qu'une espèce de canevas destiné à porter, soutenir, amener, lier, les différentes passions." Charles Batteux, *Les beaux-arts réduits à un même principe* (Paris: Durand, 1746), 258–59.

17. James Beattie, "An Essay on Poetry and Music, as They Affect the Mind. Written in the Year 1762," in *Essays* (Edinburgh and London: William Creech and E. and C. Dilly, 1776), 143.

18. For a genealogy of musical affect theories, see esp. Danuta Mirka, "Introduction," in *The Oxford Handbook of Topic Theory*, ed. Danuta Mirka (Oxford: Oxford University Press, 2014), 1–57.

19. "Wem ist die Bachische Fuge unbekannt? Mann versetze dieses Thema in $\frac{6}{8}$ also: sogleich ist die Bewegung nicht mehr dieselbe, der Gang ist weit schwerfälliger, die Töne, zumal die durchgehenden, erhalten ein zu schweres Gewicht, kurz, der Ausdruck des ganzen Stücks leidet, und ist gar nicht mehr der, den Bach darin gelegt hat." Kirnberger, *Die Kunst des reinen Satzes in der Musik*, 2:119–20.

20. "Wäre dieses als Regel angenommen, so müßte alsdenn nothwendig folgender Satz, wenn er in den Zweyzweyteltact eingekleidet wäre, z. B. . . . jederzeit in einer langsamen Bewegung, in folgender Einkleidung in den Zweyvierteltact hingegen . . . jederzeit in einer geschwindern Bewegung vorgetragen werden." Heinrich Christoph Koch, *Versuch eine Anleitung zur Composition*, vol. 2 (Leipzig: Adam Friedrich Böhme, 1787), 292.

21. "geschieht es ja zuweilen, so ist es mehr Zufall als Vorsatz, weil der Gebrauch dieser beiden Tactgattungen in Absicht auf die Geschwindigkeit der Bewegung als ganz willkürrlich angenommen ist." Ibid., 292–93.

22. See Adams, "International Dissemination of Printed Music during the Second Half of the Eighteenth Century"; Hans Lenneberg, *On the Publishing and Dissemination of Music, 1500–1850* (Hillsdale, NY: Pendragon, 2003), 85–93.

23. Augustus Frederic Christopher Kollmann, *An Essay on Musical Harmony According to the Nature of That Science and the Principles of the Greatest Musical Authors* (London: J. Dale, 1796), v.

24. Other treatises that employ this technique for their examples on meter and tempo include Friedrich Wilhelm Marpurg, *Anleitung zum Clavierspielen* (Berlin: Haude and Spener, 1755), table 1, nos. 25–45; Francesco Galeazzi, *Elementi teorico-pratici di musica*, vol. 1 (Rome: Pilucchi Cracas, 1791), table 2.

25. Kollmann, *Essay on Musical Harmony*, 72.

26. Precedents include Étienne Loulié, *Éléments ou principes de musique* (Amsterdam: Estienne Roger, 1698; facsimile edition Ann Arbor: University Microfilms, 1964), 81–88; Joseph Sauveur "Système General des Intervalles des Sons, et son Application à tous les Systèmes et à tous les Instruments de Musique," in *Histoire de l'Académie Royale des Sciences Année 1701* (Paris: Gabriel Martin, Jean-Baptiste Coignard, and Hippolyte-Louis Guerin, 1704), 299–366; Louis-Léon Pajot d'Ons-en-Bray, "Description et usage d'un Métromètre ou Machine pour battre les Mesures et les Temps de toutes sortes d'Airs," in *Histoire de l'Académie Royale des Sciences Année 1732* (Paris: De L'Imprimerie Royale, 1735), 182–95; William Tans'ur, *A New Musical Grammar* (London: Jacob Robinson for the author, 1746; revised ed. London: Robert Brown for James Hodges, 1756), 47–51.

27. Kollmann, *Essay on Musical Harmony*, 72.

28. "Es giebt Erfindungen, von deren Nützlichkeit jedermann überzeugt ist, in deren Lobe alle Welt übereinstimmt, und die doch so unbenützt bleiben, als wären sie gar nicht da. Welch eine lange Litaney könnte hier der deutsche Physiker anstimmen! Auch der Tonkünstler hat Stoff zu einer, obgleich kürzen. In diese gehört auch der Vorschlag, der schon vor mehrern Jahren, und oft gethan worden, den Grad der Bewegung eines Musikstücks durch ein eigenes Instrument so zu bestimmen, dass mit dessen Hülfe auch in den entferntesten Orten und Zeiten ein jeder im Stande ist, gerade da selbe Tempo zu fassen, das der Componist haben wollte. Der Vortheil, den ein solches Instrument bringen musste, war einleuchtend. . . . Ich hörte, um nur Eins anzuführen, Mozarts Ouvertüre zum Don Giovanni, vom Meister selbst mit der ehemaligen Guardasonischen Gesellschaft in Prag einstudirt; ich hörte sie dann, unter andern Orten, auch in Paris, Wien und Berlin. Das Adagio nahm man in Paris

um ein Unbeträchtliches langsamer, in Wien um ein Beträchtliches schneller, in Berlin fast noch einmal so schnell, als Mozart: das Allegro an allen drey Orten mehr oder weniger geschwinder, als er." Unsigned miscellaneous contribution, Leipzig, *Allgemeine musikalische Zeitung* 15, no. 18 (May 5, 1813): 305–6.

29. "Les livres purement élémentaires, les dictionnaires, les ouvrages où l'on rassemble, avec tous leurs détails, une multitude de faits, d'observations, d'expériences, où toutes les preuves sont développées, tous les doutes discutés; ces collections précieuses qui renferment, tantôt tout ce qui a été observé, écrit, pensé, sur une branche particulière des sciences, tantôt le résultat des travaux annuels de tous les savans d'un même pays; ces tables, ces tableaux de toute espèce, dont les uns offrent aux yeux des résultats que l'esprit n'auroit saisis qu'avec un travail pénible, les autres montrent à volonté le fait, l'observation, le nombre, la formule, l'objet qu'on a besoin de connoître, tandis que d'autres enfin présentent, sous une forme commode, dans un ordre méthodique, les matériaux dont le génie doit tirer des vérités nouvelles: tous ces moyens de rendre la marche de l'esprit humain plus rapide, plus sûre, et plus facile, sont encore des bienfaits de l'imprimerie." Jean-Antoine-Nicolas de Caritat de Condorcet, *Esquisse d'un tableau historique des progrès de l'esprit humain* (Paris: Agasse, 1795), 189–90.

30. Judd's book demonstrates how "the availability of printed music fundamentally altered the relationship of a theorist like Aron with the notated representation of sounding object. . . . Printed music—primarily in partbook, but also in choirbook format—available in multiple, reproducible copies (which now also included the music contained in theory treatises), was associated with profound changes in the nature of writing about music." Judd, *Reading Renaissance Music Theory*, 318.

31. "D'où l'on exerce un empire moins tyrannique sur les passions, mais en obtenant sur la raison une puissance plus sûre et plus durable; où tout l'avantage est pour la vérité, puisque l'art n'a perdu sur les moyens de séduire qu'en gagnant sur ceux d'éclairer." Condorcet, *Esquisse d'un tableau historique des progrès de l'esprit humain*, 187. See also Clifford Siskin, "Mediated Enlightenment: The System of the World," in Siskin and Warner, eds., *This Is Enlightenment*, 164–72.

32. On this particular contradiction in Enlightenment thought, see Jessica Riskin, *Science in the Age of Sensibility: The Sentimental Empiricists of the French Revolution* (Chicago: University of Chicago Press, 2002), esp. 227–81.

33. Sulzer, "Ausdruk in der Musik," 271.

Part Three

Marketing the Mundane

Chapter Five

Musical Style as Commercial Strategy in Romantic Chamber Music

Marie Sumner Lott

The mid-nineteenth-century music lover benefited from a wealth of opportunities for casual, recreational music-making. He or she could participate in community choirs, bands, and orchestras and gather around the piano with friends and family to sing and play four-hand piano works or to participate in sonatas and other chamber-music genres. Innovations in manufacturing allowed more middle-class families to purchase instruments of various kinds, and the booming publishing industry provided sheet music for performers of every level and ability. Published arrangements of operas and orchestral music made large-scale works of the past and the present available in even the most remote town or village in Europe. Although studies of music and musical life in the nineteenth century have begun to acknowledge the importance of these wildly varying musical experiences, few have examined the interdependence of consumers and producers of music in this era and the impact of that interdependence on musical style. Practically none have investigated string chamber music. Because the piano and its roles in musical life have been so influential for modern-day understandings of nineteenth-century musical culture, an important segment of the musical public—amateur string players and the composers who wrote for them—has been ignored or neglected by music historians.

This lacuna has led to two common misconceptions that I seek to correct in this chapter and to a startling opportunity overlooked until now. First, string chamber music was far more abundant and influential than most histories of the period allow. Works for three, four, or five string instruments flourished in the 1830s and 1840s and continued to be produced in ever larger numbers through the end of the century. The existence of so much musical material suggests a voracious public appetite for published string quartets and quintets that exceeds all expectations based on modern accounts. The major studies of nineteenth-century music frequently ignore chamber music composed and consumed after the 1820s (notably losing interest after the late quartets of Beethoven), except to comment on the rise of piano quartets and quintets.[1] "Light" works for solo piano—such as collections of dances and character pieces, as well as variations on popular tunes and original themes—and parlor songs were more numerous and more profitable for publishers, as the archival record clearly demonstrates. But chamber music for strings held a strong position in publishers' catalogs and apparently in the private lives of musical amateurs, since many of the works published in large numbers did not appear with much frequency on public concert programs.

Second, the musical style employed in these popular works differs in significant ways from modern-day expectations of string chamber music (especially the string quartet) in the post-Beethovenian age, and these differences are both purposeful and meaningful. Rather than describe the composers of popular string quartets as lesser contemporaries of figures like Felix Mendelssohn and Robert Schumann or their works as epigones or "watered-down" substitutes for more innovative examples, we should hear them in the context of a shared language meant to convey common interests, backgrounds, and values among communities of music lovers.

Popular string chamber music of this period addressed a completely different audience (or consumer) than the "light" works for piano and for voice produced at the same time, giving modern-day scholars an opportunity to widen and refine our understanding of domestic music and its role in nineteenth-century life. Whereas piano variations and albums of dances, for instance, were generally marketed to women—in advertisements and printed works included in women's magazines—in the nineteenth century string chamber music clearly belonged to the world of men and to specialized musical audiences. Various nineteenth-century social and pseudo-medical taboos prevented women from taking up string instruments in large numbers, and the primary participants in string ensembles were men until at least the 1880s, when women's orchestras, bands, and chamber groups became more common (though always segregated from the men). Tellingly, string quartets and quintets were advertised primarily in the music press—in reviews and announcements, for instance—and on the back covers of printed parts or scores, which frequently listed works in similar genres or instrumentations available from the same press. In part because they were easily portable, the violin and its cousins allowed men to congregate in each others' homes, in taverns or clubs, and in music halls. These semiprivate, semipublic spaces devoted to recreation fall between the clearly public concert-hall performance and the "trivial" entertainments of the parlor, centered around (stationary) instruments like the piano.[2] The music associated with these spaces likewise falls between our categories of "high art" and "ephemeral" works.

For this reason, in addition to all the high-brow associations it accrued in the nineteenth century, the string quartet provided a leisurely outlet that middle-class men needed, allowing them to engage in nonprofessional activities that were at the same time associated with learning and accomplishment. We can only know in the most haphazard way what amateur chamber groups may have played when they gathered for recreational music-making. Indeed, in an excellent study of string chamber-music culture in nineteenth-century Britain, Christina Bashford notes how frustrating this lack of information is for modern scholars.[3] Fortunately, we can know what was available to these consumers by looking at publication data. The first section of this chapter does just that, examining the archival records of two important Leipzig-based publishers to determine what music circulated and what was popular in this period (at least in German-speaking lands).[4] The second section turns to the popular works themselves for information about the musical tastes of consumers. An examination of one highly popular string quartet from this period—Václav Veit's String Quartet in D Minor, op. 3 (1836)—demonstrates the musical features that made this style appropriate for recreational domestic music-making and that helped introduce novel, "Romantic" approaches to harmony, form, and texture in the "conservative" string quartet genre.

String Chamber Music in the Marketplace

Long the center of consumer goods trading and, more important, the German printing and publishing industry, the city of Leipzig holds a special place in the intertwined histories of printed music and musical Romanticism. Unlike other large cities with an august musical establishment and history (Vienna, Paris, Dresden), Leipzig had never been the seat of a powerful monarchy or aristocratic and church leaders. Thus by the nineteenth century it represented a model of middle-class self-governance and commercial success. Without the court structures of other metropolitan centers, the city's music activities revolved around private and civic musical events. Although Leipzig did not compare favorably to Vienna's glitz and political prestige or to Paris's fashionable performance venues and concertgoers, its long-standing affinity for the printed word made it the capital of German-language music publications, including critical and academic work. (Leipzig was the home of publications such as the *Allgemeine musikalische Zeitung*, for instance.) Its universities, the historical connection to Bach's musical heritage, and, later, the prestige of hosting one of the first great German conservatories imbued Leipzig with a reputation for musical craftsmanship and learnedness.[5] Three of the most important German music publishers set up shop in Leipzig at the turn of the nineteenth century, and together, Breitkopf und Härtel, C. F. Peters, and Friedrich Hofmeister would play a significant role in the development of Romantic musical life. Although this chapter focuses on Hofmeister, the other two firms employed similar business strategies to bring music to consumers throughout Europe.

Friedrich Hofmeister made it his life's work to organize music publishers and sellers in the German lands to secure fair trading practices, serve consumers better and more efficiently, and raise the prestige of his profession. He began selling, then printing and publishing, music in 1807. Beginning in 1817, he collaborated with Carl Friedrich Whistling to publish monthly or bimonthly installments of the *Handbuch der musikalischen Literatur*, today often referred to as the "Hofmeister-Whistling" catalogs.[6] Hofmeister also established the Verein der Deutschen Musicalienhandler (Society of German Music-Sellers) to promote ethical and collegial business relationships among competitors and to lobby for copyright and other legislation to protect publishers and artists from piracy. A wealth of documents detailing the day-to-day operations of Hofmeister's business is now housed in the Sachsisches Staatsarchiv in Leipzig, and the documents shed new light on the behind-the-scenes mechanisms that drove musical consumption and popularity in the nineteenth century.[7] At least for string chamber music, public information such as listings of new publications, reviews, and public announcements or reviews of concerts indicates a narrative of declining interest and activity, but the private information preserved in these business records tells a different story.

Judging simply by the quantity of new works produced, it might seem that the potential market for published string chamber music was smaller than that for keyboard and vocal works during the long nineteenth century and considerably smaller than it had been in the late eighteenth century.[8] The Hofmeister-Whistling catalogs, for example, indicate a rapid decline in chamber-music production beginning around 1830. Publishers essentially stopped producing new works in chamber genres or produced fewer of them in the following decades, suggesting that the consumers of chamber music had moved on to other activities. The print and publication catalogs of publishers like Hofmeister, C. F. Peters, and Breitkopf und Härtel likewise show that fewer new works were published in later decades, with a precipitous drop in production in the decade between 1840 and 1850. Indeed, Robert Schumann famously lamented the deterioration of the string quartet genre in several reviews published in the *Neue Zeitschrift für Musik* in 1838 and 1842.[9]

That portrayal of decline and disinterest, though, is refuted in part by the Auflagebücher, or impression catalogs, kept by these firms, which scrupulously list each reprint of every work published by the firm beginning with the first printing and continuing into the twentieth century (see fig. 5.1). These listings show the date of each impression and the number of copies made in the right-hand column, where the text runs perpendicular to the rest of the entry. The remainder of the entry indicates, from left to right, the work's plate number (unique to the work or edition), the composer and title, the number of printing plates created for the work, and information about the title page engraving—"Stein" indicates a lithographed (Steingedruckt) title page, and the name or initial underneath indicates who engraved it. As figure 5.1 shows, some works were reprinted as often as every other year—some multiple times within the same year—and others were printed only once or twice and then abandoned. Chamber works were frequently printed in small initial runs of fifty to one hundred copies and then reprinted in increments of twenty-five, fifty, or one hundred, depending on demand. In some cases, a work was reprinted in increasingly larger print runs, presumably because the public liked it and new consumers wanted to acquire their own copies. This information suggests a continuing demand for chamber music throughout the nineteenth century, though that demand seems to have shifted to older works after about 1840, when new music became less enticing than reprints of favorite pieces and works by familiar composers.

Although works by Haydn, Mozart, and Beethoven were reprinted and distributed in the nineteenth century, they did not comprise a significant area of commercial activity until fairly late in the period. Rather, the most frequently reprinted works were by contemporaneous composers treated as "minor masters" today. Similarly, although modern discussions of Romantic chamber music frequently highlight the development of the piano quartet and quintet, focusing on the innovative works of Schumann and Brahms, these genres did not make up a large percentage of the firms' chamber-music outputs. They were far outnumbered by works for strings alone and for piano trio, both of which were reprinted regularly and therefore retained a strong position in the musical life of the age.

One of the most successful and popular composers of string music in the nineteenth century was the violin virtuoso Louis Spohr (1784–1859), who served as kapellmeister in Kassel (then the seat of power for the prince-elector of Hesse) from 1822 until his death. C. F. Peters published nine sets of string quartets by Spohr, totaling eighteen works, between 1830 and 1856 and then reprinted many of them into the 1860s.[10] Peters printed over fifteen thousand copies of string quartets by Spohr between 1830 and the mid-1860s. With the exception of his set of three quartets op. 4, though, Spohr's string quartets appear to have lost their market value quickly; Spohr's reputation declined

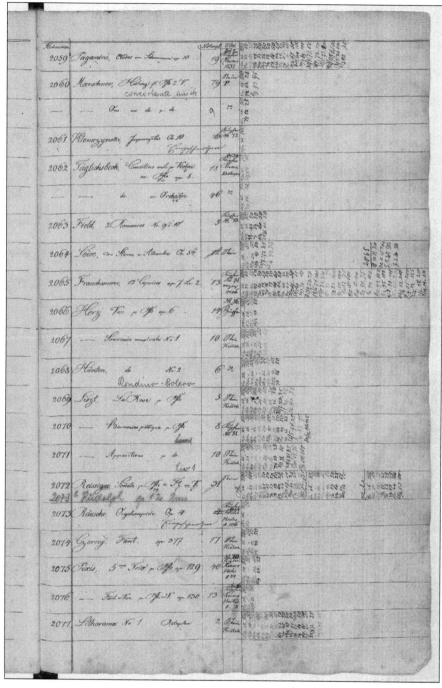

Figure 5.1. Musikverlag Friedrich Hofmeister of Leipzig, *Auflagebuch* (1832–39), 76. Courtesy of the Sächsische Staatsarchiv, Staatsarchiv-Leipzig, 21072, no. 43, F. 12963.

after his death in 1859, despite the high esteem in which musicians such as Hans von Bülow and Johannes Brahms held him.

A slightly younger contemporary of Spohr, the Czech composer Václav Jindřich Veit (1806–64), met with similar success as a composer of popular string chamber music. Although he was not as prolific as Spohr—Veit published only seven works for strings in his lifetime—his works outlasted those of the more famous composers in the nineteenth-century marketplace. Hofmeister published Veit's music under his Germanized name Wenzel Heinrich and then steadily reprinted his string quintets and quartets into the twentieth century. For example, Hofmeister printed Veit's String Quartet op. 3, twenty-four times between its introduction in 1836 and the last recorded printing in 1906 (see fig. 5.2), thus averaging a new impression almost every three years for seven decades. A total of 1,225 copies circulated over the course of the century, only slightly fewer copies than Spohr's most successful work—the *Quatuors brillants* op. 43, which were reprinted fourteen times, creating 1,380 copies. On average, each new run of a Veit quartet or quintet contained 50 new copies, ensuring that this work was always available to the music-purchasing public, though never in large quantities. Veit's subsequent works were not quite as popular, but their numbers remain impressive for the period: the two quintets opp. 1 and 2, were reprinted ten times, resulting in 500 copies of each, and the Second and Third Quartets opp. 5 and 16 (1838 and 1840), were each reprinted more than ten times, leading to over 600 copies of each. Whereas Spohr's works appear to have met with resounding success in his lifetime and then fallen quickly out of favor, Veit's works were more modestly distributed but lasted longer in the public consciousness (or at least in music shops) well after his death in 1864. As prime examples of a popular style that found favor with musical consumers throughout the nineteenth century, Veit's music serves as an excellent case study of the connections between compositional decisions and commercial success.

Musical Style

Unlike Spohr, Veit was a committed amateur rather than a professional musician. Although he received training in music and later taught piano and composition lessons in his free time, he spent his working life in the Prague judicial system, becoming the president judge in the high court there.[11] An avid string player, he composed pleasurable music for his own use, which he shared with like-minded gentlemen through publication. Veit was a model of what Germanists now refer to as the *Bildungsbürgertum*, or the upper middle classes whose position in society relied on their educational attainments and abilities. This group included government servants, teachers, scientists, writers, and intellectuals of all kinds. Music was an especially important pastime for them, as it provided the perfect opportunity to exercise the intellectual

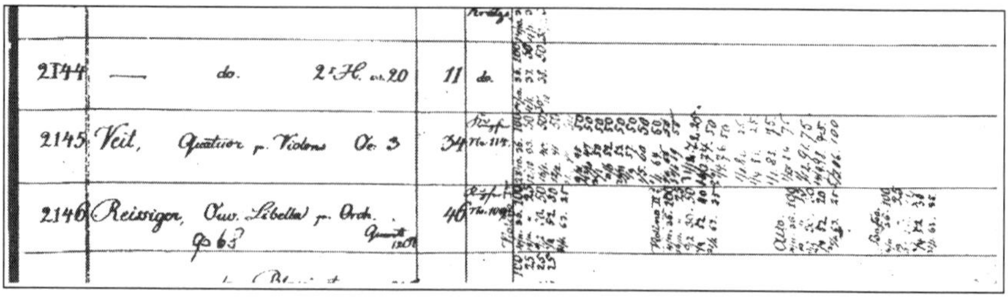

Figure 5.2. Closeup of Hofmeister's *Auflagebuch*: record of reprints for W. H. Veit, String Quintet op. 3.

and educational sophistication that set them apart from other members of the middle classes.[12]

Historian Karin Wurst has argued that the middle classes of the eighteenth and nineteenth centuries—particularly the *Bildungsbürgertum* in German-speaking lands—cultivated new entertainment industries such as fashion, reading, music-making, and theater as forms of self-expression that marked them as middle class and allowed them to exercise newfound liberty to engage in such public recreations.[13] Then as now, the conspicuous consumption of certain products and entertainment options expressed a complex web of identities including gender, marital and economic status, educational attainment, personal interest, and good taste. These industries relied on consumer demand for repeated pleasure in a favorite item or genre, such as the popular coming-of-age novel and romance novel, by balancing a familiar format with new details or characters. Wurst notes that "the reading craze [of the late eighteenth century] was propelled by this desire to repeat the sensation of pleasure. . . . Readers selected reading materials that displayed the same basic structures with only slight variations."[14] Similarly, the new musical works that most pleased recreational musicians, as far as printing data can tell us, tended to use what had become standard multimovement structures in the late eighteenth century and to incorporate memorable surprises that make each work a new adventure within acceptably familiar parameters. In music as in other entertainment commodities of the 1830s and 1840s, the ideal work still balanced references to a shared canonic ideal that demonstrated sophistication and accomplishment with references to current trends and events that showed an ability to keep up with changes in the musical and cultural scene.

The inner movements of Veit's String Quartet op. 3, for example, bear close ties to the Viennese Classical tradition, particularly as represented by Joseph Haydn, but that style is updated to reflect Romantic musical taste. Veit's slow movement clearly references the set of variations on "God Save Francis the Emperor" in Haydn's "Emperor" Quartet op. 76, no. 3 (publ. 1799). Also based on a hymn-like song in praise of an emperor, Veit's work begins with Alexei Lvov's "God Save the Tsar," which won the competition for a new imperial anthem in 1833. Veit's work capitalizes on the vogue for all things "Russian" at this time—in the musical world, sets of variations on Russian themes or tunes proliferated, and larger works incorporating Russian folk music as well as the anthem itself were popular (Tchaikovsky's "1812 Overture" is a late example of this trend). Western European interest in Russian culture was continually renewed throughout the century by revolutionary uprisings and the intermittent wars with and annexations of Poland, Lithuania, and Azerbaijan. The Crimean War, which pitted the Russian Empire against the empires of France, Britain, and the Ottomans, further increased the exotic allure of Russian culture.

Veit's string quartet incorporates the Russian theme into a Classical format that would surely have been familiar to European string players of the nineteenth century. Table 5.1 compares Veit's set of variations to Haydn's. A few significant departures from the "Emperor" model remind us that Veit's work belongs to the later Biedermeier tradition and that works like it ushered in dramatic changes in musical language. Several gestures make the work more accessible and pleasurable for players. Lvov's square, thirty-two-measure theme (two statements of an eight-measure phrase followed by a repeated eight-measure phrase: AA'BB) is simpler than Haydn's arch-like melody composed of five four-measure phrases (AABCC). Veit introduces it in a chorale-influenced, four-voice style, with the main tune played by the first violin (ex. 5.1).

Table 5.1. Comparison of variation procedures in Haydn's "Emperor" Quartet op. 76, no. 3, and Veit's "Russian" Quartet op. 3

Haydn, op. 76, no. 3: 2nd movement in G major		Veit, op. 3: 3rd movement in F major	
Theme	(AABCC form)	Theme	(AABB form)
Var. 1	theme in violin 2, filigree in violin 1	Var. 1	theme in violin 2, filigree in violin 1
Var. 2	theme in cello, countermelody in violin 2	Var. 2	theme ornamented and divided among parts
Var. 3	theme in viola	Var. 3	theme in viola, reharmonized
Var. 4 (in E minor, vi)	theme in violin 1	Var. 4 (in D-flat, flat VI)	alternates two styles viola and cello trade phrases of the theme
		(Var. 5) (in G minor, ii)	fugato on altered theme
closing	extended cadence	closing	theme returns

Example 5.1. Veit, String Quartet in D Minor, op. 3, III, mm. 1–24.

As in Haydn's quartet movement, Veit's Variation 1 gives the tune to the second violin, accompanied by decorative filigree-like writing for the first violin, and in Variation 3 the viola receives an opportunity to interpret the tune with a fresh harmonization that emphasizes the minor submediant (vi, or D minor). This variation also alternates statements of the two halves of the theme in the viola, then the cello, equitably dividing melodic materials among the four participants of the ensemble. Haydn's movement ends with a short Variation 4 that presents his theme in E minor (vi) and modulates to the tonic before the final cadence. Veit's fourth variation, in contrast, juxtaposes topical variants and uses the symmetrical design of the theme to feature different members of the ensemble in an interactive and rich "finale" to the set. Each of the tune's two halves is presented first in a martial style with *fortissimo* and staccato indications (mm. 104–11 for the A portion and mm. 120–27 for the B phrase) and then in a daintier legato style marked *piano* with arpeggiated sixteenth notes in the accompaniment. Example 5.2 shows the martial version of the A portion in measures 104–11 and the legato A' variant that follows in measures 112–19. At measure 136, a bit of fugato-style imitation progresses to a dominant seventh chord that introduces the last statement of the theme itself (mm. 152–64, "Tempo de Tema"). Unlike Haydn's example, Veit alters the theme here by adding an extended plagal cadence (B-flat minor to F major) in the last five measures, which emphasizes the reverent, hymn-like qualities of the original tune. Here as elsewhere in the quartet, Veit's free hand with modal mixture allows him to use a more varied harmonic palette than his predecessor did and to surprise listeners or players with colorful harmonizations of the otherwise straightforward hymn.

The Russian hymn is preceded in Veit's quartet by another eighteenth-century model in nineteenth-century clothes. Although the second movement is labeled a minuet, perhaps briefly bringing to mind the ancien régime and the elegant courts of the prerevolutionary era, its style is clearly that of the fashionable waltzes that characterized the Congress of Vienna and its aftermath (see ex. 5.3). With the sprightly one-beat-per-measure tempo marking of [♩.] = 76, the cello's pizzicato downbeat at the beginning of each four-measure phrase, and the first violin's swirling eighth-note gesture, the movement exemplifies the vigorous dance that took Europe by storm in the nineteenth century.[15] Veit's dance movement in D minor bears other "modern" traits, particularly in its handling of transitions. The "Minuetto" and "Trio" sections are clearly marked and bear their customary repeats to create two miniature rounded binary structures, but Veit includes a dramatic transition between the two sections. Rather than merely cadence in D minor and start fresh at the Trio, as is common in Haydn's minuet movements, Veit's minuet closes by implying minor-dominant harmony (A, C, G) in the second ending, introducing a question-like motif (E–A–A), then closing with a *pianissimo* half cadence that

Example 5.2. Veit, String Quartet in D Minor, op. 3, III, mm. 104–19.

Example 5.2.—*(concluded)*

leads smoothly into the Trio's D-major theme. Veit also dramatizes the ending of the movement as a whole by including a lengthy coda after a written-out repeat of the minuet section rather than simply indicating a *da capo* after the trio. The coda (marked *Piu moto*, mm. 238–80) is loosely based on the Trio materials, recomposed to include a discursive eight-measure section in B minor and a more conclusive and colorful approach to the final cadence (mm. 254–62). These small adjustments add up to create a "minuet" for the new age, based on the modern dance any respectable member of the middle classes would have known from parlor piano collections and from dancing in private and public social settings.

Veit's sonata-form outer movements introduce further innovations that update the form's traditional procedures and simultaneously made the work more accessible for casual players. Veit's approach to sonata form shares many

Example 5.3. Veit, String Quartet in D Minor, op. 3, II, mm. 1–24.

Example 5.3.—*(concluded)*

features with other popular string chamber works of his day, including quartets and quintets by George Onslow, Friedrich Kuhlau, Jan Kalliwoda, Carl Reissiger, and Spohr. Three musical traits set them apart from contemporaneous works by composers more familiar today:

1. They employ what had become standard structures built on Classical models without the pointed use of innovations like inter-movement allusions and cyclical forms common in quartets by their contemporaries; within that conservative framework, though, they use Romanticizing surface features such as adventurous harmonic detours rarely found in late eighteenth-century works.

2. They emphasize repetition on both large and small scales, and this repetition is designed to maximize collegial dialogue among the members of the ensemble.

3. The technical demands are high, but the writing is idiomatic enough that even the most challenging passages feel natural and manageable, unlike the more grueling works of the age that require devoted practice to master.

Veit's sonata-form first movement demonstrates all of these features. In D minor, it opens with a four-measure motif that recurs throughout the movement at important seams in the form, lending a comfortably familiar melodic cue at the same time the music often moves in an unexpected harmonic direction. The motif's stepwise descent from D to D, with an upward leap in measure 2 to emphasize the dominant, begins the work with a steady, predictable pattern that would appear to govern the movement (see ex. 5.4a). The first measure's rhythm of a dotted quarter followed by two sixteenths recalls the opening gesture of Beethoven's First String Quartet op. 18, no. 1, but the continuation down the scale to D draws out this motif and gives it a definitive and anticipated end-point, as opposed to Beethoven's playful, questioning motif followed by pauses and repetitions (compare ex. 5.4b: Beethoven, op. 18, no. 1/I, mm. 1–12, with ex. 5.4a: Veit, op. 3/I, mm. 1–4). The initial predictability of Veit's motif proves a purposeful foil just twelve measures later, when it is repeated *forte* in unison by the quartet, but the seemingly inevitable low D is replaced with an E-flat, indicating that the modulation to the secondary key—from D minor to F major by way of B-flat major (VI)—has begun.

This primary motif appears again at important junctures: it ushers in the secondary theme, and it serves as the basis for the transitional material that follows (mm. 46–49) as well as for the closing theme (mm. 61–68). In these latter examples, alterations to the motif provide novelty within a framework of familiarity. For example, added ornaments mark the leap of a minor third in the cello line (measure 46) and in the first violin line (measure 48), emphasizing a

Example 5.4a. Veit, String Quartet in D Minor, op. 3, I, mm. 1–21.

Example 5.4a.—*(concluded)*

Example 5.4b. Beethoven, String Quartet in F Major, op. 18, no. 1, I, mm. 1–12.

Example 5.5. Veit, String Quartet in D Minor, op. 3, I, mm. 45–50.

brief return to the minor mode in the midst of the secondary key area, which otherwise lies in F major (see ex. 5.5). The closing theme, rather than simply confirming the establishment of F major, also turns to the minor mode and then to the unexpected key of D-flat major (flat VI) before cadencing on F in measure 77.

The recapitulation continues to highlight a variety of distantly related tonal centers in its second half, which gives the whole movement a colorful, adventurous style in keeping with other musical works of the 1830s. The secondary theme returns in D major, for example, although new thematic transitional material provides a completely different approach to the theme and allows Veit to dramatize the arrival of the major mode at measure 157. When this theme has run its course with familiar material from the exposition, the key signature changes back to one flat for the closing theme, which begins with B-flat major (VI in the context of D minor) at the point analogous to the surprising D-flat of the exposition. The coda turns toward the key of the Neapolitan (E-flat major) briefly before the movement closes in D minor with a final ominous-sounding statement of the primary motif. These short harmonic surprises lend a Romantic flair to an otherwise Classically oriented work.

Perhaps because the exposition and recapitulation contain so much quasi-developmental repetition and modulation, the development section itself is short (just fifty-six measures) and straightforward. This tendency to highlight the presentation and repetition of thematic material at the expense of a rigorous development section is evident in the recreational works of other composers from this era, including chamber works by Spohr and Onslow. Veit's development is especially concise and collegial. For example, after a unison statement of the primary motif in D minor, which allows the ensemble a good place to regroup if needed, the music moves to G minor for a series of melodic and harmonic sequences. The three lower voices accompany the first violin in a decorated version of the primary motif, then the two lower voices accompany the same material played by the second violin in A minor. The viola picks up the second half of this theme in E major (mm. 108–10), then the cello takes over, moving the harmony through A major to tonic D minor. The last twenty measures of the development section allow the first violin to engage in acrobatic passagework over sustained dominant harmonies in the lower voices before dropping out again to allow each of those voices a brief imitation of the scalar runs that acted as the foundation for that brilliant-style display. The development closes with a descending chromatic scale set to a pulsing dotted rhythm in all four voices and a gradually diminishing dynamic (mm. 131–35). In this way, Veit brings the mood of the work back to the brooding style of the opening and back to the musical teamwork that made this style so popular with sheet-music purchasers.

Veit's quartet closes with a sonata-form finale that features many of the accessible characteristics described above in a lighter style. Although it begins and ends in D minor, the movement spends more time in the major mode, with the secondary theme/key area dominating much of the form. The airy secondary theme is presented as a duet between the two violins; their leaping two-note gesture provides a rustic, dance-like partnership over an open-fifth drone in the cello and a repeated leaping sixth in the viola (see ex. 5.6). The topical lightness adds a degree of gaiety noticeably absent from the first movement but appropriate for this fun-filled closer. The emphasis here on a collegial exchange between members of the ensemble and the many opportunities for the players to repeat that pleasant interaction demonstrates how Veit's specific use of musical language naturally fit the recreational domestic scenarios in which his works were performed. Outside of the secondary key area, modulations and closing sections in this movement highlight brilliant-style scalar and arpeggiated passages (especially for the first violin) that give the whole a sparkling, buoyant quality.

As in the first movement, some choices indicate a composer seeking to strike the right balance between a reverence for Classical models, on the one hand, and Romantic innovations on the other, which may have led to these works' long-term popularity, or their ability to "age well" in the public marketplace. The finale opens with a bombastic introduction that quickly moves the ensemble through three separate thematic units with distinctive textures and moods before settling in D minor (at the downbeat of m. 23) for the violin's presentation of the primary theme in a simpler homophonic style (pickup to m. 24). The movement begins with a loud, tense unison phrase (see ex. 5.7) that returns at significant junctures in the form, as did the first movement's primary motif. This striking opening also provides the memorable head-motif for the primary theme: the sixteenth-note anacrusis moving up by half-step to a long held tone. In measures 10–14, syncopated entrances briefly divide the ensemble into two duos and propel the music forward. A longer section of ascending passagework for the first violin follows, while the three lower instruments

Example 5.6. Veit, String Quartet in D Minor, op. 3, IV, mm. 79–113.

Example 5.6.—*(concluded)*

accompany in gasping eighth-note chords separated by rests. The breathless rush of ideas must have felt "modern" and exciting for sheet-music purchasers and their indulgent listeners when the work was new in the 1830s, but it surely still felt current in later decades, alongside public works like the symphonies and tone poems of the 1850s and 1860s and newly published chamber music by the likes of Brahms and Dvořák that emphasized a similarly impassioned style.

The finale's off-tonic recapitulation of the primary theme materials provides another example of Veit's Romantic inclination in this otherwise conventional work. The short development section explores the primary head-motif from the introduction at a variety of pitch levels, ending at D-flat major in measure 202. Here, as in the first movement, harmonic motion toward flat-side major keys allows Veit to incorporate abundant harmonic variety in a mostly consonant, rosy style. The use of so many flattened tones, moreover, allows the players to incorporate much vibrato and emotive ornamentation that simultaneously solves practical intonation issues and allows for greater personalization of the experience. A series of half-note chords followed by ascending chromatic motion leads the ensemble back to C major (V of III, in the context of the

Example 5.7. Veit, String Quartet in D Minor, op. 3, IV, mm. 1–47.

Example 5.7.—(concluded)

work's tonic) in measure 212, where the primary theme returns. This off-tonic return allows Veit to continue developmental procedures with a series of sequences that travel through G minor, D minor, and E minor to arrive at A major. Measures 257–77 prolong this dominant harmony in a long, decisive preparation for the return of the tonic major and the secondary theme at measure 280. From here, the recapitulation largely covers the same ground traversed in the exposition, with no significant alterations.

❧   ❧   ❧

Situated stylistically between familiar, exemplary works by Mozart and Haydn on one side and the wild experiments of Beethoven's or Schubert's late works on the other, Veit's recreational string quartet catered to consumers seeking a middle ground during the early decades of musical Romanticism and to those seeking to relive those more certain times in later decades. Works like this one scripted interactions between players that mirror the collegial, recreational gatherings for which they were intended. The individual parts use common, easily learned figuration patterns and accompanimental textures that allow the melody-carrying soloist to "sing" without fighting to overcome the volume and bustle of a polyphonic texture in the other three voices. Seductively simple melodies alternate with brilliant figuration to create a lively, lighthearted atmosphere. This accessible style lies well under the hand and brings pleasure to the performer without requiring much study or practicing. Like other consumable commodities, this work and others like it remained repeatable because the tunes and figuration are simply fun to play; the parts fit together well and easily, providing hours of enjoyment to the players. The shared domestic-centered style employed by numerous composers in the first half of the nineteenth century allowed casual performers to enjoy new works with a leisurely approach—once a group had played one Spohr or Veit quartet, the next work and the next would have felt comfortable and familiar enough to sight-read. That sense of playability distinguishes many of these popular works from the more revered pieces of the period—works by Beethoven, Schubert, Schumann, and Brahms—which were often more difficult for both players and listeners. The domestic style cultivated by Veit and his counterparts was directed at performers who would play the work for pleasure but who possessed enough musical training and discernment to appreciate connections between these new compositions and the Classical models they updated and emulated.

These traits made works by Veit, for instance, appropriate for everyday musical use during an age when domestic music-making was a commonplace activity—they are the "qualities," to use Ralph Locke's term, that made the period and its music distinctive, in contrast to the various innovations and irregularities that make an extraordinary work stand out and that have come to signal compositional "quality" for later generations.[16] The archival evidence that documents publication and reprinting practices of the long nineteenth century shows that this music resonated with Veit's peers in his lifetime and with similar musical enthusiasts well after his death in 1864. Through frequent reprinting, this recreational music continued to influence musicians and musical practice into the twentieth century. Surely composers such as Smetana and Dvořák, both of whom were active in Prague and were string players, encountered quartets and quintets by Veit and his contemporaries when they played among friends and visited music shops. Members of the Brahms-Joachim circle and Viennese musicians like Joseph Hellmesberger interacted regularly with amateur musicians and music lovers who must have enjoyed this music as well.

The characteristics that make this style perfectly suited for its consumers and their specific uses of chamber music also led to its decline in the last decades of the nineteenth century and its near absence from twentieth-century musical consciousness, as represented by performances and histories of music. Modern listeners tend to find these works repetitive, boring, or uneventful because they often lack rigorous development or surprising formal and harmonic innovations. In short, works designed to appeal to an audience of active, if amateur, performers do not always appeal to concert-hall listeners. But when we consider the narrative of musical life in the nineteenth century, we must include music outside the concert hall, including music like this that falls in the uncomfortable cracks between works of high art and trivial commercial products. One of the reasons the nineteenth century is held up as a sort of golden age of musical engagement, when a variety of new institutions were established for amateur and professional musicians and thriving audiences seemed to flourish for them all, is that composers like Václav Veit and his contemporaries wrote recreational music to engage those audiences, and the commercial viability of that product reflected a wide range of musical tastes. Works like the amicable string quartets of Veit and his contemporaries demonstrate the diversity and richness of musical life during the long nineteenth century and the important role commerce and the music business played in that culture.

Notes

1. For representative examples, see Carl Dahlhaus, *Nineteenth-Century Music*, trans. J. Bradford Robinson (Berkeley: University of California Press, 1989), 75–81; Leon Plantinga, *Romantic Music: A History of Musical Style in Nineteenth-Century Europe* (New York: W. W. Norton, 1984); Jim Samson, ed., *The Cambridge History of Nineteenth-Century Music* (Cambridge: Cambridge University Press, 2002). Discussion of chamber music after Beethoven is even more sparse in general histories and textbooks that treat multiple periods, such as J. Peter Burkholder, *A History of Western Music*, 9th ed. (New York: W. W. Norton, 2014); Douglass Seaton, *Ideas and Styles in the Western Musical Tradition*, 3rd ed. (Oxford: Oxford

University Press, 2010); Richard Taruskin and Christopher H. Gibbs, *The Oxford History of Western Music, College Edition* (Oxford: Oxford University Press, 2013).

2. The concert harp, also an acceptable instrument for young ladies, is a similarly unwieldy, furniture-like installment.

3. Christina Bashford, "Historiography and Invisible Musics: Domestic Chamber Music in Nineteenth-Century Britain," *Journal of the American Musicological Society* 63, no. 2 (2010): 291–360.

4. The first section of this chapter summarizes findings about the publication of chamber music available in greater detail in Marie Sumner Lott, *The Social Worlds of Nineteenth-Century Chamber Music: Composers, Consumers, Communities* (Urbana-Champaign: University of Illinois Press, 2015). The larger second section provides an analytical case study explored here for the first time in print. An earlier version of this chapter was presented at the 2013 meeting of the American Musicological Society in Pittsburgh, Pennsylvania, and in other conference venues. I am grateful to Douglas Shadle, Cindy L. Kim, Kristen Meyers Turner, and Christina Bashford for their comments on earlier versions of this work.

5. Franz Liszt and his associates would mock that learnedness (understood by the "New German School" adherents as conservatism) in his well-known comments made to Robert Schumann. Liszt described Schumann's Piano Quintet op. 44, as "too Leipzigerisch" upon first hearing it, upsetting the composer and rending their friendship.

6. These catalogs record what music was published by whom and at what cost to the consumer, providing an invaluable tool for modern-day researchers. In the nineteenth century, they allowed music sellers and publishers to advertise their music (and music by foreign publishers distributed in German lands) and to acquire new works for their shops, promoting collegial distribution and greater variety for the consumer. See Rudolf Elvers and Cecil Hopkinson, "A Survey of the Music Catalogues of Whistling and Hofmeister," *Fontes Artis Musicae* 19 (1972): 1–7. In 2004, a research team based at Royal Holloway of the University of London created a searchable online database called Hofmeister XIX with the complete Hofmeister-Whistling catalogs at http://www.hofmeister.rhul.ac.uk/2008/index.html (accessed July 18, 2016).

7. See James Deaville, "Publishing Paraphrases and Creating Collectors: Friedrich Hofmeister, Franz Liszt, and the Technology of Popularity," in *Franz Liszt and His World*, ed. Christopher Gibbs and Dana Gooley (Princeton: Princeton University Press, 2006), 255–88. I am grateful for his guidance at the early stages of my investigation of this treasure trove.

8. Throughout this discussion, references to copies of chamber music and individual musical works will indicate a set of parts for performance. Music for multiple players in this era was rarely printed in score format, which was typically reserved for study scores of "Classical" works, such as Ignaz Pleyel's series of pocket scores (Bibliothèque Musicale, begun in 1802), which included quartets by Haydn alongside the composer's symphonies and works by Mozart, Beethoven, Hummel, and Onslow. In exceptional cases, a score might be produced several years after the parts were published, as was the case for Mendelssohn's and Schumann's string quartets. In the 1870s, the printing of "score and parts" became more common, though not the normal expectation.

9. See Robert Schumann's series of "Quartett-Morgen" reports in the *Neue Zeitschrift* published between June and September 1838 (vol. 8, nos. 46, 49; vol. 9, nos. 10, 13, 20) and his review "Preis-Quartett Julius Schapler" from May 3, 1842 (vol. 16, no. 36: 142–43).

10. Peters reissued Spohr's quartets op. 4 in a Peters Edition volume later in the century. The Peters Edition used a new lithographic process that allowed the publisher to generate very large print runs of several thousand copies from a single set of plates, printed on lighter, cheaper paper. Thus works included in that series of publications were frequently new editions of very popular works that could sell between five thousand and ten thousand copies in a few years' time. For the role of chamber music in this series, see Sumner Lott, *Social Worlds*, 38–42.

11. For a brief and somewhat "rosy" biography of Veit, see the memoir by Wilhelmine Cartellieri, "Erinnerungen an Wenzel Heinrich Veit," *Deutsche Arbeit* 3 (1903–4): 820–45.

12. See William Weber, *Music and the Middle Classes: The Social Structure of Concert Life in London, Paris, and Vienna between 1830 and 1848*, 2nd ed. (Burlington, VT: Ashgate, 2002). In the 1990s, social scientists and cultural historians began to revise their collective understanding of the "middle classes," which had actually focused mainly on the working class, or laborers, and ignored the more affluent nonaristocratic groups in European society up to that point. Following the fall of the Berlin Wall in 1989, research on the bourgeoisie expanded considerably. Germanist Jonathan Sperber noted at the time that "the workers are out; the Bürger are in." See Jonathan Sperber, "Burger, Bürgertum, Bürgerlichkeit, Bürgerliche Gesellschaft: Studies of the German (Upper) Middle Class and Its Sociocultural World," *Journal of Modern History* 69, no. 2 (1997): 271–97. Scholars of French, Italian, Russian, and other European societies have also embraced the bourgeoisie in the past twenty-five years. See Pamela Pilbeam, *The Middle Classes in Europe, 1789–1914: France, Germany, Italy, and Russia* (London: Macmillan, 1990); Jürgen Kocka and Allan Mitchell, eds., *Bourgeois Society in Nineteenth-Century Europe* (Oxford: Berg, 1993); Hartmut Kaelble, ed., *The European Way: European Societies during the Nineteenth and Twentieth Centuries* (New York: Berghahn, 2004).

13. Karin Wurst, *Fabricating Pleasure: Fashion, Entertainment, and Cultural Consumption in Germany, 1780–1830* (Detroit: Wayne State University Press, 2005), esp. chapter 2 ("The Differentiation of the Middle Class"), 23–40.

14. Ibid., 96.

15. For an extended discussion of the waltz and its importance for nineteenth-century musical culture, see Eric McKee, *Decorum of the Minuet, Delirium of the Waltz: A Study of Dance-Music Relations in $\frac{3}{4}$ Time* (Bloomington: Indiana University Press, 2011).

16. Ralph P. Locke, "Nineteenth-Century Music: Quantity, Quality, Qualities," *Nineteenth-Century Music Review* 1, no. 1 (2004): 3–41. See also Marie Sumner Lott, "Changing Audiences, Changing Styles: String Chamber Music and the Industrial Revolution," in *Instrumental Music and the Industrial Revolution: Proceedings of the International Conference, Cremona, 1–3 July 2006*, ed. Roberto Illiano and Luca Sala (Bologna: Ut Orpheus, 2010), 175–239.

Chapter Six

In Vienna "Only Waltzes Get Printed"

The Decline and Transformation of the *Contredanse Hongroise* in the Early Nineteenth Century

Catherine Mayes

In Vienna at the turn of the nineteenth century, the enjoyment of music and dances of various national origins was both common and unsurprising, as subjects from lands throughout the Habsburg Empire flocked to the city to make their living. In Viennese author Joseph Ferdinand Kringsteiner's 1807 farce *Der Tanzmeister*, a chorus of guests at a private ball provides humorous confirmation of the multitude of dances that could be included in such an event. I reproduce the text of the chorus here, both in its original dialect and in an approximate English translation.

> Der Anfang, so ists Etikett,
> der geschieht mit einem Menuett.
> Dann wirbeln gleich die Pauken drein
> Und's fallen halt die Deutschen ein;
> Dann gehts erst, so ist's der Brauch,
> Uiber d'Landlerischen auch
> Ist das vorbey, so weiß man eh,
> Da kömmt sodann das englische,
> Dann wechseln wir mit türkischen,

Bald wieder mit Kosakischen;
Damit man endlich alls probirt,
Wird Ungarisch auch produzirt;
Und habn wir g'nug tanzt, dann erst
gehn wir nach Haus,
Doch vorher, versteht sich, kömmt noch
der Kehraus.[1]

[The opening, according to etiquette,
takes place with a minuet.
Then the kettledrums roll in
And the German dances just break right out;
Then next come, according to custom,
The Ländlers too[;]
When those are over, as one knows,
Then come the English dances,
Then we switch to the Turkish dance,
Soon again to the Cossack dance;
Finally[,] so that one tries everything,
The Hungarian dance is also cranked out;
And once we've danced enough, only then
do we go home,
But before that, of course, comes
the Kehraus.]

Most of the dances mentioned in this chorus—the minuet; the German dance and Ländler, whose names were often used interchangeably; the English dance, or longways contredanse; the Cossack dance; and the Kehraus, or last dance of the ball—were common at the turn of the nineteenth century, and references to and descriptions of them appear in numerous contemporary sources. The allusion to a Turkish dance, however, is more unusual; Turkish dances were sometimes imitated in stage works, but Turkish music and the militaristic *alla turca* style that evoked it for Western European consumers were not typically associated with social dancing.[2]

Yet of all the dances to which this chorus alludes, the Hungarian is undoubtedly the least familiar, least studied, and consequently least well understood today, despite the fact that beginning in the early 1780s, published representations of Hungarian-Gypsy music flooded the Viennese music market.[3] Example 6.1, reproduced from an anonymous 1788 collection titled *Contredanses hongroises*, is typical of this repertoire, featuring repetitive figurations within four-square parallel periods combined in an additive fashion and departing only briefly from the home key of F major, modulating to the subdominant for the final period before the *da capo*. Its duple meter, murky bass, and alternating tonic and dominant harmonies are also characteristic of Viennese representations of Hungarian-Gypsy music.

Example 6.1. Anonymous [probably Stanislaw Ossowski], *Contredanses hongroises,* no. 5 (Vienna: no pub., 1788); in Géza Papp, ed., *Hungarian Dances 1784–1810,* Musicalia Danubiana 7 (Budapest: Magyar Tudományos Akadémia, Zenetudományi Intézet, 1986), 125–27. Reproduced by permission of the Institute for Musicology of the Hungarian Academy of Sciences, Budapest, Hungary.

Example 6.1.—*(concluded)*

Da Capo

Although the sheer number of such pieces attests to their commercial success, their use in social dancing has remained largely unexplored. Rebecca Harris-Warrick, for instance, has noted that "Hungarian dances, such as the Gypsy-inflected *verbunkos,* began having a musical impact in Vienna in the last third of the [eighteenth] century," yet her qualification of their impact as purely "musical" undermines the possibility of their use as an accompaniment to dancing.[4] More recently, Jonathan Bellman has declared that the "*ongherese,*" like the fandango and polonaise, "would either have had specialized choreography (when performed in European centers) or been observed by relatively few western Europeans when danced *in situ.*" He elaborates that "because the *ongherese* was never part of the conventional dance suite, the only steps associated with it were those described by travelers or those choreographed for Hungarian-themed ballets."[5] Yet Géza Papp has suggested that in the twilight of the eighteenth century, the Hungarian dance was well-known in Europe and enjoyed by performers, listeners, and dancers alike.[6] By drawing on contemporary and more recent writings about social dancing in Vienna and about Hungarian-Gypsy dances in particular, I argue that publications such as example 6.1 would have been used as accompaniments to contredanses around the turn of the nineteenth century. Moreover, even in the absence of an explicit title such as the one under which example 6.1 was issued, the perceived affect and simplistic style of Hungarian-Gypsy dances were consonant with the contemporary understanding of the contredanse.

Nevertheless, as fashions in dancing changed and the contredanse lost ground to the increasingly popular waltz, the consumer appeal of these publications waned. They were gradually replaced by representations of a different kind, which capitalized on the growing cult of instrumental difficulty and virtuosity, as well as a developing affinity for more pronounced music-stylistic exoticism, as demonstrated by example 6.2—reproduced from a different anonymous collection issued in Vienna, the third volume of *Originelle ungarische Nationaltänze* of 1810 or 1811. Example 6.2 is markedly different from example 6.1: the figuration is more varied, combining straight with triplet sixteenth notes; the specified, slow tempo allows for melodic ornamentation through grace notes, trills, and a thirty-second-note turn; and perhaps most striking, the harmony manifests what Shay Loya has referred to as a fascination with the "alien exotic."[7] Over the course of the first four measures, the dance modulates from G minor to F major; slips into E-flat major after the repeat sign, only to cadence again in F major in measure 8; and takes up G minor again at the beginning of the last phrase, which ultimately cadences in B-flat major.

Although 1810 has long been recognized as an approximate turning or tipping point around which Hungarian-Gypsy dances became melodically, harmonically, and rhythmically much richer, the cause of this stylistic change has always been traced to what Loya has summarized as "shifting socio-political conditions that affected cultural-translation strategies," including the rise of Hungarian political nationalism.[8] In fact, Loya himself has attributed the transformation to what he has termed "authorial *verbunkos*": pieces of Hungarian-Gypsy music emblematic of the art of a specific celebrated musician or composer, most notably including János Bihari (1764–1827), János Lavotta (1764–1820), and Antal Csermák (1774–1822).[9] Loya ascribes the relative simplicity of early representations such as example 6.1—as compared to the greater complexity of later publications such as example 6.2—to what he calls the "quasi-Ossianic" ideology and "intellectual austerity" underlying the earlier repertoire rather than to actual changes over time in the melodic, harmonic, and rhythmic richness of the music performed by ensembles of Hungarian-Gypsy musicians themselves.[10] Similarly, Loya's explanation of the advent of greater stylistic complexity in published dances—"authorial *verbunkos*'s" stamp of individuality—highlights a particular manifestation of the much more widespread Romantic cult of uniqueness and originality in the nineteenth century.

Example 6.2. Anonymous, *24 originelle ungarische Nationaltänze für das Clavier*, vol. 3, no. 10 (Vienna: Chemische Druckerey, 1810 or 1811); in Papp, *Hungarian Dances 1784–1810*, 258. Reproduced by permission of the Institute for Musicology of the Hungarian Academy of Sciences, Budapest, Hungary.

Thought-provoking as this account may be, it fails to consider representations of Hungarian-Gypsy music as products and reflections of their function within Viennese society, not simply as objects whose style evolved independent of particular consumer demands and social practices. By investigating these social practices and, as David Gramit has argued, by approaching music as "an activity in which people engage," we gain a fundamentally different perspective on how, when, and why stylistic changes happen.[11] Given the centrality of social dancing to Viennese life in the early nineteenth century, the stylistic transformation we witness in representations of Hungarian-Gypsy music around 1810 may productively and convincingly be linked to specific changes in the popularity of certain dances rather than only to the much more generalized "celebration of creative individualism" proposed by Loya.[12] Thus although I consider a narrow repertoire at a particular moment in history, the broader significance of this case study lies in its exploration of the intersection of musical style with the status of music as a social activity and commercial product.

❧   ❧   ❧

The only detailed description of the choreography of the Hungarian dance as a specialized and distinct Western European social dance of which I am aware appears in Carl Joseph von Feldtenstein's treatise *Erweiterung der Kunst nach der Chorographie zu tanzen, Tänze zu erfinden, und aufzusetzen*, published in Braunschweig in 1772. Feldtenstein's explanation merits a lengthy quotation:

> The Hungarian dance has the same affects as the three previously introduced, namely the *Hannakischer*, *Masurischer*, and *Kosakischer*, and these go so well together that those who dance them (even when they must dance them on command—these are always the dullest dances) dance them nonetheless with feeling because they are carried away by the composition of the charming and comical music. The affects expressed through this dance are, as it were, divided, and each sex is allocated its role, so that the flirtatious affect is given to the female dancer and the free, comical wildness is given to the male dancer.
>
> I would still need to have various copper engravings made of choreographic symbols if I wanted to work with the steps and figures of this dance, but because I am writing mostly for my own pupils so they can remember the information they received, I will make do with a demonstration. I mention as a caveat that the female dancers must avail themselves of flirtatious manners and the steps associated with these [manners], as well as *solid* turns, just like the male dancers, higher, and with confused positions, whereby regular and irregular [false positions] are mixed together, which can be seen on the second copper plate . . . so that every trained dancer must adopt a comfortable wildness (if I may say so). However, he must also spin his female partner in a certain, *solid* manner and at the same time unite himself with her in the flirtatious affect, revealing the apparent wildness as a boisterous and somewhat exaggerated joy only when each partner dances figures alone. Thus will the beautiful be granted also to this nation in its dance.[13]

The figures on the copper plate to which Feldtenstein refers show only the male dancer's initial foot positions in Feuillet notation, many of which are what French dancing treatises refer to as false positions, typically associated with theatrical dances. Feldtenstein's figures thus lend further weight to Eva Campianu's assertion that many national dances became popular social dances only after first having been displayed in the theater.[14]

Although it would admittedly be very difficult to perform a Hungarian dance based solely on Feldtenstein's description of it, in his commentary on the *Hannakischer*, Feldtenstein suggests an approach to performing both

dances that would require very few instructions. The *Hannakischer*, he speci-
fies, "possesses the ease of the *Schwäbischer*, that each couple can dance
according to their own expression without it being necessary to follow [what]
others [do]."[15] Given the similarity in affect Feldtenstein noted between the
Hungarian and the Hanakian dances at the beginning of his description of
the former, they likely also shared the same freedom of performance in his
view. As Kurt Petermann has emphasized, exhortations to improvised or
quasi-improvised performance of national dances are common throughout
Feldtenstein's treatise and reflect his broader support of naturalism in dance,
which he believed was hindered through the imposition of too many rules.
Feldtenstein's position, according to Petermann, was that "where national
dances are concerned[,] the ability and taste of the dancers should take prece-
dence over the structure and choreography of the dance."[16]

This attitude reflects the broader democratization of dance especially in
the second half of the eighteenth century, manifested in practical terms by
the remarkable ascendancy of the contredanse during this time, which Curt
Sachs has interpreted as "analogous with the rise of bourgeois society and the
decline of the aristocratic culture."[17] In almost every respect, the contredanse
was the opposite of the minuet, whose position of prominence in ballrooms
it quickly overtook: the minuet was danced by a single couple, whereas the
contredanse could be enjoyed by as few as six or eight dancers or by "as many
as will," to use John Playford's phrasing in *The English Dancing Master*.[18] The
minuet was performed for the enjoyment of onlookers, specifically the *présence*
(the highest-ranking person or persons toward whom the *révérences*, or opening
and closing bows and curtsies, were directed), while the contredanse was primarily intended to give pleasure to the dancers themselves. Further, the minuet's steps, choreography, and etiquette required extensive training to master,
whereas the contredanse was much simpler, "essentially a walk or alternation
of steps," as Wye Jamison Allanbrook has aptly described it, or in Adolph
Bernhard Marx's words, a "dancelike movement" performed by couples tracing a series of figures.[19]

Sachs has noted that to ensure their accessibility, dancing manuals devoted
to contredanses were typically much simpler than those explicating the minuet.[20] The walking and gliding steps of the contredanse achieved the same
accessibility, as did the dance's adaptability to varying numbers and arrangements of dancers: linear columns or the circular or square formations for two
to eight couples favored in France and known as *cotillons* or *contredanses françaises*. As Freda Burford and Anne Daye have explained, "Figures were executed
with any suitable steps familiar to the company or chosen by individual dancers," leaving ample room for improvisation and personal expression as well
as current fashion.[21] Steps were also imported from other eighteenth-century
dances, including the gavotte, bourrée, and rigaudon. Yet the plain walking

steps called for in various editions of Playford's *Dancing Master* remained very attractive to dancers, especially in Vienna, as Herbert Lager and Hilde Seidl have documented in their study of the contredanse in the Habsburg capital. As they relate, the nineteenth-century Viennese dancing master Eduard Rabensteiner recommended that modest dancers cultivate walking or gliding steps in performing contredanses, signaling a departure from the more complicated steps favored in the previous century, especially in France. Yet even there, simpler steps eventually prevailed, leading the Sieur De La Cuisse to admonish his pupils by 1762 that dances should consist of dance steps, not simply "promenading."[22]

Thus Feldtenstein's instructions pertaining to the "English dance," or longways contredanse, which allow for freely improvised variations insofar as the music and the skill and number of dancers permit, clearly reflect widely held notions about this dance's versatility and adaptability.[23] Indeed, Friedrich Schiller upheld the contredanse as a symbol of an ideal society in which "each seems only to be following his own inclination, yet without ever getting in the way of anybody else. It is the most perfectly appropriate symbol of the assertion of one's own freedom and regard for the freedom of others."[24] Although it would be impractical for the couples performing a contredanse, or any group dance, for that matter, to dance entirely "without following what others do," as Feldtenstein suggested for the Hanakian dance, the freedom inherent in the enjoyment of the contredanse resonates strongly with that which he suggested was appropriate for many national dances.

The perceived similarity between the contredanse and the Hungarian dance, furthermore, was suggested long before Feldtenstein wrote his dancing manual and before *contredanses hongroises* such as the one given as example 6.1 were published. When the Silesian composer and music theorist Daniel Speer (1636–1707) traveled through Hungary, he observed that "Hungarian dances were similar to Western dances but more orderly and charming." More specifically, Louis XIV's ambassador to Hungary, Abbé Révérend, described in his memoirs the dances he encountered there as "similar to French *branles* and *contredanses*."[25] By then, the contredanse was well established as a popular dance not only in France but elsewhere in Europe as well; Lager and Seidl date the emergence of the longways contredanse in Vienna to approximately 1700, with the *cotillon* appearing slightly later, ca. 1720.[26]

It seems only natural that visitors to Hungary would interpret and compare the dances they witnessed there to those with which they were already familiar; in the case of the Hungarian-Gypsy *verbunkos*, used in Hungary both for military recruiting and as a social dance, the similarities to the contredanse may have been particularly striking. As László Kürti has explained, *verbunkos* exists in versions for solo, couple, and group performance, the latter variant of which is performed in a circular formation, undoubtedly reminiscent of the formation in which couples faced each other when performing a *cotillon*. The circular types of the dance, called *karéj* or *körverbunkos*, were particularly common in the western regions of Hungary and, like the contredanse, featured simple but organized steps and figures, determined by the leading dancer.[27] It is unsurprising, therefore, that in Vienna especially, with its close proximity to western Hungary, *contredanses hongroises* such as the one reproduced as example 6.1 arose as one type of contredanse with mildly exotic-sounding music; in addition to the *Contredanses hongroises* that appeared in manuscript copy in Vienna in 1788, from which example 6.1 is excerpted, a *Contradanza all'Ungarese* was included in the July 15, 1809, issue of the *Musikalisches Wochenblatt*.[28] Yet the paucity of instructions in social dancing manuals about the performance of Hungarian dances outside Hungary suggests that the hundreds of examples of Hungarian-Gypsy dances published for Western European or specifically Viennese consumers in the late eighteenth and early nineteenth centuries were in fact enjoyed as familiar contredanses—for which no further or special directions were necessary—regardless of whether their status as such was made explicit through specific titles.

This contention is strongly supported by comparing the musical characteristics of representations of Hungarian-Gypsy dances issued from approximately 1784 to 1810 to contemporary descriptions of the defining traits of the contredanse. In his *Dictionnaire de musique* of 1768, Jean-Jacques Rousseau explains that the contredanse is

> executed by four, six, [or] eight persons and usually danced at balls after the minuets because it is more gay and involves more persons. The melodies of contredanses are most often in duple meter; they must be well articulated, brilliant, and gay, yet quite simple; since they are repeated so often, they would become intolerable if they were overly ornate. As with all things, those that are the simplest are those of which one tires the least.[29]

Johann Georg Sulzer echoes much of Rousseau's definition in his *Allgemeine Theorie der schönen Künste* while providing additional musical details in his treatment of "English dances":

> These are also called contredanses, from the English word "Country-dances." . . . These dances . . . may be performed together by four, six, eight, or more persons; therefore after minuets are danced for a certain period of time at balls, most of the remaining time is spent performing contredanses since they occupy more persons at once and since one can alternate between them indefinitely, for there are innumerable contredanses. They exist in a variety of duple and triple meters, but all are similar in that they are very lively and for the most part they are moderately comical, thereby uniting pleasure and decorum. . . . The music of English dances, which are called *Angloisen* in

Germany, is in general very simple and lively, divided into very clearly notice-able sections, and [it] displays through varied [means] the particular [characteristic] that its cadences fall on the upbeat.[30]

Both Daniel Gottlob Türk and Heinrich Christoph Koch emphasize many of the same features in their discussions of the contredanse as do Rousseau and Sulzer, notably liveliness, simplicity and artlessness, and a moderately comical affect; a generally upbeat tempo; duple or triple meter; and sectional divisions of the music. Türk adds that "the first note of every measure is strongly accented."[31]

The affect of the contredanse highlighted by these authors maps well onto the "flirtatiousness" and "comical wildness" of the Hungarian dance described by Feldtenstein, a dance that also treads a middle ground between the "pleasure" and "decorum" Sulzer identified as defining the contredanse. The simplicity and artlessness of the music that accompanied contredanses mirrored the unpretentiousness and freedom of execution of the dance itself and may have reflected its purportedly rustic or pastoral origins; as Koch reminded his readers, English dances are "also called *Contretänze*, an expression that originated from the English word 'Country-dances' and that refers to dances that are customary to the peasantry of the various provinces."[32] Similarly, Hungarian dances—and indeed Eastern European national musics in general—were widely understood by Western Europeans to be the product of a realm of largely rural and vernacular, as opposed to urban and cultivated, music-making, and the plainness of the musical style of representations such as example 6.1 translates this perceived lack of sophistication.[33]

The specific music-stylistic features of contredanses have been further explored in recent scholarship, and, as I've suggested, these characteristics are also clearly reflected in many representations of Hungarian-Gypsy dances from the turn of the nineteenth century. They include:

1. Duple meter, whether simple or compound. In Vienna, $\frac{2}{4}$ meter was predominant.[34] In the 1790s, contredanses in $\frac{3}{8}$ or $\frac{3}{4}$ meter began to appear as well.[35]
2. "Clarity and symmetry," which were reflected through "regular hypermetric patterns."[36]
3. Four-measure phrases with a narrow range combined to form eight-measure (or sometimes sixteen-measure) periods, most of which were enclosed within repeat signs and followed one another in a chain-like fashion.
4. Predominance of major keys and simple harmonic structures.
5. Composition and publication in sets, often of four, six, or twelve dances.

In addition, further attributes distinguish the three main types of contredanses: the *contredanse anglaise, contredanse française,* and *contredanse allemande.* Whereas the *contredanse anglaise* was performed by two columns of dancers, with men and women facing each other and each couple executing a series of figures with the successive couple down the line until the original leaders had regained their place at the head of the formation, the *contredanse française* was performed by couples in a square arrangement dancing a series of nine, ten, or twelve *entrées* that were the same for all contredanses and alternated with a refrain particular to each individual contredanse, resulting in a rondo-like structure. The music of the *contredanse française* responded to this structure as well as to the preference for French dance steps, especially the rigaudon and gavotte, the latter of which required a half-measure upbeat. This upbeat was also characteristic of the music accompanying *contredanses anglaises.*[37]

The *contredanse allemande,* in contrast, was characterized by phrases beginning on the downbeat, a turn figure or other ornament in measure four, and a formal structure following the pattern AA BB CC XX.[38] The music reproduced here as example 6.1, for instance, has all the features of a *contredanse allemande*: $\frac{2}{4}$ meter; simple melodies rarely exceeding the range of an octave; symmetrical four-measure phrases combined to form eight-measure periods and one eight-measure sentence, each of which is repeated; major home key with only a brief excursion to the subdominant; virtually exclusive use of tonic and dominant chords within each key area; phrases beginning on downbeats; turn figures ornamenting the melody typically every fourth measure; a formal structure corresponding to the pattern AA BB CC DD AA BB; and publication as part of a set of twelve dances.

Indeed, each of the dances in the 1788 *Contredanses hongroises* collection is of the *contredanse allemande* type, yet seven of the dances also appeared in other contemporary collections—the *Zingarese* of 1792 (distributed in manuscript copy by Johann Traeg) and the *VI Danses hongroises* of 1791 (published by Hoffmeister), for instance—whose titles in no way identify them as including contredanses. Similarly, all twenty-eight of the *Ausgesuchte ungarische Nationaltänze,* purportedly notated from the playing of Gypsies from Galanta (the region surrounding Pozsony, or Pressburg in German; now Bratislava, the capital of Slovakia) and published by Ignaz Sauer in 1803, are *contredanses allemandes.* Each of these collections, furthermore, was scored for solo keyboard, and a version of the *VI Danses hongroises* for two violins and bass was also published in 1791.[39] These two instrumentations were the most common ones used to accompany dancing at small, domestic balls in the late eighteenth and early nineteenth centuries; in addition, keyboard arrangements of dances were used as accompaniments to dance practice. As dancing among the middle and upper classes in Vienna became increasingly oriented toward small gatherings rather than large balls around 1800, reflecting a reaction against the overcrowding of public ballrooms after they were opened to all classes of society in the 1770s and 1780s, collections of dances that could easily be performed by soloists or small chamber ensembles in the home held great consumer appeal.[40]

Although we lack specific information about the purchasers who acquired the particular collections of keyboard dances from which the examples I've discussed are excerpted, it is reasonable to assume that they were primarily the same ones who bought other music of similar difficulty and function: women and girls. As numerous scholars have documented, women were the principal consumers of keyboard music in the eighteenth and early nineteenth centuries, regardless of whether a given publication was overtly marketed to them; in this sense, as Matthew Head has observed, explicit dedications to women on the title pages of music scores were redundant.[41] Rather, the stylistic simplicity of keyboard music was the primary indication that women were its intended market, for "easiness," with its associations with beauty, charm, and naturalness, was synonymous with femininity. The markers of "easiness" Head has identified—"keys without many sharps and flats, melody-centered styles, and avoidance of both figuration (however easily it might fall under the hands) and thick, reinforced textures"[42]—are nowhere more evident than in collections of Hungarian-Gypsy dances arranged for the pleasure of Viennese amateurs. Given that publishers knew and understood their buying public, issuing music with an eye to sales, this observation is unsurprising, as is the inclusion of words such as *"Danses," "Contredanses,"* or *"Tänze"* in the titles of many of these collections, promising an agreeable pastime for the purchaser and her family and friends.

What is perhaps most remarkable about such collections, then, is their reference to Hungarian and Gypsy styles, which tantalized consumers through the suggestion of music that was exotic on many levels: not only nationally foreign but foreign to the domestic sphere of amateur women, for *verbunkos* was originally performed in public by ensembles of professional male Gypsy musicians. In an age when public and private realms were rigorously demarcated and gendered, such promised exoticism may explain how these collections enticed consumers, even though the music they contained was ultimately a very far cry from actual *verbunkos* and not necessarily even particularly exotic in style.[43] Thus although references to dances in Hungarian and Gypsy styles were largely false advertisement, they functioned and succeeded as advertisement nonetheless, for they lured purchasers through the evocation of a sphere of music-making—and of life—very different from their own, yet still enjoyable and understandable as familiar contredanses.

But the preferred types of dances at gatherings large and small were changing. According to Reingard Witzmann's study of *Ländler* in Vienna, the earliest references to the ancestors of the waltz—lively, rustic triple-time dances such as the *Deutscher, Ländler,* and *Steyrischer*—emerged around 1750, and the development of the waltz continued unabated until about 1815, by which point it had essentially attained the form with which we are still familiar today.[44] Just as stylistic changes in music occur gradually, fashions in dancing also change progressively, and it is difficult to identify exactly when—or precisely why—the waltz attained its position of preeminence in Vienna and elsewhere. In 1812, Lord Byron apostrophized the "Endearing Waltz" in his hymn to the dance, declaring that "to thy [more] melting tune / bow Irish Jig, and ancient Rigadoon. / Scotch reels, avaunt! and Country-dance forego / your future claims to each fantastic toe! / Waltz—Waltz alone—both legs and arms demand[s], / liberal of feet, and lavish of her hands."[45] Reports from Vienna attest to the rising popularity of the waltz by 1790, yet the contredanse continued to hold its own, especially in the domestic balls of the middle and upper classes, often with waltz steps and arm movements mixed into its figures.[46]

Gradually, however, the appeal of the contredanse waned, perhaps for the very reason it was initially so beloved: its ease of execution and openness to variation were interpreted, in the words of one contemporary commentator, as "nothing but a characterless tripping. . . . The beautiful art has sunk to the level of ordinary physical exercises. They stamp around and leap to the rhythm and call that dancing."[47] As Peter van der Merwe has noted, during approximately the years 1815–30, the waltz, in various forms, extended its reach into music of all kinds, from the salon pieces of Schubert and Chopin to Berlioz's depiction of it in his *Symphonie fantastique,* much as the contredanse had in the previous century, appearing in everything from anonymous *Hausmusik* to Haydn's symphonic finales.[48] Indeed, writing to his teacher József Elsner from Vienna on January 26, 1831, Chopin complained that in the Habsburg capital, "only waltzes get printed."[49] Eventually, the quadrille and polka became sensations, taking Vienna by storm around 1840 and filling the gap for duple-meter dances engendered by the decline of the contredanse.

Thus in waltz-crazed Vienna in the first decades of the nineteenth century, collections of Hungarian-Gypsy contredanses no longer held the appeal they once had, and as consumer products, they needed to respond to the demands of a changing market. Example 6.2, in fact, was originally issued in 1788 as the ninth dance of the *Contredanses hongroises;* as example 6.3 demonstrates, a brief examination of the first eight measures of the original dance alone reveals how a change in tempo, harmonization, and figuration turned a simple and lively contredanse strain into a much more complex and foreign-sounding phrase (cf. ex. 6.2). The transformation of these few measures of music between 1788 and 1810 or 1811 is representative of a widespread shift toward greater difficulty and exoticism in representations of Hungarian-Gypsy music in the nineteenth century, as exemplified, for instance, by Schubert's *Divertissement à l'hongroise,* D. 818, as well as by works in the *style brillant* such as Carl Georg

Example 6.3. Anonymous [probably Stanislaw Ossowski], *Contredanses hongroises,* no. 9, mm. 1–8 (Vienna: no pub., 1788); in Papp, *Hungarian Dances 1784–1810,* 130. Reproduced by permission of the Institute for Musicology of the Hungarian Academy of Sciences, Budapest, Hungary.

Lickl's *Les Charmes de Presbourg: Rondeau brillant à l'hongroise* (Vienna, 1825) and ultimately by Liszt's *Hungarian Rhapsodies.*[50] The *style brillant* itself, which peaked in popularity in the 1820s and 1830s, responded to the desires of consumers, now for displays of what Ignaz Moscheles described in his diary as "amazing powers of execution, overwrought sentimentality, and the production of piquant effects by the most rapid changes from the soft to the loud pedal, or by rhythms and modulations, which if not to be completely repudiated, are only allowable on the rarest occasions."[51]

Although Moscheles himself rejected empty virtuosity, his personal taste as a composer was likely ultimately of less consequence as a determinant of musical style than were the preferences and demands of consumers. In his day as in ours, music existed within and responded to a wider culture not only of ideological, intellectual, and aesthetic trends but also of concrete social practices, of which it was but one strand. As Rupert Ridgewell reminds us (chapter 2 of this volume), a Viennese *Kunsthandlung* around the turn of the nineteenth century sold not only music but books, maps, various artwork, scientific "gadgets," games, supplies for leisure activities such as needlework and sketching—in short, "everything regarded as 'cultural.'" Changes in musical style, as this case study demonstrates, can therefore only be fully understood when they are placed in the context of music's function as a commodity and a social activity enjoyed together with many others.

Notes

1. In Reingard Witzmann, *Der Ländler in Wien. Ein Beitrag zur Entwicklungsgeschichte der Wiener Walzers bis in die Zeit des Wiener Kongresses* (Vienna: Arbeitsstelle für den Volkskundeatlas in Österreich, 1976), 83; the chorus is also reproduced in Walburga Litschauer and Walter Deutsch, *Schubert und das Tanzvergnügen* (Vienna: Verlag Holzhausen, 1997), 12–13. Unless otherwise noted, all translations are my own.

2. I have discussed the cultural associations of the *alla turca* style in more detail in my chapter "Turkish and Hungarian-Gypsy Styles," in *The Oxford Handbook of Topic Theory*, ed. Danuta Mirka (Oxford: Oxford University Press, 2014), 214–37. Rebecca Harris-Warrick, "Dance §5. 1730–1800," in *Grove Music Online* (Oxford: Oxford University Press, 2001–), accessed July 24, 2013, http://www.oxfordmusic online.com/subscriber/article/grove/music/45795, provides the most succinct treatment of Turkish stage dances: "Turkish music and dance, which had been imitated on stage as far back as Lully's *comédie-ballet*, *Le bourgeois gentilhomme* (1670), featured in numerous works in the 18th century including Rameau's *opéra-ballet*, *Les Indes galantes* (1735, Paris), Starzer and Hilverding's pantomime ballet, *Le Turc généreux* (1758, Vienna), Favart's *opéra comique*, *Soliman Second, ou Les trois sultanes* (1761, Paris), Gluck's *opéra comique*, *Le cadi dupé* (1761, Vienna), and Salieri's *Tarare* (1787, Paris). Just as composers developed musical markers for the Turkish style while remaining within the parameters of European art music, so dancers probably put a veneer of gestures characterized as 'Turkish' on top of the basic ballet step vocabulary. The single extant choreography called a 'Turkish dance,' set to music from 'La Turquie' in Campra's *opéra-ballet*, *L'Europe galante* and published by the English choreographer Anthony L'Abbé in 1725, uses certain character steps such as planting the foot flat on the floor and hopping backwards to mark the dance as exotic."

3. I refer to Viennese *representations* of Hungarian-Gypsy music to distinguish this published repertoire from the one actually performed by Gypsy musicians in Hungary and elsewhere, including Vienna; I have explored some of the differences between the two traditions in "Reconsidering an Early Exoticism: Viennese Adaptations of Hungarian-Gypsy Music around 1800," *Eighteenth-Century Music* 6, no. 2 (September 2009): 161–81.

4. Harris-Warrick, "Dance §5. 1730–1800."

5. Jonathan Bellman, "*Ongherese*, Fandango, and Polonaise: National Dance as Classical-Era Topic," *Journal of Musicological Research* 31, nos. 2–3 (2012): 71–72.

6. Géza Papp, *Hungarian Dances 1784–1810*, Musicalia Danubiana 7 (Budapest: Magyar Tudományos Akadémia, Zenetudományi Intézet, 1986), 23, 25: "In the last two decades of the 18th century . . . a new dance, the Hungarian dance (*Magyar, Hongroise*) had been added to the favourite national dances widely known to European music. . . . Dance melodies . . . were not only for dancing to or listening to being performed by others, but a source of pleasure to those who could play them themselves."

7. Shay Loya, *Liszt's Transcultural Modernism and the Hungarian-Gypsy Tradition* (Rochester, NY: University of Rochester Press, 2011), 79.

8. Ibid., 78–79. Bence Szabolcsi first suggested 1810 as a dividing point between "early verbunkos" and "culminating verbunkos" in *A Concise History of Hungarian Music*, trans. Sára Karig and Fred MacNicol (n.p.: Corvina, 1974), 63. Other scholars who agree with this approximate chronology include Géza Papp, "Stilelemente des frühen Werbungstanzes in der Gebrauchsmusik des 18. Jahrhunderts," in *Musica Antiqua III: Acta Scientifica*, ed. Jerzy Wisniowski (Bydgoszcz: Bydgoskie Towarzystwo Naukome, 1972), 641; Csilla Pethő, "Style Hongrois: Hungarian Elements in the Works of Haydn, Beethoven, Weber and Schubert," *Studia Musicologica* 41, nos. 1–3 (2000): 199. It is important to remember that 1810 is not an exact date to which any specific development can be traced. As Papp's research attests, some early collections of Hungarian-Gypsy dances were reissued decades later, presumably because they remained popular—the twenty-eight *Ausgesuchte ungarische Nationaltänze im Clavierauszug von verschiedenen Ziegeunern aus Galantha*, published in 1803 by Ignaz Sauer and again in 1822 by Sauer and Leidesdorf, for instance—while other collections from the turn of the century already betray stylistic developments that would only later become commonplace—Franz Paul Rigler's *12 ungarische Tänze* of ca. 1800 is a case in point. Papp's *Hungarian Dances 1784–1810* is a modern edition of these and several other collections and contains invaluable information about their publication histories.

9. Loya, *Liszt's Transcultural Modernism*, 78. For further information on "authorial *verbunkos*," see also pp. 14, 65, 78–81. Loya defines *verbunkos* on p. xvii.

10. Ibid., 78–79. I have explored the ideological underpinnings of the early repertoire further in "Eastern European National Music as Concept and Commodity at the Turn of the Nineteenth Century," *Music and Letters* 95, no. 1 (February 2014): 70–91.

11. David Gramit, "Musicology, Commodity Structure, and Musical Practice," in *Crosscurrents and Counterpoints: Offerings in Honor of Bengt Hambraeus at 70*, ed. Per F. Broman, Nora A. Engebretsen, and Bo Alphonce (Gothenburg: University of Gothenburg, 1998), 25. My approach to this repertoire was also inspired by David Gramit, "Music Scholarship, Musical Practice, and the Act of Listening," in *Music and Marx: Ideas, Practice, Politics*, ed. Regula Burckhardt Qureshi (New York: Routledge, 2002), 3–22.

12. Loya has not ascertained what role, if any, such an outlook may have played in determining what music a consumer purchased and in turn what music a publisher issued. He writes (*Liszt's Transcultural Modernism*, 79): "The early *verbunkos* literature appears simplistic because of the aesthetic ideology and limited technical means already discussed, and not because Gypsy-band music before 1800 was stylistically less diverse, texturally poorer, harmonically less adventurous, or technically less demanding. Likewise, the literature produced between 1810 and 1840 was more serious and complex because of the celebration of creative individualism and because transcriptions of *verbunkos* also increasingly assumed the function of art music during this period."

13. Carl Joseph von Feldtenstein, *Erweiterung der Kunst nach der Chorographie zu tanzen, Tänze zu erfinden, und aufzusetzen; wie auch Anweisung zu verschiedenen National-Tänzen; Als zu Englischen, Deutschen, Schwäbischen, Pohlnischen, Hannak-*

Masur- Kosak- und Hungarischen; mit Kupfern; nebst einer Anzahl Englischer Tänze (Braunschweig: no pub., 1772; reprint ed. Kurt Petermann, Leipzig: Zentralantiquariat der deutschen demokratischen Republik, 1984), 103–4 (italics original): "Der Ungarische Tanz hat von den vorherangeführten dreyen, als den Hannakischen, Masurischen, und Kosakischen Tänzen die Affekten zugleich, und diese sind so angenehm zusammen geseßet, daß die, so ihn tanzen (und wann sie auch auf Befehl tanzen müßten, welches allemal der matteste Tanz ist,) wegen der Einrichtung der reizenden und komischen Musik hingerissen werden, daß sie dennoch aus Affektion tanzen würden. Dann die Affekten in der Declamation dieses Tanzes sind gleichsam getheilet, und jeden Geschlecht seine Rolle angewiesen, so daß der tändelnde Affekt der Tänzerin, und der Freye, und in das komische Wilde fallende dem Tänzer zugeeignet ist. Ich würde, wann ich nach chorographischen Zeichen von denen Schritten und Touren dieses Tanzes handeln wollte, noch verschiedene Kupfer müssen stechen lassen, und da ich großtentheils für meine Lernenden schreibe, damit sie sich an die erhaltene Information erinnern können: so will ich es diesmal bey einer Demonstration bewenden lassen. Ich sage also zur Nachricht, daß die Tänzerinnen sich in ihrem Tanz eines tändelnden Anstandes, und damit verknüpften Schritts, wie auch *solider* Umdrehung oder *Tournées* bedienen müssen, so wie die Tänzer höher, und mit verwechselnden Positionen, wobey sie regulaire, und irregulaire zusammen mischen, welche sie auf der zweyten Kupfertafel (T. 2. Fig. 9 bis 18.) zu sehen haben, wobey ein jeder gebildeter Tänzer doch ein angenehmes Wildes (wann ich so sagen kann und darf) anzunehmen hat, doch muß er auch seine Tänzerin im drehen mit einen gewissen *soliden* Anstand führen, und gleichsam sich mit ihr in dem tändelnden Affekt vereinigen, das anscheinende Wilde aber als eine ausgelassene, und in etwas übertriebene Freude nur zeigen, wann jedes allein figuriret. Dadurch wird auch dieser Nation in ihren Tanze das Schöne bestimmet." My translation of this passage originally appeared in "Turkish and Hungarian-Gypsy Styles," 219–20, in which I suggested that the Hungarian dance may have been performed as a contredanse, but I did not elaborate this hypothesis.

14. Eva Campianu, "Langaus, Quadrille, Zingarese: Joseph Haydn und der Tanz," *Morgen* 6, no. 23 (June 1982): 174. Christian Friedrich Daniel Schubart, *Ideen zu einer Ästhetik der Tonkunst* (1806; reprint with index and preface by Fritz Kaiser and Margrit Kaiser, Hildesheim: Georg Olms Verlagsbuchhandlung, 1969), 352, also confirms the suitability of the Hungarian dance to the theater, writing that "dieser Tanz verdient sehr auf das Theater gebracht zu werden."

15. Feldtenstein, *Erweiterung der Kunst nach der Chorographie zu tanzen*, 101: "Er hat das bequeme von Schwäbischen an sich, daß jedes Paar nach ihren eigenen erfindenden Wendungen . . . tanzen kann, ohne genöthiget zu seyn, sich nach andern zu richten."

16. Petermann's quotation in ibid., xx: "Bei den Nationaltänzen soll Geschicklichkeit und Geschmack der Tanzenden über die Struktur und den Verlauf des Tanzes entscheiden."

17. Curt Sachs, *World History of the Dance*, trans. Bessie Schönberg (New York: W. W. Norton, 1963), 398.

18. John Playford, *The English Dancing Master; or, Plaine and Easie Rules for the Dancing of Country Dances, with the Tune to Each Dance* (London: Thomas Harper, 1651).

19. Wye Jamison Allanbrook, *Rhythmic Gesture in Mozart: Le Nozze di Figaro and Don Giovanni* (Chicago: University of Chicago Press, 1983), 61; trans. from Adolf [Adolph] Bernhard Marx, *Die Lehre von der musikalischen Komposition*, 2 vols. (Leipzig: Breitkopf and Härtel, 1837–38), 2:57.

20. Sachs, *World History of the Dance*, 400–401.

21. Freda Burford and Anne Daye, "Contredanse," in *Grove Music Online* (Oxford: Oxford University Press, 2001–), accessed July 24, 2013, http://www.oxford musiconline.com/subscriber/article/grove/music/06376.

22. In Herbert Lager and Hilde Seidl, *Kontratanz in Wien: Geschichtliches und Nachvollziehbares aus der theresianisch-josephinischen Zeit* (Vienna: Österreichisches Bundesverlag, 1983), 36, 42.

23. Feldtenstein, *Erweiterung der Kunst nach der Chorographie zu tanzen*, 96–97.

24. Friedrich Schiller to Christian Gottfried Körner, February 23, 1793, in Friedrich Schiller, *On the Aesthetic Education of Man in a Series of Letters*, ed. and trans. with an introduction, commentary, and glossary of terms by Elizabeth M. Wilkinson and L. A. Willoughby (Oxford: Clarendon, 1982): "I can think of no more fitting image for the ideal of social conduct than an English dance, composed of many complicated figures and perfectly executed. A spectator in the gallery sees innumerable movements intersecting in the most chaotic fashion, changing direction swiftly and without rhyme or reason yet *never colliding*. Everything is so ordered that the one has already yielded his place when the other arrives; it is all so skillfully, and yet so artlessly, integrated into a form, that each seems only to be following his own inclination, yet without ever getting in the way of anybody else. It is the most perfectly appropriate symbol of the assertion of one's own freedom and regard for the freedom of others" (italics original).

25. Both quotations are from László Kürti, "Hungary," in *International Encyclopedia of Dance*, ed. Selma Jeanne Cohen (Oxford: Oxford University Press, 1998), 3:409. I assume that Kürti is referring to the *Mémoires historiques du Comte Betlem-Niklos: contenant l'histoire des derniers troubles de Transilvanie* (Amsterdam: Jean Swart, 1736); I have not been able to examine this material myself. According to WorldCat, the only extant copy is housed in Spain's Biblioteca nacional. The branle was a group dance, performed either in a line or in a circle and characterized by a sideways stepping motion; it was popular from at least the fifteenth through the late seventeenth or early eighteenth centuries, and the few choreographic examples in Feuillet notation resemble contredanses. See Daniel Heartz and Patricia Rader, "Branle," in *Grove Music Online* (Oxford: Oxford University Press, 2001–), accessed July 26, 2014, http://www.oxford-musiconline.com/subscriber/article/grove/music/03845.

26. Lager and Seidl, *Kontratanz in Wien*, 21. The authors also quote a letter of January 1, 1717, from Lady Mary Wortley Montagu confirming the presence of English longways contredanses (*anglaises*) in Vienna by that time.

27. Kürti, "Hungary," 409.

28. Much of the music of the 1788 publication appeared in slightly varied versions in numerous other publications in the late eighteenth and early nineteenth centuries; for a discussion of these versions, see Mayes, "Eastern European National Music," 90. The *Musikalisches Wochenblatt* was published in Vienna by Johann Cappi during the years 1806–9.

29. Jean-Jacques Rousseau, *Dictionnaire de musique* (Paris: Chez la Veuve Duchesne, 1768; reprint Geneva: Editions Minkoff, 1998), 121: "Contre-danse. Air d'une sorte de Danse de même nom, qui s'exécute à quatre, à six & à huit personnes, & qu'on danse ordinairement dans les Bals après les Menuets, comme étant plus gaie & occupant plus de monde. Les Airs des Contre-Danses sont le plus souvent à deux tems; ils doivent être bien cadencés, brillans & gais, & avoir cependant beaucoup de simplicité; car comme on les reprend très-souvent, ils deviendroient insupportables, s'ils étoient chargés. En tout genre les choses les plus simples sont celles dont on se lasse le moins." My translation is based in part on Leonard G. Ratner, *Classic Music: Expression, Form, and Style* (New York: Schirmer Books, 1980), 13. The definition of the contredanse in Charles Compan's *Dictionnaire de danse* (Paris: Cailleau, 1787) is almost identical to Rousseau's.

30. Johann Georg Sulzer, *Allgemeine Theorie der schönen Künste* (Leipzig: Weidmann, 1792; reprint Hildesheim: Georg Olms, 1967), 2:66: "Englische Tänze: Sie werden auch Contretänze genennt von dem englischen Wort Country-dances. . . . Diese Tänze . . . können von vier, sechs, acht und noch mehr Personen zugleich getanzt werden. Deßwegen wird insgemein bey den Bällen, nachdem eine Zeitlang Menuetten getanzt worden, die meiste übrige Zeit damit zugebracht, weil sie mehr Personen auf einmal beschäfftigen, und weil man bis ins unendliche damit abwechseln kann; denn man hat unzählige Contretänze. Sie sind von verschiedenen Bewegungen von zwey und von drey Zeiten; alle kommen darinn überein, daß sie sehr lebhaft sind, und größtentheils etwas mäßig comisches haben, dadurch sie Vergnügen und Artigkeit mit einander vereinigen. . . . Die Musik zu den englischen Tänzen, die man in Deutschland insgemein Angloisen nennt, ist insgemein bey einer großen Einfalt sehr lebhaft, mit ungemein deutlich bemerkten Einschnitten, und hat vielfältig das besondere, daß die Cadenzen in den Aufschlag fallen."

31. See Daniel Gottlob Türk, *School of Clavier Playing, or Instructions in Playing the Clavier for Teachers and Students*, trans. with introduction and notes by Raymond H. Haggh (Lincoln: University of Nebraska Press, 1982), 393; Heinrich Christoph Koch, *Musikalisches Lexikon* (Frankfurt am Main: August Hermann dem Jüngern, 1802; reprint Hildesheim: Bärenreiter, 1964), col. 536. The definition Koch provides of the contredanse in his *Versuch einer Anleitung zur Composition* (3 vols.; 1782–93) is even more clearly heavily indebted to Sulzer; see Heinrich Christoph Koch, *Versuch einer Anleitung zur Composition*, ed. Jo Wilhelm Siebert (Hannover: Siebert, 2007), 425, 427.

32. Koch, *Musikalisches Lexikon*, col. 536: "Man nennet diese Art Tänze auch Contretänze, ein Ausdruck, der von dem englischen Worte Country-dances entstanden ist, welches so viel bedeutet, als Tänze, die unter dem Landvolke, in den verschiedenen Provinzen, gebräuchlich sind."

33. I have explored this perception in much more depth in "Eastern European National Music," 70–91.

34. Lager and Seidl, *Kontratanz in Wien*, 111.

35. Günter Mössmer, "Kontretänze," in *Mozart in der Tanzkultur seiner Zeit*, ed. Walter Salmen (Innsbruck: Helbling, 1990), 100.

36. David Neumeyer, "The Contredanse, Classical Finales, and Caplin's Formal Functions," *Music Theory Online* 12, no. 4 (December 2006), http://www.mtosmt.org/issues/mto.06.12.4/mto.06.12.4.neumeyer.html.

37. The information on *contredanses anglaises* and *françaises* is closely based on Eric McKee's very clear discussion of these dances in "Ballroom Dances of the Late Eighteenth Century," in Mirka, ed., *The Oxford Handbook of Topic Theory*, 164–93. See also Richard Semmens, "Branles, Gavottes and Contredanses in the Later Seventeenth and Early Eighteenth Centuries," *Dance Research: The Journal of the Society for Dance Research* 15, no. 2 (Winter 1997): 35–62.

38. Sarah Reichart, "The Thuillier Contredanses," *Proceedings of the Society of Dance History Scholars* 8 (1985): 103; Sarah Reichart, "The Influence of Eighteenth-Century Social Dance on the Viennese Classical Style" (PhD diss., City University of New York, 1984), 302–9.

39. These collections, as well as extensive information about their authorship and publication histories, are included in Papp, *Hungarian Dances 1784–1810*.

40. For information on domestic dance gatherings in Vienna, see Lager and Seidl, *Kontratanz in Wien*, 44; Walter Salmen, "Tanzinstrumente und -ensembles," in Salmen, ed., *Mozart in der Tanzkultur seiner Zeit*, 58; Witzmann, *Der Ländler in Wien*, 13, 54; Monika Fink, *Der Ball: Eine Kulturgeschichte des Gesellschaftstanzes im 18. und 19. Jahrhundert* (Lucca: Libreria musicale italiana, 1996), 86, 89–91, 169.

41. Matthew Head, "'If the Pretty Little Hand Won't Stretch': Music for the Fair Sex in Eighteenth-Century Germany," *Journal of the American Musicological Society* 52, no. 2 (Summer 1999): 208. Head's article is reprinted with slight revision in his monograph *Sovereign Feminine: Music and Gender in Eighteenth-Century Germany* (Berkeley: University of California Press, 2013), 48–83. Multiple scholars have provided evidence that women and girls were the primary performers of domestic keyboard music in the eighteenth and early nineteenth centuries, including Bianca Maria Antolini, "Publishers and Buyers," in *Music Publishing in Europe 1600–1900: Concepts and Issues, Bibliography*, ed. Rudolf Rasch (Berlin: Berliner Wissenschafts-Verlag, 2005), 234–35; William Weber, *Music and the Middle Class: The Social Structure of Concert Life in London, Paris and Vienna* (New York: Holmes and Meier, 1975), 35–36; Jeffrey Kallberg, *Chopin at the Boundaries: Sex, History, and Musical Genre* (Cambridge, MA: Harvard University Press, 1996), 35–38; Richard Leppert, "Music, Domestic Life, and Cultural Chauvinism: Images of British Subjects at Home in India," in *Music and Society: The Politics of Composition, Performance, and Reception*, ed. Richard Leppert and Susan McClary (Cambridge: Cambridge University Press, 1987), 85; Arthur Loesser, *Men, Women and Pianos: A Social History*, preface by Jacques Barzun (New York: Simon and Schuster, 1954), esp. 64–67. The *Contredanses hongroises* were dedicated to Archduchess Elisabeth, and the French title and dedication

reflect the linguistic preference of the nobility, especially of noble women. For a facsimile of the ornamental title page, see Papp, *Hungarian Dances 1784–1810*, 58.

42. Head, "If the Pretty Little Hand Won't Stretch," 214. Head elaborates that "Johann Mattheson's remarks on the foundations of melody in *Der vollkommene Capellmeister* (1739) furnish a close to comprehensive inventory of what was musically at stake in 'easiness' in music for the fair sex: the avoidance of excessive melodic embellishment and of rapid changes in meter, tempo, and register; restriction to diatonic harmony; uniformity rather than diversity; and cultivation of 'noble simplicity.' A rejection of conspicuous compositional artifice underwrites these elements."

43. Mayes, "Reconsidering an Early Exoticism."

44. Witzmann, *Der Ländler in Wien*, 1.

45. In Werner Bachmann, *Musikgeschichte in Bildern: Tanz im 19. Jahrhundert* (Leizig: VEB Deutscher Verlag für Musik, 1989), 5.

46. See Witzmann, *Der Ländler in Wien*, esp. 50–51, 54, 82; Fink, *Der Ball*, 169–70; Lager and Seidl, *Kontratanz in Wien*, 26; Andrew Lamb, "Waltz (i)," in *Grove Music Online* (Oxford: Oxford University Press, 2001–), accessed June 11, 2014, http://www.oxfordmusiconline.com/subscriber/article/grove/music/29881.

47. In Sachs, *World History of the Dance*, 428; Sachs identifies his source as *Tanzkalender* (1801).

48. Peter van der Merwe, *Roots of the Classical: The Popular Origins of Western Music* (Oxford: Oxford University Press, 2004), 239.

49. In Eric McKee, *Decorum of the Minuet, Delirium of the Waltz: A Study of Dance-Music Relations in $\frac{3}{4}$ Time* (Bloomington: Indiana University Press, 2012), 181, from Frédéric Chopin, *Chopin's Letters*, collected by Henryk Opieński, trans. with a preface and editorial notes by E. L. Voynich (New York: Dover, 1988), 137: "Here, waltzes are called works! And Strauss and Lanner, who play them for dancing, are called *Kapellmeistern*. This does not mean that everyone thinks like that; indeed, nearly everyone laughs about it; but only waltzes get printed."

50. I have explored virtuosic works in the Hungarian-Gypsy style, with particular attention to Liszt's *Hungarian Rhapsodies*, in chapter 4 of my doctoral dissertation—see "Liszt's *Des Bohémiens et de leur musique en Hongrie*: *Verbunk* in Defense of Virtuosity," in "Domesticating the Foreign: Hungarian-Gypsy Music in Vienna at the Turn of the Nineteenth Century" (PhD diss., Cornell University, Ithaca, NY, 2008), 164–205.

51. In Mark Kroll, *Ignaz Moscheles and the Changing World of Musical Europe* (Woodbridge, UK: Boydell & Brewer, 2014), 162–63, from Charlotte Moscheles, *Recent Music and Musicians as Described in the Diaries and Correspondence of Ignaz Moscheles*, trans. A. D. Coleridge (New York: Henry Holt, 1873; reprint New York: Da Capo, 1970), 255.

Chapter Seven

The Power to Please

Gender and Celebrity Self-Commodification in the Early American Republic

Glenda Goodman

Before the careers of audacious promoters like P. T. Barnum, sensational black-face minstrel performers, and renowned authors such as Washington Irving and Mark Twain brought about an entertainment boom in the nineteenth century, the cultural phenomenon of mass-marketed celebrity had a slow start in America. For much of the eighteenth century, the colonies lacked the infrastructure to foster a cultural environment in which professional performers could flourish. The shuttering of venues during the Revolutionary War hampered what entertainment did exist in cities such as Charleston, Philadelphia, New York, and Boston. The age of American musical celebrity dawned only in the 1780s and 1790s, but its essential features were not native to the new nation. Musical life in the early American republic relied heavily on European performers and repertory, and transatlantic émigré performers nurtured the marketplace for celebrity in America.[1] Borrowing conventions from Britain, transatlantic performers engaged in savvy self-commodification to whet audiences' appetites not just for the latest music from Europe but for renowned performers as well.

Yet the United States was not a tabula rasa; performers found themselves engaging in an active, often contentious public sphere in which the comportment of public figures—especially women—fed into larger debates about what society in the new republic would be like. Female performers learned to pick careful paths across the potentially treacherous public stage. Reputations and livelihoods were at stake. Yet even in the midst of fulminating debates over whether and how women should participate in the public sphere, the visible presence of female performers was undeniable proof of women's agency. Occasionally, female actors and playwrights used their position in the public eye to participate actively in political debates. Most notably, Susanna Rowson used her renown as a playwright, an actress, and the author of the bestselling novel *Charlotte Temple* to advocate for women's education and equality in the 1790s. Yet Rowson was exceptional compared to the many other performers who elected to be more circumspect in the way they crafted their public personas. Indeed, many performing women obfuscated their power on the stage—and thus mitigated possible censure—by hiding behind conventions of demure femininity. Ironically, by sublimating their agency, female performers were able to earn livings for themselves, empowered by their astuteness in making career decisions and deft ability to manipulate their public images.[2]

Adding to the complexity of early American gendered celebrity culture is the fact that many of the performers were emigrants from England. Performers often came from less populous cities, were older, or had otherwise reached a ceiling in their performing careers in Britain.[3] As transatlantic immigrants their cosmopolitan sheen contributed to their allure for American audiences, but their presence also raised questions about whether the United States was being culturally recolonized by Britain. In truth, postrevolutionary imports from Britain were part of a decades-long trend of American consumption of British products. Beginning in the mid-eighteenth century, colonists were offered an increasing array of British goods, and importation extended far beyond the musical realm: all things British were in high demand, from porcelain and furniture to books and maps.[4] This consumer trend resumed after the Revolution; despite achieving independence from Britain, the process of "unbecoming British" was torturously slow.[5] The cultural dimension of nation formation in particular lagged behind political and economic sovereignty, as Americans continued to desire British music, British plays, British literature, and British material goods.[6] Yet British performers in the United States in the 1780s and 1790s were required to cultivate the marketplace for their wares and mollify any concerns about bringing an aristocratic sensibility to the new republic. Female performers were thus triply charged: they had to create a commodified image of themselves as enticing entertainers who undermined neither American political ideals nor the nation's changing social imperatives pertaining to gender.

This chapter unpacks the workings of celebrity in the early American republic and dissects the way female performers managed to succeed in public in a period in which women's social and political roles were contentious. Denied equal legal rights when the nation was formed, women nevertheless found myriad ways to participate in civil society.[7] Debates about the role of women in the public sphere following the American Revolution have consumed historians' interest for several decades, and some scholars have located political agency in the onstage actions of female performers, but missing is an analysis of how exactly these performers managed to build successful careers in the public eye.[8]

No one negotiated the challenges of a public professional life with greater adroitness than Mary Ann Wrighten Pownall, a tireless singer-actress-composer whose career is emblematic of the careful path picked by female performers who wished to market themselves as celebrities in America.[9] A seasoned performer on London stages, Pownall (1751–96) immigrated to America in 1792 and worked there until her death in 1796. She brought expertise in concert and comic opera performance as well as a keen understanding of the importance of self-promotion in print. Pownall was not the most famous or the most highly praised performer of her generation, but what fame she possessed was carefully cultivated. Pownall mastered the art of self-commodification and modeled a type of celebrity persona that was successful because it was unfailingly polished and professional. Whereas other star performers competed with each other as "rival queens," Pownall carefully cultivated her image as a generous, maternal, and engagingly accessible woman.[10] An examination of the tangible record of her accomplishments allows us to understand how celebrity culture developed in early America. In particular, by analyzing Pownall's multimodal approach to self-commodification, we see through the glossy surface of celebrity culture to the dogged labor on which successful careers were based. Ultimately, a good deal of that labor came in the form of negotiating gender expectations in the early republic.

Pownall successfully navigated the troubled waters of the early American public stage by using familiar and nonthreatening tropes of womanhood. In particular, she cultivated an image as a capable and generous collaborator and a caring mother—she was both unstintingly professional and thoroughly domesticated. Pownall balanced these roles publicly, appearing onstage and publishing music that bore her name (in an era when most women published anonymously). By publishing her songs, Pownall showed herself to be no mere wallflower; she adhered to the conventions of female behavior but was not overly restricted by them. But what is perhaps most noteworthy about Pownall is how *unexceptional* she was. She was well-known in her time but is largely unknown today, forcing us to consider how celebrity is not only gained and preserved for posterity but lost. What is more, she defies the scholar's wish to identify her as a progressive feminist, inspiring further inquiry into the overlooked histories of women in music. Instead, she demands that we pay attention to the mundaneness of earning a living as a female celebrity. Her achievements are noteworthy not because they are remarkable but because they are indicative of a broader celebrity culture as it emerged in the early republic.[11] Taking Pownall as a case study, we find that the careful balance of her image not only teaches us about self-commodification and the rise of celebrity culture in America but also illuminates how women in public were expected to both sell themselves and deny that they were working to do so. In short, by studying Pownall, we can better understand the contradictions confronted and reflected by women in the public sphere in early America.

The Transatlantic Underpinnings of American Celebrity

The American Revolution ushered much newness into the world, but the young nation's entertainment and celebrity culture was not particularly novel.[12] The model for American celebrity culture came from Britain, where this culture was fostered by industrialization and the emergence of a robust public sphere fueled by new media for disseminating images and news.[13] The rise of print media in particular promoted the celebrity as an authority figure, one who, as Joseph Roach has suggested, was split between public image and corporeal and biographical reality.[14] Renowned British actors such as Colley Cibber, David Garrick, Lavinia Fenton, and Sarah Siddons were dexterous in manipulating their images by blurring the line between their public and private lives. For example, Cibber, a loquacious actor-manager, penned an entertaining autobiography in 1740 that ostensibly offered readers access to his personal experiences but in fact was purposefully unreliable, self-serving, and obscuring.[15] Such performers presented highly sculpted and scrupulously maintained personas to audiences and fans. Their mechanisms for maintaining celebrity were manifold and served as a template for performers who followed in their footsteps: being associated with particular roles, circulating news and gossip about romantic attachments or other scandals, publishing memoirs, and engaging in real or manufactured rivalries. Thus the celebrity conventions American audiences experienced in the late eighteenth century were built on a solid foundation of tried-and-true techniques.

Eighteenth-century Americans came into contact with multiple forms of celebrity, but in the colonial period civic leaders and religious reformers provided most of the focal points of public attention, and these figures harnessed the growing power of print to broadcast their fame. Patriot printer Benjamin Franklin's *Poor Richard's Almanack* and autobiography and charismatic evangelical minister George Whitefield's sermons are examples of printed material that spread their creators' fame throughout the North American British colonies. Following the Revolution, another class of celebrity emerged: the virtuous and selfless political leader, embodied by George Washington. In many ways, Washington's fame was a direct rebuttal of the celebrity of the British royalty. Whereas royals were renowned because of who they were, American civic, religious, and political leaders sought to be famous for what they did.[16]

Transatlantic émigré performers, too, were famous because of what they did rather than who they were; theirs was an achieved rather than an ascribed celebrity.[17] The similarities between eminent figures like Franklin, Whitefield, and Washington on the one hand and professional musicians like Pownall on the other are noteworthy. Each harnessed the power of print to promote themselves, and each understood the vital importance of appearing to present an authentic and sincere persona to the public. This latter task was easier for politicians than performers, for while in the eighteenth century leaders were believed truly to embody the ideals they represented, performers' sincerity was called into question. Simply put, when George Washington shed a tear, it was taken as a sign of his authentic sensibility; when an actor shed a tear onstage, it was interpreted as artifice, for the crafts of acting and singing were understood to be fundamentally crafts of dissimulation.[18] Yet Pownall, through her benevolent works and publications, strove to convince her fans that she was showing them her "true self" both on and off stage.[19] Her livelihood depended on it.

The transatlantic performers who flooded American stages in the early national period had colonial antecedents. The first public concert was held in Boston in 1731, the first operas were performed in Charleston in 1735, and in 1752 Lewis Hallam established the first permanent touring theater company: the American Company, initially based in Williamsburg.[20] By the 1760s, colonial audiences could expect to hear English operas within a few years of their London premieres. Although religious authorities considered secular entertainment an impious luxury, no objection could stifle the growing popularity of imported European plays, operas, and concert repertory in colonial cities.[21] Only with the hostility born of the Revolutionary War did American consumption of British cultural imports temporarily break down, a rupture codified by the Continental Congress resolution banning public performances in October 1774. It took nearly a decade for American entertainment to rebound from the war, and it did so by settling back into its British mold. Not only repertory but scenery, costumes, and American theaters were copied from British models and imported from Britain. For example, Thomas Wignell, a theater company manager in Philadelphia, hired a carpenter to copy scenery and machinery based on models from London stages.[22] As the British traveler Henry Wansey declared after an evening out in Philadelphia in 1794, "I should have thought I had still been in England."[23]

The resolution that closed venues during the war was repealed on a state-by-state basis in the late 1780s and early 1790s, and as theaters reopened and theater companies resurfaced or were newly formed, all concerned tried to ascertain the tastes of the new nation. After the patriotic rhetoric of the Revolution, in which all things British were equated with tyranny, it was up to theater troupes to convince American audiences that operas, plays, and concerts could be enjoyed as entertainment without exposing the infant nation to the risks of Britain's so-called dissipated culture of luxury.[24] In this they were successful: the last decade of the eighteenth century was marked by growth, as theater troupes recruited transatlantic performers to occupy America's increasing number of stages. It was also marked by competition, as the proliferating troupes fought for territory and audiences. Two companies in Philadelphia—Hallam's Old American Company, returned from its wartime exile in Jamaica and with a new partner, John Henry, onboard, and the upstart company formed by Thomas Wignell and Alexander Reinagle in 1791—vied for the same audiences, until the Old American Company shifted its focus northward. Both Hallam and Henry as well as Wignell and Reinagle realized that they needed to replenish their supply of British talent to compete with each other, so both traveled to London to scoop up performers.[25] It was there that John Henry recruited Mary Pownall.

Pownall's career looked to be over in 1792, the year she immigrated to the United States. She had just turned forty-one, and although she had nearly two decades of experience on the stage, she had not performed in England for six years—not since she left her actor husband James Wrighten, instigating something of a scandal by living with another man, Hugh Pownall. Mary had had an early start onstage: apprenticed as an adolescent and married at eighteen, as a young woman she was hired by the famed actor and manager David Garrick to appear in the Theater Royal on Drury Lane. She performed there for sixteen years, and beginning in 1777 she spent summers on the outdoor stage at the Vauxhall pleasure gardens. She had a pleasing soprano voice, and both the comic opera composer Charles Dibdin and the Vauxhall tunesmith James Hook wrote songs for her. But in 1786, after seventeen years of marriage and sixteen years onstage (while managing to have six children, at least three of whom survived), she separated from her husband, abandoned her career, and moved in with the apothecary Hugh Pownall. She then disappeared from public view.[26]

Yet when Pownall disembarked from the ship *Betsey* in New York with her family on September 29, 1792, she stepped into a new life.[27] No longer "Mrs. Wrighten," the aging and semidisgraced actress who was estranged from a drunkard husband, she assumed the name "Mrs. Pownall" and embraced her role as a star in the small constellation of American celebrities.[28] She collaborated with musicians and actors in Philadelphia and New York, performing in operas, on subscription concert series, and on benefit concerts. From 1792 to 1796 Pownall lived the seasonally peripatetic life typical of performers, traveling up and down the eastern seaboard. She had steady employment and regular benefit evenings that sustained her and her family.[29] She was successful.

In the fall of 1795, Pownall relocated her family to Charleston, by far the most culturally sophisticated southern US city. It was to be Pownall's last stop. She made a successful debut that November, and for the next nine months she occupied a prominent place in Charleston theater life. Pownall spoke epilogues from stage, was given leading roles, and received warm reviews.[30] She began to assume the role of producer, organizing a successful "Grand Concert Spiritualé," or sacred concert, on March 24, during Passion Week.[31] Yet like that of many performers of the period, Pownall's financial security was likely tenuous, and in Charleston she may have faced financial decline; by the summer she began to announce an impending retirement, to be preceded by a "final" appearance and a raffle of her professional accouterments, including her piano.[32] Such announcements were a useful strategy for drumming up interest in a performer and could be used to bolster a fading career. The true reason for Pownall's announcement cannot be known with certainty because she died suddenly before she could sing in public for the last time. The Charleston *City Gazette* alluded to an "unnatural change which has taken place in her family" as the cause of her rapid decline, referring to the elopement of her seventeen-year-old daughter Charlotte. The real cause, however, was probably yellow fever.[33] Despite her quick decline, the four years Pownall spent in the United States are a veritable template for a successful, professional celebrity in early America, and the second wind Pownall's career received on this side of the Atlantic was boosted in no small part by the energetic welcome of critics.

Tame Renown: Satisfying the Critics

Pownall's critical reception illustrates how smoothly she mobilized conventional tropes of femininity to appear as a nonthreatening public figure. Anonymous writers (whose credentials and experiences are unknown) introduced Pownall to American audiences and endorsed her appearances onstage in blurbs that circulated in newspapers throughout the United States. Her skills were widely touted, but the unspecific and rather tame language used to describe her suggests mostly that there was nothing objectionable about her—that she met all the requirements for a female performer. This is not to say that her critics' admiration was false. For example, the witnesses of her Philadelphia debut in 1792 were clearly impressed, causing her to be trumpeted as "one of the finest singers Europe can boast of."[34] Further, we must not question the American-born dancer John Durang's sincerity when he wrote in his memoir that Pownall was "a singer and actress of superior merit; I have not seen another lady to equel [*sic*] her on the stage."[35] But when Durang went on to describe Pownall as "graceful" and "a most accomplished and excellent performer," he was slotting her into a paradigm of femininity in which her physical comportment mattered as much as her skills as a singer.[36]

In addition to assessing Pownall's skills as a performer, items about Pownall in newspapers were instrumental in solidifying her personal reputation. Here the coverage becomes more interesting, for writers projected onto Pownall their concerns about the proper behavior of women in public. By the time Pownall died, she was renowned in the United States, and her reputation and legacy were cemented by press coverage that praised her accomplishments and personal qualities. For example, in a poem dedicated to Pownall published in a newspaper soon after she arrived in Charleston, she was praised as a "sweet Warbler" who had a heaven-given "power to please . . . to raise the smile, to charm the list'ning ear; / To cause the sigh, or start the gushing tear; / To rouse th' insensible, from a torpid state / To admiration, and their hearts elate."[37] Emphasizing her charm and her ability to inspire emotion (thus tapping into prevalent eighteenth-century discourses about sensibility that privileged emotional responsiveness), the poet locates Pownall's power in the realm of sentimentality.[38] The habit of attributing to Pownall acceptable traits of convention-bound femininity is also evident in her death notices that appeared in cities from Savannah to Boston in 1796. Pownall was commemorated in neutral terms as a performer "at the head of her profession," but feminine conventions were promptly evoked when she was described as a woman in whose "private deportment her benevolence stood conspicuous" and whose "manners were refined, her language chaste and classical, and her conversation amusing and instructive."[39] Pownall's personal traits were weighted equally with her decades-long career on both sides of the Atlantic. No matter how excellent a singer (or composer—a fact that went unmentioned in the notices) she was, her reputation as a virtuous woman mattered more.

It would be a mistake to see Pownall's reception as proof that women in the public sphere were simply disempowered when they were praised as much for their virtue as for their skills, for Pownall benefited from the critical responses to her performances. The scribblers who filled the pages of American newspapers were quick to identify Pownall as a bona fide celebrity and thus bolstered her career. Critics expressed enthusiasm at witnessing a "much celebrated and highly admired" professional working in their midst who had "for many years performed at different royal theaters in London; and always with unbounded applause."[40] As her reputation in America grew, accounts of her talents added to reports of her transatlantic accomplishments (which were perhaps inflated).

Critics were fond of using the term *celebrity* to describe her status in Britain and Europe. "Her *celebrity*, on the boards of the Continent, has as far outstripped the emulation of her Sister performers, and surpassed the eulogiums of her panegyrists, as her *merit* has exceeded the most sanguine *expectations*, and gratified the most exalted *wishes* of the Operatic Connoisseur," gushed a Boston writer in 1794. "In her, we behold the Columbian Billington," he added, referring to one of the leading opera singers of the day, Elizabeth Weichsell Billington.[41] When she arrived in Charleston, her achievements in Philadelphia, New York, and Boston were added to the record of her London career; one newspaper referred to "the celebrity which [Pownall has] acquired on the stages of the Northern states."[42] Another "correspondent, and lover of drama," using Pownall's previous married name, claimed to have "been often entertained by the comic powers of Mrs. Wrighten, on the other side of the Atlantic" and enjoined Charleston to embrace "the same lady in the person of Mrs. Pownall" in her role as Madge in Thomas Arne's comic opera *Love in a Village*, "in which character she shone *unequalled* on the British stage."[43] While some statements about Pownall's celebrity and skill were almost certainly publicity ploys engineered by the performer herself or by the troupe manager, they nonetheless indicate the importance of reputation in early American celebrity culture—and how necessary it was for women who were in the public eye to stay on the correct side of the line between admiration and admonishment.

Pownall's celebrity rested in part on her stature as a virtuous and benevolent woman, an image she cultivated by regularly donating her services. In fact, there is an ironic twist to her charitable image: self-servingly, she took to the public stage to neutralize whatever scandal may have lingered from her complicated marital history and to stave off criticism that she sought public approbation too much. Performing in benefit concerts was a key way Pownall built her reputation during the four years she lived in America, and she excelled at using these events to advance her career. Such concerts were a coveted part of a performer's season—a boon to both finances and reputations. Benefits were a way for performers to make money: the proceeds from the evening went to the featured performer, who called on his or her colleagues to lend their talents to the program. In Britain, star performers could compete with each other to see who made the most money from ticket sales, but the success of an evening in America usually hinged on solidarity among musicians simply because there weren't that many performers to turn to when one's night arrived. An experienced singer-actress such as Pownall earned the goodwill of her fellow performers by appearing frequently in benefit evenings, and she could count on them to pitch in when it was time for her own benefits, which regularly took place in New York, Philadelphia, Boston, and Charleston.

More advantageous to one's reputation than singing on other performers' benefit concerts was the chance to donate to charity, and Pownall was quick to grasp the positive publicity associated with donating her singing skills to worthy causes. For example, in 1793 she sang on a concert for the New York Episcopal Church's Charity School. When a fire coincided with her benefit evening in Boston in 1794, she donated the proceeds to the victims. And she and her daughters donated their services to the Charleston Freemasons in 1796.[44] When Pownall appeared on French musicians' benefit concerts in Philadelphia in 1793, this charitable impulse overlapped with professional courtesy.[45] Coinciding with the upheavals of both the French and Haitian Revolutions, the French benefits drew attention to the very real sacrifices made by musicians who escaped the uncertainties of both France and the Caribbean island. Pownall's contribution to their evenings thus made her both a colleague and a benefactor to a pressing cause, adding to her image as a generous and virtuous woman. In general, by manipulating her reputation to appear as both an accomplished performer and a benevolent woman, Pownall focused audiences' attention on the irreproachable nature of her recent deeds rather than on the scandals of her past.

Pownall's amiable and respectable persona was aided by the fact that she often appeared onstage with her children. She began performing with her two teenage daughters, Mary and Charlotte Wrighten, in 1794. Her young son Felix, born from her partnership with Hugh Pownall, also appeared onstage at least once in 1795.[46] Felix was too young to become a professional performer, but Mary and Charlotte began to appear regularly in the years 1794–96. The two young women performed vocal and piano duets together, and both also appeared next to their mother in minor comic opera roles. When Charlotte held a benefit concert in Charleston, naturally, her mother sang on it.[47] Mary and Charlotte did not garner the level of praise given to their mother—one critic graciously noted that their debut in Boston could be deemed good "when considered as their first attempt at acting"—but audiences were pleased by them.[48]

In Britain, acting dynasties were not unusual, but in America the spectacle of two generations appearing onstage together was something of a novelty. Pownall's strategy of performing with her children served at least two purposes: it reminded audiences of her role as a mother, thus playing into her public persona as a mature and caring woman; and by contrasting herself with her less experienced daughters, she appeared to be the consummate professional. Indeed, bringing motherhood to the stage was a deft maneuver, allowing audiences to feel like they were seeing a private side of Pownall even as she performed her professional parts. Her success in wedding the two roles was evidenced in the publicity that followed her death: critics blamed Pownall's collapse on her daughter's professional and personal betrayal by eloping with another performer.

Playing Neutral: The Politics of Pownall's Repertory

Mary Pownall's repertory bolstered her public persona as an agreeable performer and uncontroversial woman. Although no great beauty, Pownall was a talented performer who could handle a range of comedic roles. Her repertory was almost entirely drawn from well-known British comic operas, some of which were decades old by the time she appeared on US stages. In postrevolutionary America, where aristocratic themes ran contrary to the nation's explicitly democratic (and ostensibly nonhierarchical) ideals, Pownall's tendency to play supporting or secondary roles was appealingly ecumenical and nonelite. Importantly, by performing chestnuts of the theater and the concert world, Pownall did not engage with the increasingly partisan political atmosphere of the 1790s.[49] The stage, at first a forum for debates about whether America could uncouple from Britain's consumer luxuries, after the Revolution became a venue for a different kind of fight over America's national identity. Specifically, in the early republic the theater became a site for proxy battles between the two sides in the emerging two-party system. Federalist and Republican partisans routinely scrutinized plays and operas for their potential partisan meanings, and performers were requested to sing songs co-opted by one side or the other.[50] In this potentially tense atmosphere, Pownall's choice of innocuous roles kept her outside the fray. Moreover, the songs she sang associated her with accessible yet lofty images and emotions that were in keeping with the era's culture of sensibility. The nearly sixty roles Pownall played in America helped her to cultivate her celebrity image as collaborative, warm, and accomplished while avoiding direct involvement with politics.[51]

Nearly all the roles Pownall played came from British comic operas that had been popular for decades by the time she performed them in America, yet on US stages they took on new connotations. Some parts carried over from when she performed as "Mrs. Wrighten" at Drury Lane and Vauxhall. For example, she played the lead role of Peggy in *The Gentle Shepherd*, a pastoral ballad opera adapted from Allan Ramsay's 1725 publication of the same name. The opera premiered in 1729 but was popular in London and America in the late eighteenth century (in America, all things Scottish were supported both by a robust immigrant community and a general fascination with the region). An engraving from 1777 of Pownall as Peggy shows a plain but pleasant woman, bedecked in flowers (fig. 7.1).

Rustic secondary roles suited Pownall. She possessed a pleasing voice but lacked the beauty to command star parts very often. In addition to being associated with Ramsay's Scottish pastoral character, Pownall also performed frequently in Thomas Arne and Isaac Bickerstaff's popular pasticcio opera *Love in a Village*. This work, which premiered at London's Covent Garden on December 8, 1762, was beloved in both England and America. Pownall performed the minor comic role of the rustic servant Margery (or Madge) in London in 1781, as well as in America with the Old American Company (fig. 7.2). The pastoral and rustic roles in which Pownall appeared in England and America bolstered her image as an accessible woman to whom audiences could easily relate.

Pownall was as closely tied to particular songs as she was to specific roles, which also supported her agreeable brand of celebrity. As noted, she appeared frequently on subscription series and in benefit concerts, and the

THE GENTLE SHEPHERD.

M.ʳˢ WRIGHTEN in the Character of PEGGY.

Figure 7.1. Mrs. Wrighten as Peggy in *The Gentle Shepherd* (1777). Reproduced by permission of the Harvard Theater Collection, Cambridge, MA.

T.Roberts del.   Publish'd for Bells British Theatre March 29ᵗ 1782.   Thornthwaite Sc.

Mʳˢ WRIGHTEN in the Character of MADGE.
Since Hodge proves ungrateful no farther I'll seek.

Figure 7.2. Mrs. Wrighten as Madge in *Love in a Village* (1782). Reproduced by permission of the Harvard Theater Collection, Cambridge, MA.

advertisements for these events reveal that her performance of certain songs was believed to be a major draw. Published sheet music identified the songs as "sung by Mrs. Pownall," following the convention of linking a publication to a famous personage to increase sales.[52] The two songs most closely tied to Pownall were "Tally Ho," a highly popular hunting song composed by the Irish songwriter Thomas Carter, and "The Primrose Girl," or "Primroses" as it was sometimes called, a sentimental song written by the New York musician James Hewitt.[53] Both songs are in the British *galant* style associated with Vauxhall and the comic opera houses, and both helped solidify Pownall's image as an accessible celebrity in America.

"Tally Ho" and "The Primrose Girl" were complementary songs that offered audiences the illusion of having a direct view into Pownall's personality. "Tally Ho" connected Pownall to images of vigorous outdoor activities, while the aristocratic connotations of hunting were tempered by lyrics that explicitly welcomed people of all classes and professions to the chase. Such democratic sentiment resonated strongly in early national America, and the music was catchy, too. Composed in a rollicking $\frac{6}{8}$ meter and the key of E-flat major, the piece employs typical idioms of hunting songs. Pownall had a facile voice well suited to the repeated calls of "Tally ho" in rising arpeggiated intervals that pervade the song (fig. 7.3).

"The Primrose Girl," in contrast, was a sweetly sentimental song about a virtuous but poor flower seller. The song solicits sympathy for the hardworking but unfortunate maiden, with lines such as "My dress is quite plain, and my parentage low" and "All wicked temptations I ever will fly." The music is simple yet tuneful, in a major key that softens the plaintive tenor of the lyrics. It was not particularly challenging to sing, and the sheet music was reprinted often in the 1790s and early 1800s. Hewitt included the song in a collection he published with Pownall in 1794. At least five of the reprints indicated that the song was "as sung by Mrs. Pownall," which indeed it was.[54] Pownall performed "The Primrose Girl" often, along with "Tally Ho," and was applauded for her interpretation. As the Boston *Mercury* reported in 1795, "The refined simplicity of 'Primroses,' and the lofty execution of 'Tally ho,' were each equally inimitable."[55]

American music aficionados knew about transatlantic celebrities from reading about them and buying music written for them, but in Pownall they had the chance to establish a more tangible connection to that elusive phenomenon. Whether witnessing her perform onstage or purchasing the sheet music for songs "as sung by Mrs. Pownall," Pownall's audiences had access to their own "Columbian Billington." Pownall's strengths in playing supporting comedic roles and her association with rustic and sentimental songs made her seem accessible to her fans while also eschewing the divisive politics common elsewhere in the public sphere. Her fame hinged on her appearance as

Figure 7.3. "Tally Ho" (Gilfert, n.d.). Reproduced by permission of the Newberry Library, Chicago, IL.

good-natured and collaborative rather than demanding, partisan, or competitive. Pownall's roles and repertory were remarkably unremarkable—neither overly virtuosic nor particularly showy.

"A Desire to Peruse the Productions of Her Pen": Female Authorship as Compromise[56]

Mary Pownall was a woman of letters. As with other aspects of her life in the public sphere, she found the world of publishing to be one in which women's activities were closely monitored and carefully prescribed. In the late eighteenth century, female writers' intellectual abilities and reputations were on trial when women endeavored to put their words in print. Ironically, the Enlightenment ideals of equality and intellectual progress that helped fuel the booming print trade did not eradicate the patriarchal belief that women were naturally subordinate. Yet it was in print that advocates for gender parity and greater educational resources for women found a powerful new outlet on both sides of the Atlantic. Judith Sargent Murray published her groundbreaking essay "On the Equality of the Sexes" in *Massachusetts Magazine* in 1790, predating Mary Wollstonecraft's notorious *A Vindication of the Rights of Woman* by two years. Female authorship increased in the 1790s as periodicals aimed at women solicited their readers to contribute letters, comments, and poetry. However, strictures regarding women's reputations demanded that they publish anonymously, using a pseudonym or even adopting a male penname. Women could participate in the public print sphere, but they faced considerable headwinds and risked condemnation when they did so, unless they adhered to expectations of feminine demureness.[57]

Operating in the convention-bound world of print, female performers had a little leeway that nonperforming women lacked. Already known as public figures (and having already taken the risk of participating in a profession that was not always viewed as reputable), actresses', singers', and playwrights' publications were extensions of their public personas. The connection between publication and persona is illustrated clearly in the practice of including a singer's name on published sheet music, as seen with "Tally Ho" and "The Primrose Girl." However, being associated with a piece as a performer was far more benign than being its author, since the former treated women as a means of conveying a (presumably male) creator's products to the audience, while the latter granted women agency and a measure of expressive autonomy. Nonetheless, some women in the theater world took advantage of their relative freedom to advance controversial views about gender inequality. Such was the case with Susanna Rowson, whose play *Slaves in Algiers* (1794) used the themes of slavery and liberty to call for a reevaluation of women's restriction to the domestic realm.[58] Scholars have pointed to such instances as important signs of women's participation in political life, and for that reason greater attention has been paid to women authors like Rowson. Pownall's approach represented another strategy for harnessing the power of print, one that demonstrates a less controversial mode of self-commodification.

Pownall's print output was small, but it clarifies her conciliatory approach to being a public figure. In 1793 she published a volume titled *Mrs. Pownall's Address*, a collection of original song lyrics and songs performed at a benefit concert held in Philadelphia earlier that year.[59] In 1794 she released a collection of songs in collaboration with James Hewitt, the New York violinist, composer, and publisher. All told, eight songs by Pownall have been identified, five of which survive. Both publications featured her name in the title or prominently displayed on the title page. Her compositions were emblematic of the style common among the rising number of secular compositions flooding the market: light, tuneful *galant*-style songs for keyboard and voice featuring sentimental or topical lyrics.[60] Though modest in size, Pownall's publications are significant because they refined her celebrity image, marking her as both a performer and a composer and thus as something of a novelty. They also serve as evidence of her deft self-commodification—in particular her awareness that audience members might wish to own something tangible associated with her.[61]

The collection of songs Pownall published with Hewitt best displays her compositional style and her gifts as a singer. The volume was simply titled *Six Songs*, and Pownall's contributions reveal her command of the musical idioms that were popular at the time. Her songs tend to feature first-person narratives, often in the voices of country girls who sing of the swains who wronged them. They are simple and easy for an amateur to sing. For example, in her song "The Straw Bonnet," one finds an undemanding Alberti bass set at an easy *allegretto* pace, over which the singer recounts the duplicity of a ploughboy. Lingering ornamentation on the words "deceived" and "treason" is completely in keeping with the *galant* style of British comic opera songs (fig. 7.4). Some of her songs became quite popular, including "Jemmy of the Glen." Adopting the snap rhythms of the Scottish style that was in vogue in the late eighteenth century, this song was reprinted in Boston, Philadelphia, Baltimore, and New York and was frequently copied by hand.[62] Pownall performed it in concerts, thus promoting her compositions with her own voice.[63]

Pownall's collection of song lyrics is an altogether more complex publication, one that illustrates her astute avoidance of politically tumultuous waters. Titled *Mrs. Pownall's Address* and printed in Philadelphia in 1793, the collection—or songster, as it should be called—is a multifaceted vehicle for self-promotion. It is also a bit of a hodgepodge. The conceit is that the songster was published to commemorate her benevolence toward French refugees

Figure 7.4. "The Straw Bonnet," in *Six Songs* (Hewitt, 1794). Courtesy of the New York Public Library, New York, NY.

fur'd the same Vows were be--leiv'd, by Pat-ty and Ruth he for-
-took and de--ceiv'd yet his words are so sweet and like
truth so ap--pear that I par-don the Treason the Traitor so
dear. for

2

I saw the straw Bonnet he bought at the Fair
    With Rose colour'd Ribbon's, to deck Sally's Hair
    The Shoe ties of Bridget, and more then all this
    The Gloves he gave Peggy for granting A Kiss
    All these Did I see and with Heart rending Pain
    Swore to part, yet I know when I see him again
    That his words and his looks will like Truth so appear.
I shall Pardon the Treason the Traitor so dear.

Figure 7.4.—(concluded)

recently arrived in Philadelphia. Yet rather than engage with the topic of the revolutions in France and Haiti—or the implied partisan leaning toward the Republicans, who were vastly more sympathetic toward the French than were the Federalists—the volume eschews politics entirely. In it Pownall offers lyrics to five of her own songs, including "Jemmy of the Glen," followed by the lyrics to nine songs by other composers. A separate title page demarcates the section of Pownall's songs, declaring them "Pastoral Songs" written by "Mary A. Pownall." The other nine songs do not have their own title page and are simply designated at the start of the section as songs recently performed in concert. Someone—presumably the publisher or Pownall—penned anonymous prefatory material praising Pownall for her great skill as a performer, mentioning in particular her generosity in participating in recent benefit concerts in Philadelphia. Next is a rhyming speech Pownall delivered at one such benefit—the "address" to which the volume's title refers. (The volume's full title is *Mrs. Pownall's Address, in Behalf of the French Musicians, Delivered on Her Benefit Concert Night, at Oeller's Hotel, Chestnut-Street, Philadelphia.*) It seems likely that Pownall had planned to publish only a pamphlet of her song lyrics, but upon receiving a salutary response to her appearance in benefit concerts, she expanded the venture by including more song lyrics and the front matter. What began as a small project grew into a more robust form of self-commodification through print.

Instead of voicing a political opinion, Pownall used *Mrs. Pownall's Address* to announce her presence in America and introduce herself as a gracious woman. This point is made clear in the volume's prefatory material. She had only recently immigrated when the volume was published in March 1793, and the texts demonstrate her canny sense of how to present herself. The anonymous editor's note to the reader espouses her as a singer who for years had been the "Favorite Singer at Vauxhall" and heaps praise on the audience (and presumably the purchasers of the volume) for their good taste. In a long sentence that twists from complimenting Pownall to commending the audience, the preface mentions her participation in benefit concerts for French musicians and drums home the point that her talent more than matches her virtue: "Her Benevolence of Conduct, respecting the *French Performers*, may in the eyes of *Philadelphians* have given additional *Grace* to her exertions at their Concerts, yet the applauses bestowed on her *Performances*, by a very crowded and respectable audience, when for her own *Benefit*, shew a just appreciation of *Merit*, even when unaided by Circumstances, adapted to silence the voice of Criticism and excite the Feelings of *Philanthropy*."[64] Everyone who had attended, performed in, or strategically issued a publication following the benefit concerts deserved accolades, according to the editor. The "address" that follows the editor's note continues the tactic of praising the reader and Pownall equally but this time in Pownall's own voice. The address is a consummate performance of humility and virtue. She begins by comparing herself to Mary Queen of Scots, who was much in vogue in the late eighteenth century: "'Twas said of Queen Mary, when she died, and was Anatomiz'd, the Word *Calais* was found engraved on her *Heart*." Pownall continues to state that, because of her kindly reception in Philadelphia, "*Die when I may*, the Names of GRATITUDE and PHILADELPHIA will be found on *Mine*."[65] These charming words flattered the city in which she had recently arrived and emphasized her humility.

Pownall next turned to cajoling. Her "address" continues with twenty-two sets of rhyming couplets, a lengthy verse that could well have been spoken from the stage in a direct address to the audience. In it she enjoined her public to turn out their pockets for the benefit of the French refugee musicians. The verse is stuffed with solicitous niceties ("If Ladies you'll forgive this faint endeavor"[66]), glancing acknowledgment of her audience's political inclinations and recent history ("What say you Sirs;—but put it to the vote" and "Shall it be said, *Collumbia*'s [*sic*] Sons forgot / That *Frenchmen* in their cause once bravely fought?"[67]), and sly allusions to her performances in popular shows (a current hit was the farce *No Song, No Supper*, which Pownall referenced with the line "I cou'd not Sing, if I had eat [*sic*] no Dinner"[68]). Under the guise of soliciting the audience's approval and sympathy, the couplets were also engineered to showcase Pownall as a practiced performer and self-sacrificing celebrity who used her renown for the good of others—then made it available for sale at the local bookseller's shop.

As in other areas of her career, Pownall's publications eschew innovation and embrace convention. No controversial topics jump off the pages of her works—no claims for women's rights and education, no statements about partisan politics, no opinions about the revolutions in France and Haiti. Instead, her publications demonstrate her entrepreneurialism as she crafted her image as a kindhearted performer who was also a cultured woman of letters. In doing so, she illustrated how publishing was an important mode of self-commodification to an audience eager to emulate the model of cosmopolitan sophistication she represented.

⅔ ⅔ ⅔

The importance of transatlantic influences on early American musical life cannot be underestimated; neither can the significance of transatlantic performers like Pownall. The complexity of Pownall's model of celebrity, manufactured through shrewd self-commodification, accounted for her success: she presented herself in the roles of experienced professional, virtuous and accessible mother, and woman of letters. She was able to help foster a taste for celebrity among early American audiences, and her career served as a template for how performers could take advantage of the new American entertainment market. In doing so, however, she avoided entirely any controversial stances that might have undermined her career or disrupted the fragile fabric out of which performers' careers were weaved in the early republic. Taking stock of her career shows that celebrity culture emerged through the savvy and multimodal self-commodification engineered by transatlantic performers and draws attention to the surprising importance of mundaneness for achieving success.

Notes

1. The substantial bibliographical work on early American music bears testament to this transatlantic influence. See Oscar G. T. Sonneck, *Early Opera in America* (New York: G. Schirmer, 1915); Oscar G. T. Sonneck, *A Bibliography of Early Secular Music, 18th Century*, ed. William Treat Upton (New York: Da Capo, 1964); Irving Lowens, *A Bibliography of Songsters Printed in America before 1821* (Worcester, MA: American Antiquarian Society, 1976); Richard J. Wolfe, *Early American Music Engraving and Printing: A History of Music Publishing in America from 1787 to 1825 with Commentary on Earlier and Later Practices* (Urbana: Published in cooperation with the Bibliographical Society of America by University of Illinois Press, 1980).

2. Such skillful professional navigation was not unique to women in early national America. For example, see Paula Gillett's assessment of the opportunistic approaches of professional women musicians in Britain in the long nineteenth century. Paula Gillett, "Entrepreneurial Women Musicians in Britain: From the 1790s to the Early 1900s," in *The Musician as Entrepreneur, 1700–1914*, ed. William Weber (Bloomington: Indiana University Press, 2004), 198–220.

3. Susan L. Porter, "English-American Interaction in American Musical Theater at the Turn of the Nineteenth Century," *American Music* 4, no. 1 (1986): 8; Nicholas Temperley, *Bound for America: Three British Composers* (Chicago: University of Illinois Press, 2003), 4.

4. T. H. Breen, *The Marketplace of Revolution: How Consumer Politics Shaped American Independence* (New York: Oxford University Press, 2004).

5. Kariann Akemi Yokota, *Unbecoming British: How Revolutionary America Became Postcolonial* (New York: Oxford University Press, 2011).

6. On nation formation and the theater, see Heather Nathans, *Early American Theatre from the Revolution to Thomas Jefferson: Into the Hands of the People* (New York: Cambridge University Press, 2003); Jason Shaffer, *Performing Patriotism: National Identity in the Colonial and Revolutionary American Theater* (Philadelphia: University of Pennsylvania Press, 2007).

7. On the usefulness of understanding women as participating in "civil society" rather than the "public sphere," see Mary Kelley, *Learning to Stand and Speak: Women, Education, and Public Life in America's Republic* (Chapel Hill: University of North Carolina Press, 2006), 5–8. Kelley's formulation is important, but since I am concerned with the overtly public world of theater and concert entertainment, I continue to use the term *public sphere*, which I employ in a generic and not explicitly Habermasian sense.

8. Catherine Allgor, *Parlor Politics in Which Ladies of Washington Help Build a City and a Government* (Charlottesville: University of Virginia Press, 2000); Susan Branson, *These Fiery Frenchified Dames: Women and Political Culture in Early National Philadelphia* (Philadelphia: University of Pennsylvania Press, 2001); Simon P. Newman, *Parades and the Politics of the Street: Festive Culture in the Early American Republic* (Philadelphia: University of Pennsylvania Press, 1997); David Waldstreicher, *In the Midst of Perpetual Fetes: The Making of American Nationalism, 1776–1820* (Chapel Hill: University of North Carolina Press, 1997); Rosemarie Zagarri, *Revolutionary Backlash: Women and Politics in the Early American Republic* (Philadelphia: University of Pennsylvania Press, 2007). On female performers in particular, see Branson, *These Fiery Frenchified Dames*, 106–23; Nathans, *Early American Theatre*.

9. Judith Tick has assessed Pownall's contributions as a composer. See Judith Tick, *American Women Composers before 1870*, 2nd ed. (Rochester, NY: University of Rochester Press, 1995), 58–59.

10. Felicity Nussbaum, *Rival Queens: Actresses, Performance, and the Eighteenth-Century British Theater* (Philadelphia: University of Pennsylvania Press, 2010).

11. I borrow this formulation of the importance of case studies (or microhistories) from Jill Lepore, "Historians Who Love Too Much: Reflections on Microhistory and Biography," *Journal of American History* 88, no. 1 (June 2001): 129–44.

12. Nearly every study of celebrity takes pains to distinguish among "celebrity," "fame," and "renown," among other terms. Definitions vary but hew to general distinctions based on the extent to which an individual was known and degrees of separation between the individual and the public, how acclaim was gained, and the mechanisms by which acclaim was distributed. I am using celebrity to mean a well-known personage whose actions were chronicled in print and observed by audiences in public. When I use "fame" or "renown," it is to vary the terminology, not because I am referring to a distinct and separate category from celebrity. On the rise of commercialized celebrity culture in the nineteenth century, see Thomas Nelson Baker, *Sentiment and Celebrity: Nathaniel Parker Willis and the Trials of Literary Fame* (New York: Oxford University Press, 1999).

13. The eighteenth-century evolution of celebrity culture in Britain is well studied. See, for example, Mary Luckhurst and Jane Moody's introduction to *Theatre and Celebrity in Britain, 1660–2000*, ed. Mary Luckhurst and Jane Moody (New York: Palgrave Macmillan, 2005), 3. Classic studies of celebrity in general include Leo Braudy, *The Frenzy of Renown: Fame and Its History* (New York: Vintage Books, 1997); Chris Rojek, *Celebrity* (London: Reaktion, 2001); Joseph Roach, "It," *Theatre Journal, Theorizing the Performer* 56, no. 4 (2004): 555–68; Fred Inglis, *A Short History of Celebrity* (Princeton: Princeton University Press, 2010). Further developments in celebrity culture in the nineteenth century are adumbrated in Edward Berenson and Eva Giloi, eds., *Constructing Charisma: Celebrity, Fame, and Power in Nineteenth-Century Europe* (New York: Berghahn Books, 2010). See esp. Berenson and Giloi's introduction for a discussion of the connection of celebrity to the mass press in the nineteenth century (6).

14. Joseph Roach, "Public Intimacy: The Prior History of 'It,'" in Luckhurst and Moody, eds., *Theatre and Celebrity in Britain*, 24.

THE POWER TO PLEASE 〜 199

Colley Cibber, *Apology for the Life of Colley Cibber* (London: John Watt, 1740).

On Whitefield, see Jessica Parr, *Inventing George Whitefield: Race, Revivalism, and the Making of a Religious Icon* (Jackson: University of Mississippi Press, 2015); on the cult of Washington's celebrity, see Barry Schwartz, *George Washington: The Making of an American Symbol* (New York: Free Press, 1987).

17. I take the terminology of ascribed and achieved celebrity from Rojek, *Celebrity*, 18.

18. Sarah Knott, *Sensibility and the American Revolution* (Chapel Hill: Published by the Omohundro Institute for Early American History and Culture by the University of North Carolina Press, 2009).

19. Nussbaum calls this relationship between audience and performer the "interiority effect." Particularly noteworthy is how this effect encompasses the commodification of the performer, as one of the ways the audience members are made to feel as though they have access to the celebrity is by purchasing souvenirs, tickets, publications, and similar items. Nussbaum, *Rival Queens*, 20–22.

20. Oscar G. T. Sonneck, *Early Concert-Life in America (1731–1800)* (New York: Da Capo, 1978 [1907]), 251; Porter, "English-American Interaction," 6. The American Company was subsequently rechristened the Old American Company and recruited Pownall in 1792.

21. Shaffer, *Performing Patriotism*, 11; Dorothy T. Potter, *Food for Apollo: Cultivated Music in Antebellum Philadelphia* (Bethlehem, PA: Lehigh University Press, 2011).

22. Porter, "English-American Interaction," 11.

23. Quoted in Susan L. Porter, *With an Air Debonair: Musical Theatre in America 1785–1815* (Washington, DC: Smithsonian Institution Press, 1991), 126.

24. Shaffer discusses the "cultural incongruity" of British plays dominating American stages after the revolution as a significant hurdle British-staffed troupes had to overcome. Shaffer, *Performing Patriotism*, 168.

25. Other cities had theaters and troupes as well. In Boston, the Federal Street Theater was built and opened in 1794 and was soon rivaled by the Haymarket Theater, which opened in 1796. In Charleston, the Virginia Company of John Bignall and Thomas Wade West opened the Broad Street Theater in 1793. French refugees from the revolutions in France and Haiti took over Charleston's City Theater on Church Street in 1794. By 1797 the United States was divided into three theatrical domains: in Boston and New York, the Old American Company dominated; Charleston, Richmond, and the South had Monsieur Solee's Company; and Philadelphia, Baltimore, and Annapolis was Wignell and Reinagle territory. Porter, *With an Air Debonair*, 10–11.

26. Olive Baldwin and Thelma Wilson, "Wrighten, Mary Ann (1751–1796)," in *Oxford Dictionary of National Biography*, online ed., ed. Lawrence Goldman (Oxford: Oxford University Press, October 2005); online ed., ed. Lawrence Goldman (May 2008), http://www.oxforddnb.com/view/article/61886.

27. Pownall's arrival was reported in *The Diary or Loudon's Register* (New York City), October 1, 1792.

28. Her backstory was not unknown in America, and she was referred to in print as "Mrs. Pownall," "Mrs. Wrighten," and "the former Mrs. Wrighten."

29. Pownall's benefit concert in May 1793 was reported in *The Diary or Loudon's Register* (New York City), May 21, 1793; her June benefit was in the *Daily Advertiser* (New York City), June 4, 1793.

30. *City Gazette and Daily Advertiser* (Charleston, SC), November 9 and 23, 1795.

31. Pownall filled the program with repertory from Handel's oratorios, particularly *Messiah, Judas Maccabeus, Esther*, and *Sampson*, and advertised that a "synopsis of the concert" was for sale in advance of it. *City Gazette and Daily Advertiser* (Charleston, SC), March 22, 1796; synopsis also advertised in *City Gazette and Daily Advertiser*, March 23, 1796. The reprised concert was again advertised in *City Gazette and Daily Advertiser*, March 25, 1796.

32. *Columbian Herald or, the New Daily Advertiser* (Charleston, SC), July 14 and 30, 1796.

33. *City Gazette and Daily Advertiser* (Charleston, SC), August 4, 1796. See also Baldwin and Wilson, "Wrighten."

34. *The Mail; or, Claypoole's Daily Advertiser* (Philadelphia, PA), October 18, 1792.

35. John Durang, *The Memoir of John Durang, American Actor 1785–1816*, ed. Alan S. Downer (Pittsburgh: University of Pittsburgh Press, 1966), 36.

36. On accomplishment and its gendered connotations, see Tick, *American Women Composers*; Richard D. Leppert, *Music and Image: Domesticity, Ideology, and Socio-Cultural Formation in Eighteenth-Century England* (New York: Cambridge University Press, 1988); Candace Bailey, *Music and the Southern Belle: From Accomplished Lady to Confederate Composer* (Carbondale: Southern Illinois University Press, 2010).

37. *The Mail; or, Claypoole's Daily Advertiser* (Philadelphia, PA), October 18, 1792; *City Gazette and Daily Advertiser* (Charleston, SC), January 13, 1796.

38. G. J. Barker-Benfield, *The Culture of Sensibility: Sex and Society in Eighteenth-Century Britain* (Chicago: University of Chicago Press, 1992).

39. *Columbian Herald or, the New Daily Advertiser* (Charleston, SC), August 13, 1796. Similar notices appeared in Savannah, Baltimore, Philadelphia, New York, Providence, and Boston.

40. *The Mail; or, Claypoole's Daily Advertiser* (Philadelphia, PA), October 18, 1792.

41. *Columbian Centinel* (Boston, MA), July 19, 1794 (italics original).

42. *City Gazette and Daily Advertiser* (Charleston, SC), November 6, 1795.

43. Ibid., November 7, 1795 (italics original).

44. The Charity School concert was advertised in the *Daily Advertiser* (New York City), June 22, 1793; the Boston concert in the *Columbian Centinel* (Boston, MA), August 9, 1794; on the Freemasons concert, see *Columbian Herald or, the New Daily Advertiser* (Charleston, SC), June 17, 1796.

45. The first French benefit appeared in the *General Advertiser* (Philadelphia, PA), January 4, 1793; the second benefit in the *Federal Gazette, and Philadelphia Evening Post*, January 11, 1793. The French musicians had been in Philadelphia since at least a few months before Mrs. Pownall's arrival. Their periodic benefit concerts began in September 1792; see *Dunlap's American Daily Advertiser* (Philadelphia, PA), August 31, 1792.

46. *Federal Orrery* (Boston, MA), October 12, 1795.

47. *City Gazette and Daily Advertiser* (Charleston, SC), April 2, 1796.

48. The *Mercury* (Boston, MA), October 16, 1795.

49. Richard Hofstadter, *The Idea of a Party System: The Rise of Legitimate Opposition in the United States, 1780–1840* (Berkeley: University of California Press, 1969).

50. For example, a letter in the January 23, 1794, issue of Boston's *Independent Chronicle and Universal Daily Advertiser* complained: "ÇA IRA! However 'jarring' the sound of *God Save the King* may be to the Republicans, it is presumed that the tune of *Ça Ira* will be agreeable to every Citizen who wishes well to the cause of France, and to the Rights of Man—it is therefore requested that the Theatre may be opened with the animating tune of *Ça Ira* accompanied with a FULL BAND; and it will be re-echoed by the loudest acclamations from every friend, to the tune of YANKEE DOODLE"; quoted in Nathans, *Early American Theater*, 79.

51. For a list of all of Pownall's roles in America, see George O. Seilhamer, *History of the American Theatre: New Foundations* (Philadelphia: Globe, 1891), 294–95.

52. For example, George Gilfert published sheet music for several comic opera songs with the subtitle "A favorite song, sung by Mrs. Pownall," including James Hook's "Ma Belle Coquette" (New York: George Gilfert, ca. 1795).

53. "Tally Ho" was published in London by William Randall sometime after 1777. George Gilfert printed and sold it in New York ca. 1795.

54. Sheet music for the song was published nine times in the 1790s and also appeared in several collections during the years 1800–1828. See Sonneck, *Bibliography of Early Secular Music*, 346–47.

55. The *Mercury* (Boston, MA), October 16, 1795.

56. *Mrs. Pownall's Address*, note "to the reader," n.p.

57. On the pervasiveness of female authorship and publications aimed at women, see Branson, *These Fiery Frenchified Dames*, 24–26; Zagarri, *Revolutionary Backlash*, 51–53. On equality and education, see Linda Kerber, "The Republican Mother: Women and the Enlightenment—an American Perspective," *American Quarterly* 28, no. 2 (Summer 1976): 187–205.

58. On Rowson's performing career, see Peter Leavenworth, "The Pursuit of a 'Just Proportion of Public Approbation': Rowson in Her Musical Context," *Studies in American Fiction* 38, nos. 1–2 (2011): 33–56. On the controversy stirred up by *Slaves in Algiers*, see Branson, *Fiery Frenchified Dames*, 115–16.

59. *Mrs. Pownall's Address* was advertised in *Dunlap's American Daily Advertiser* (Philadelphia, PA), April 5, 1793. Pownall was likely responsible for financing at least part of the printing, as it was common practice for an author to write prose and pay a typesetter to print it. In the case of *Mrs. Pownall's Address*, the printer was Enoch Story.

60. Pownall's compositional activities predated her arrival in the United States. She wrote lyrics for songs she performed on British stages, several of which were published between 1783 and 1785. See Michael Kassler, comp., *Music Entries at Stationers' Hall, 1710–1818* (Burlington, VT: Ashgate, 2004), 35, 44, 54.

61. For a comparative look at how collecting memorabilia fed into celebrity culture, see Eva Giloi, *Monarchy, Myth, and Material Culture in Germany, 1750–1950* (New York: Cambridge University Press, 2011).

62. Examples of manuscript copies of the song are included in the Herreshoff Music Collection, MSS 490, box 2, item 8, Rhode Island Historical Society, Providence; and in the Lucy Sheldon Beach Music Books, vol. C (1910-11-0), Litchfield Historical Society, Helga J. Ingraham Memorial Library, Litchfield, CT.

63. *The Diary or Loudon's Register* (New York City), May 28, 1793.

64. *Mrs. Pownall's Address* (Philadelphia: Printed and sold by Enoch Story, 1793), 3–4 (italics original).

65. Ibid., 1 (italics original).

66. Ibid., 2.

67. Ibid. (italics original).

68. Ibid., 3.

Part Four

Cultivating Communities

Chapter Eight

Exchanging Ideas in a Changing World

Adolph Bernhard Marx and the *Berliner allgemeine musikalische Zeitung* in 1824

Patrick Wood Uribe

If I may begin with an understatement, music journals of the eighteenth and nineteenth centuries offer a wealth of material for scholarly study. Essays and reviews of musical works in periodicals such as the *Allgemeine musikalische Zeitung* and the *Neue Zeitschrift für Musik* are rich sources for exploring a variety of topics: music criticism, as in the work of Mary Sue Morrow, Sanna Pederson, and Barbara Titus; and reception histories of individual composers, as in Robin Wallace's work on Beethoven or the volumes of contemporaneous criticism of Beethoven edited in English by Wayne M. Senner and in German by Stefan Kunze.[1] The content of these journals can also tell us a good deal about the societies and institutions that published, performed, and enjoyed the music they discuss.

The periodicals in which these texts appear, however, are not documents that existed in a vacuum. They were, rather, part of a dynamic and competitive commercial market, an aspect of these publications that this volume sets into relief. Not only were they destined for a paying readership, but most journals were produced by publishing houses whose primary business was selling music. I suggest that considering this wider commercial context as more than a mere backdrop in fact materially changes the way we read these texts.

As a brief example, we might look to the *Allgemeine musikalische Zeitung,* in which E. T. A. Hoffmann's famous groundbreaking essays on Beethoven appeared in 1810.[2] Although Hoffmann's insightful writing naturally absorbs our attention, the commercial context of the reviews is by no means neutral; compelling as they are, the essays served a range of other interests. Most significant, the journal itself was issued by Breitkopf und Härtel, which also published and sold the scores Hoffmann was discussing. In a basic way, Hoffmann's essays served as advertising, generating or increasing demand for publications Breitkopf und Härtel could then supply. For modern readers, this function should at the very least raise questions about the selection of works reviewed in the journal and, perhaps more important, about works whose omission for commercial reasons has left them with a less prominent contemporaneous documentary history. Certainly, we ignore these considerations at our peril: the relationship between reviews and publishers was plainly evident to contemporary readers and open to cynical interpretation, so much so, in fact, that Schumann's *Neue Zeitschrift* laid claim to a higher degree of critical independence precisely as a specific exception to this model, since it was not connected to a music publisher.

My focus here will be the *Berliner allgemeine musikalische Zeitung.* Published by A. M. Schlesinger, the journal was as obviously aimed at securing business as was the *Allgemeine musikalische Zeitung.* The journal's pages clearly demonstrate the competitive marketplace for printed music in reviews and advertisements, which, on the one hand, make a study of the publication especially apposite to the topic of this volume. On the other hand, however, many of its most prominent articles are overwhelmingly not concerned with either marketing or the kind of appraisal of works that we might expect. Instead, a great many of the articles are dedicated to raising self-conscious—and more fundamental—questions about criticism itself, including, what are the standards to which new works are held? How do we evaluate what is genuinely new, since it is necessarily unlike what we already know? What actual purpose is served by reviews and by criticism in general? What is a journal supposed to do for its public? For a publication that seems so evidently designed to drive sales through advertising, these are surprisingly philosophical, idealistic, and existential lines of inquiry. That such reflexive questions should appear alongside commercial concerns suggests that the music marketplace was not just a competitive one but one in which competition itself brought a number of deeper interpretive insecurities. Battles in the marketplace were not just over which scores consumers bought and where they bought them; also at stake was how readers approached, absorbed, and understood the works they purchased.

These questions, all of which appear in the pages of the *Berliner allgemeine musikalische Zeitung,* are telling precisely because they are ones an established journal might think are so fundamental and obvious that they do not require answers. The fact that the *Berliner allgemeine musikalische Zeitung* asked them suggests either that they were worth revisiting or that there were readers for whom those unspoken answers could not be taken for granted. As I outline in greater detail below, the market for the consumption of music grew larger as it added music lovers, but many of this journal's articles seem aimed at readers of even more limited expertise or knowledge than those who were the targets of earlier publications. In part, this is a reflection of the often-cited expansion of the German middle class, but it also implies an underlying worry about the consumption of music: what if music lovers want to love bad music?[3] Or good music for the wrong reasons?[4] How these readers are treated by the journal offers an important perspective on the way new consumers participated in their market.

These issues surfaced in part because the market itself was growing, and it seems that in Berlin, growth was particularly fast-paced. In the 1820s the city was rapidly becoming a cosmopolitan center, and part of its transformation was reflected in its music publishing landscape. In 1806, there were only four music publishers in Berlin, one of which closed that year; another dwindled until it was shuttered in 1822. But only six years later, in 1828, ten music publishers were in business, not counting the increasing number of bookshops that also sold music—some of which sporadically published musical works. By midcentury, in addition to these stores, Berlin boasted seventeen music publishers.[5] In 1824, in the midst of this great expansion, Adolph Martin Schlesinger founded the *Berliner allgemeine musikalische Zeitung*. He appointed the young and energetic Adolph Bernhard Marx as its first and only editor. Marx is now principally known as a music theorist and more specifically as the person who named sonata form and first discussed it at length. In this early stage of his career, Marx edited the journal for its entire six-year run, during which he contributed a vast number of essays and articles.

Although most modern scholarship on Marx focuses on his work as a theorist in the four-volume *Die Lehre von der musikalischen Komposition* (1837–47), his criticial writings in the *Berliner allgemeine musikalische Zeitung* have received occasional attention. Marx was a tireless and enthusiastic champion of Beethoven, and his work on this composer in particular has drawn scholars to him. Marx's criticism is featured in Robin Wallace's *Beethoven's Critics* as well as in Thomas Sipe's monograph on the *Eroica* Symphony. Neither book, however, represents Marx completely, as the scope of their readings is limited to some (but nowhere near all) of Marx's writing on Beethoven, itself only a fraction of a voluminous body of work that encompasses and combines criticism, theory, philosophy, and politics.[6] More broadly, a portion of Marx's writing in the *Berliner allgemeine musikalische Zeitung* is central to Sanna Pederson's work on concert life in Berlin, in particular to her argument that Marx's championing of German music formed "an exclusionary ideology directed at other nations."[7] In response, four years later Celia Applegate pointed out several misleading aspects of Pederson's rationale, most importantly the anachronism of failing to distinguish the twentieth-century catastrophe of German nationalism from early nineteenth-century efforts to understand German identity. In Marx's day, Germany remained a loose collection of states, so the very idea of German nationalism, or "German-ness" compared to other European identities, must necessarily be more complex. As Applegate puts it, nationalism in the early nineteenth century was "an emergent cognitive model . . . a way of ordering experience, of looking at the world and making sense of one's place and identity in it."[8]

As I have argued elsewhere, Marx is among the most influential and important musical thinkers of both his age and ours, although, as Ian Bent put it, he is "perhaps the most maligned—the most *unjustly* maligned—of all nineteenth-century writers on music."[9] His views, particularly as a critic, are frequently misrepresented and oversimplified. Much as it might be overdue, however, it is not my intention here to offer a comprehensive assessment of or apology for him.[10] My focus, rather, is on a specific but enlightening aspect of Marx that is seldom considered: his editorship of the *Berliner allgemeine musikalische Zeitung*, in particular what his choices as contributor and editor can tell us about the commerce and exchange of ideas in his changing musical world.

It is plainly evident that one of the journal's important functions was to enhance the publisher's sales of books and scores. Every third or fourth issue— or about one issue a month—included advertising supplements in which Schlesinger's new music publications were announced. The title of the supplements, "Musical Advertiser" (*Musikalischer Anzeiger*), was followed immediately by the words "Catalog of scores on offer at the Schlesinger book and music shop, Unter den Linden No. 34." The first supplement was only two pages long, but the second took up four complete pages—a substantial addition to an eight-page issue. It was followed by another supplement, a "*Literarisch-artistisch-musikalischer Anzeiger*," which was also included in *Der Freimüthige*, another journal published by Schlesinger. It is not surprising that in this supplement, too, all the books advertised are found at the Schlesinger shop: every listing contains the reference "in Berlin at the Schlesinger book and music shop" (*In Berlin in der Schlesingerschen Buch- und Musikhandlung*). By dint of sheer persistence, the phrase almost takes on the character of a refrain. More than that, however, there is something very deliberate about its appearance: not only is it phrased slightly differently each time, but it is always part of a grammatical sentence. Whereas unchanged or unthinking repetitions might make it seem like a habit or a reflex, these varied appearances convey a different quality: although faint, there is a voice, and it is not dogged but rather solicitous, even anxious. For example:

The fifth edition of the second section of Friedrich Kohlrausch's History has just been issued and dispatched to all bookstores (in Berlin to the Schlesinger Book and Music Shop).

Published by G. Braun in Karlsruhe, and on offer at all bookstores (in Berlin at the Schlesinger Book and Music Shop): The History of Two Somnambulists along with Some Other Commentaries from the Field of Magical Healing Arts and Psychology, by Dr. Justinus Kerner.

Just published by us, and on offer in all bookstores (in Berlin at the Schlesinger Book and Music Shop): A Collection of Drawings for Silversmiths and Silver Merchants.[11]

And so it continues in the pages that follow, with slight changes in format: "Musical scores from H. A. Probst publishers in Leipzig, which can be obtained at the Schlesinger shop"; "an edition of the complete novels of Walter Scott in English has been published by the Schlesinger Book and Music Store in Berlin"; "New French Books, which just now have arrived at the Schlesinger Book and Music Store in Berlin."[12]

Since these supplements were intended as advertisements, this persistence is not surprising, and we might expect the journal's main substance to be less sales-oriented. Strikingly, however, the contents pages of the journal itself sketch a scene that in many ways is equally relentless. A brief look at the list of reviews in the journal's first year reveals an overwhelming emphasis on Schlesinger publications: sixty-five works or collections were reviewed, of which thirty-eight were printed by Schlesinger. Twelve different publishers issued the remaining twenty-seven pieces or sets. In effect, Schlesinger publications occupied 60 percent of the journal's coverage, while the remaining 40 percent was unevenly distributed among the twelve others. These proportions alone created a world for the journal's readers in which most roads led to Schlesinger, and the choice of works to review served Schlesinger's interests by steering readers to the bookshop. At the same time, this sales-boosting technique suggests a note of caution to any scholar aiming to understand the musical—or historical—landscape through contemporary criticism: although publications like these promise a wealth of material, it is surely naive to trust implicitly that they aimed to be neutral, uncolored, or disinterested.

It is ironic that the *Berliner allgemeine musikalische Zeitung* should so brazenly have steered its readers toward the Schlesinger shop, since in its very first issue its editor claimed specifically that this was not its function. In an article addressing the role of critics directly, Marx claims that the majority of reviews serve readers as "nothing more than a higher category of bookshop advertisements, providers of advice for their purchases."[13] He adds that this kind of writing fails to represent readers' true interests, to which he wants to turn his attention.[14] Marx continues by stating a goal for criticism—speaking to those "true interests"—that is far more ambitious than mere purchasing advice. "Any effort," he writes, "that does not aim toward a refinement, toward a broadening of view, toward a spiritual enrichment of the reader, must be regarded by the writer as futile and lost."[15]

While these aims are both idealistic and sincere, they are not free of commercial motivations. Without a readership prepared to pay for the journal, Marx would have had no one to enrich, broaden, or refine; no journal can survive for long unless it supplies something in which the market has an interest. At the same time, the spiritual or intellectual enrichment of his readers was one of Marx's lifelong pursuits: from his work as a theorist to his biography of Beethoven, all of his writing exhibits a bustling, enthusiastic engagement with his—and his readers'—intellectual surroundings.

In the *Berliner allgemeine musikalische Zeitung*, Marx worked toward that "spiritual enrichment of the reader" in two principal ways. First, in his editorial decisions, he encouraged debate in the journal's pages, which often presented dramatically opposing views. In the later years of the journal, there are reviews in three or four installments to which another author responds, also in three or four installments. Second, as a writer, his contributions to the journal are not just spirited and engaging but also go to some length to guide and sharpen readers' thinking, particularly their sense of history. Each article positions its topic within a historical context, not as mere background but as a means of understanding the present through the past that brought the topic about. As a result, the commercial function served by the journal is effectively overshadowed by Marx's deliberate efforts to make the journal itself a different kind of marketplace, namely a forum for voicing and exchanging ideas.

In his first article in 1824, Marx characterizes the *Berliner allgemeine musikalische Zeitung* as a community, specifically one that grants freedom of expression to its contributors. He asks, "Who indeed would demand of any organization that all its participants behave in a completely concurrent way? Or of a scientific society that all members profess absolutely the same views and opinions? The society of contributors and the editor—may one never lose sight of it—is as free as any scientific organization or one dedicated to other purposes."[16] It was imperative for Marx that the journal invite and welcome multiple views, so much so, in fact, that he went out of his way to enact debate, sometimes by fairly elaborate means. Two examples from the journal's first year stand out. His review of Beethoven's Piano Sonata op. 111, for instance, begins as a letter to the editor from a fictional contributor, who opens with "Dear Sir, you will be surprised to receive, instead of the review of the 111th Sonata [*sic*] by Beethoven (published by Schlesinger) you kindly assigned to me, this same returned to you. I cannot review it."[17] (Schlesinger's role as the sonata's publisher is acknowledged—indeed, advertised—even in this fictional refusal to review it.) The unsigned letter goes on to describe how this man's perplexed consideration of the work was interrupted by a visit from a local music director, accompanied by a young man named Edward. The anonymous author transcribes a discussion that took place among these three characters. Edward is profoundly affected by the sonata, while the anonymous author, unbending and old-fashioned, cannot see its virtues since it fails to follow the rules he knows. The director and the author contend that only the recognized rules of harmony and counterpoint can provide a sound basis for aesthetic judgment. In contrast, Edward insists that there is something else at work, that art is not merely a pretty consolation for life's vicissitudes but rather that artworks are creations that reflect the way we experience life itself: "Art is life, it is the world created again by men. . . . Why should not art express what reality impresses upon us with an iron stamp?"[18] Although the reviewer has given voice to Edward's opinion, the letter closes with an appeal: "May you, dear editor, find the point from which the universally acknowledged rules of aesthetics can defend against these novelties. . . . Because when the first grasp of works detracts from reason and it is left to the senses to determine the standpoint of judgment, when works that mock all our rules gain such ardent followers, then I am silent."[19]

In another letter to the editor, almost certainly fabricated by Marx, a pedantic and conservative music lover holds forth on the topics reviews in the journal should discuss.[20] The letter is signed "Schimmel"—German for "mold." He takes the editor to task for his efforts to come to terms with Beethoven's sonatas and symphonies and asks if he really supposes the journal's readers are constitutionally fit for that kind of critical diet. After demonstrating the type of fare he would have preferred, namely a traditional discussion of parallel fifths, Schimmel argues—like the music director we just met—that it is only by consulting established and existing rules that works can be reliably evaluated. He closes by admonishing Marx: "Convert, young man, before it is too late. . . . It is wicked indeed to disturb the customary calm of wise composers and proven theorists, and since I do not think you wicked, it shall make me glad if I have brought you to the right path."[21]

These views are diametrically opposed to those Marx actually held, but they raise a question the journal intended to answer: if new works are genuinely new and thus do not resemble what we already know, then how do we evaluate them? Marx's first contribution to the journal confronts this question directly, in an article titled "On the Demands of Our Time on Music Criticism." In it, he argues that traditional criteria—such as those of Schimmel and the anonymous opus 111 reviewer—are outdated and insufficient for grasping the emotional depth of new works. The use of consonance as a standard for aesthetic judgment has filtered out works that do not follow the rules but that have more to say. Thus it occurred that artworks, which had set themselves "only this goal [consonance], corresponded far more with experience already gained and with the rules that were formed out of it than those works in which richer and deeper conceptions were set down."[22] In other words, by adhering to standards we already know, we miss an opportunity for finding and understanding greater depth and richness achieved by new compositional means, and in the pages of the journal, Marx dramatized the shortcomings of these views by creating these old-fashioned, fictitious personas.

Even taking into account Marx's stated intention to encourage freedom of opinion in the journal, in the passages above he goes well beyond merely fostering different perspectives: he actually fabricates them to make sure they are present. At first, this may seem like putting up straw men to knock down—a type of orchestrated crisis merely for rhetorical purposes. It might also remind us of Hoffmann's Johannes Kreisler or Robert Schumann's Florestan and Eusebius personas: for both writers, their essays are to a degree also fiction and serve the function of criticism while at the same time offering some of the freedom and appeal of creative writing. Although Marx's use of fictional mouthpieces shares a great deal with these examples and may stem from similar impulses, I argue that Marx's alter-egos are a deliberate expression of his convictions as to a journal's function.

In the journal's later years, Marx had no difficulty securing articles from actual contributors who held differing views, but in this first year he felt the need to contrive them. Curiously, he mentions that it was hard to find likeminded correspondents in other cities, offering this as a reason why there are rather few "Korrespondenzen" in the journal's first year.[23] It seems he was prepared to accept fewer reports from other music centers but could not forgo fewer perspectives in the journal's discussions. Even assuming that it was difficult to find contributors, however, I suggest that Marx's fabrications tell us something more, namely that debate itself was indispensable to him. But why go to such lengths? The reason is implicit in one of his initial claims for the journal's community of contributors: a free society allows for differences of opinion. In fact, Marx expected nothing less. As a result, the multiple views we read are not providing fair or unbiased perspectives; rather, they often express extremes, but that is precisely how their presence makes the freedom of Marx's community visible. Debate mattered to Marx because it proved that the society gathering in the journal's space was free.

The idea that the "society of contributors" and readers should be free was an important and very real concern in Berlin in the 1820s. The Carlsbad Decrees of 1819 had imposed stringent restrictions on the press, and, as Florian Edler has argued, it was a time during which Prussian "public life was controlled by authorities in drastic ways and censorship harshly clamped down."[24] Freedom of the press, as we understand it, was neither commonplace nor easily secured. Indeed, censorship was tight enough that Edler has suggested that music journalism served as an outlet for implicitly politicized debate not possible in the mainstream press: one could argue political views no censor would otherwise allow to be printed through—or disguised by—music.

With this in mind, when Marx refers to the "true interests" of readers, it is not without a political dimension. In his first article in the journal, Marx describes most journalists' writing as irrelevant to the needs of readers, most reviews as edicts as to the quality of a work based on equally irrelevant factors, and many readers as passive recipients who read "just to read."[25] Using language reminiscent more of parliaments than of writers, he continues: "We do not recognize all these vocalizers as representatives of the world of readers and wish to keep in mind the true interests of the latter instead of the former."[26] Those true interests are served not by being told what to think or buy but rather by awakening debate in the context of a free exchange of ideas.

Debate alone might demonstrate that freedom of exchange, but it would not be enough to offer readers "spiritual enrichment" or to "aim toward a refinement, toward a broadening of view."[27] Consequently, while Marx encouraged—and even manufactured—debate as an editor, as a writer he took every opportunity to offer his readers specific guidance. Compare, for instance, the basic strategies in two reviews of Mendelssohn's Piano Quartet op. 1, one from the Leipzig *Allgemeine musikalische Zeitung* and the other from the *Berliner allgemeine musikalische Zeitung*. The Leipzig reviewer essentially takes the reader on a guided tour of the work's features, briefly describing each movement in turn. Having done so, he remarks that Mendelssohn made an excellent choice by taking Mozart as his model. Mozart, he writes, remains the paragon: "This radiant star outshines all neighboring suns."[28] The article closes with advice for the reader that actually sounds like one of Marx's caricatures: "May the idle thirst for glory and flattery never remove him [Mendelssohn] from the road of truth and beauty in art, so as to worship fashionable tastes."[29] Marx's review in the *Berliner allgemeine musikalische Zeitung* also points out the relationship to Mozart, but in contrast it immediately adds that to understand that relationship, it is necessary to know what features are so characteristic of Mozart as to make the composer's style instantly recognizable; the review eventually arrives at Mendelssohn's work but only after first guiding the reader through Mozart's style.

The premise of Marx's article is to place the work under consideration at the end of a historical trajectory. In this case it's a short one, but the same gesture launches a great many of the journal's essays. A review of Beethoven's choral setting of "Meeres Stille" by Goethe begins with a discussion of some of Goethe's other poems and the relationship of poetry to music before moving on to a critical assessment of Beethoven's work.[30] Another essay, on Beethoven's achievements as a symphonist, spends two of its three substantial installments on the history of the symphony from Handel's overtures through Mozart and

Haydn before eventually coming to Beethoven.[31] In one way or another, these articles all begin by taking a step backward and guiding the reader through a learning process. The goal is neither a mere acquaintance with the features of a work nor a recommendation to buy it but the sale of something nobler: a fuller understanding of the work's place among or outside existing traditions. If the journal's space offers freedom, it does so without abandoning its readers to fend for themselves unguided.

A historical understanding of this kind is a vital part of Marx's goals for the journal, as he argues in the last article of 1824, titled "The Position of the Journal": "As we strive to the best of our abilities to fathom more deeply the essence of music, if we succeed, more and more light will fall on the creations of earlier periods. Too often and for too long, the works of old masters have been neglected in this respect and like corpses only anatomically . . . explored."[32] Using the concept of fugue as an example, he goes on to ask, "And how did it come about that art evolved this way? What must have preceded so that it could reach its present position?" His next sentence offers a concise argument for the importance of the journal's historical perspective: "The present can only be grasped in a completely satisfactory way from its past, and even if a journal is dedicated primarily to the former, the counsel and teaching of the latter ought not to be neglected."[33] One can draw a distinction between this attention to history and Marx's caricatures of "established rules" and the "customary calm . . . of proven theorists." Earlier in the journal's pages he argued that traditional criteria are insufficient for evaluating new works, and he firmly opposed clinging to the criteria and standards of a bygone era. Indeed, his argument here is that the *Allgemeine musikalische Zeitung*, whose aesthetic judgment is appropriate to the age of Mozart and Haydn, is no longer relevant because a new era is beginning. The *Berliner allgemeine musikalische Zeitung*, in contrast, is answering the call of its time while recognizing that without knowledge of existing traditions, its readers cannot completely make sense of new works.

Marx's antitraditionalism and historicism are not necessarily difficult to reconcile. In one, the past acts as the standard against which the present is measured, and this is the view Marx caricatures as utterly inadequate. In the other, the present can be fully understood only by first understanding the past that brought it about, and this is the need Marx intends to answer. Such an understanding is much more than a matter of being familiar with the chronology of events, and, as a result, the journal's historical perspective has somewhat deeper ambitions. As Marx puts it, "An arts journal must provide information not just on what happened but also on the spirit [*Geist*] in which it was undertaken and accomplished."[34] His choice of the word "Geist" is important, and it signals precisely the greater depth he has in mind: far more than the style of historical artworks, it expresses rather the human efforts and concerns to which they testify.[35] In the journal's first issue, Marx had already argued this position on a grander scale, outlining a narrative in which each successive age struggles to create art that accurately reflects its preoccupations:

> Have not all artworks the past consigns to us the same origin, the same goal? Has not the human spirit, with the totality of its powers, everywhere and in all times struggled to represent to the senses its perception of mankind, of life, of nature, its ideas? For no artist, for no period of art, is there a different task. Thus the totality of artworks represents in sensual images a history of the human spirit and its unfolding in different times, in different places; and as the human spirit expands, so art has also always created new means and tools for itself and always advances to further boundaries.[36]

This history of the human spirit is the context in which new works—that is, the "new means and tools" that mark the growth of the human spirit—are to be evaluated. Consequently, Marx's concern is less with increasing his readers' knowledge or even keeping them informed and more with nurturing a particular way of contextualizing and organizing the knowledge they acquire.

As a result, the journal's aspirations were vastly more ambitious than either advertising or edification. In place of recommendations, it sought to broaden readers' views; instead of mere chronology, it offered a historical trajectory, presenting the past not simply as what had come before but as a key to grasping something deeper and more fundamentally human. Readers who could take mental hold of this underlying narrative would not just understand art; they would know the untold chronicle of how we have struggled to understand ourselves and the changing world around us.

The idea that beneath contingent historical events lies a coherent narrative of the human spirit is one that Marx presented elsewhere and that has overwhelming resonance with Georg Wilhelm Friedrich Hegel's sense of history as it appears in his *Aesthetics*, as well as in *The Phenomenology of Spirit* and *The Philosophy of History*.[37] An examination of those resonances would be too much of a detour to take here, but the Hegelian tenor of Marx's journal is significant to my argument because it speaks directly to the intellectual atmosphere of Berlin ca. 1820. Hegel was appointed to the University of Berlin in 1818 and lectured there through the 1820s; not only were his lectures well attended, but informal transcripts of them circulated widely. On the one hand, the evident popularity of Hegel's lectures—in person and in those informal transcripts— gives the *Berliner allgemeine musikalische Zeitung*'s Hegelian resonance something of a "home field" feel, as Berlin was the obvious epicenter of Hegel's ideas; on the other hand, it is also clear that there was a willing market for those ideas and that the journal might have aimed to reach those Berliners already reading or attending Hegel's lectures.

It is striking that the journal should present both the insistent advertising with which I began and the unabashed idealism Marx offers in his writing;

one might even be tempted to see them as contradictory, especially taking at face value Marx's aim to enrich and refine his readers' views. The framework of the marketplace, however, makes more nuanced interpretations possible. Features like the advertising supplements and the relentless promotion of Schlesinger products make it very clear that the marketplace was both competitive and growing. More and more people were buying scores and taking them home for private consumption. One consequence of this was that previously public genres such as symphonies or large-scale choral works were being separated from the places and occasions of their performance and consumed in domestic settings. Once a score was purchased, the responsibility for its interpretation fell out of the hands of its original performers and into those of its new owners, and we might imagine questions arising among musicians and critics as to how seriously that responsibility would be taken and how—or even if—music would be adequately understood in these new private settings. This rationale would reconcile Marx's solicitude over interpretive guidance with the constant awareness of Schlesinger's commercial enterprise.

Beyond merely reconciling the idealistic and commercial aspects of the journal, however, it is possible to unite them as features of the same endeavor. Marx's idealistic goals for his readers need not stand in contrast to Schlesinger's interests; rather, Marx's seemingly infinite idealism and energy were precisely what appealed to the journal's readers. The marketplace is a forum in which both goods and ideas are exchanged, and in both instances, sellers make no transactions without willing buyers.

This context also begins to present the journal's readership in a different light: if we see Marx as an editor responding to a market need rather than as a proselytizer, it becomes clear that his audience was not just growing but increasingly included a new kind of participant. In the example above, the Leipzig journal felt no need to clarify which features of Mozart's style or technique Mendelssohn emulated; in contrast, Marx offered a summary of what he believed made Mozart unique. Marx's essay on Beethoven's symphonies spends two of its three installments placing Beethoven at the end of a Hegelian path of historical development. If we see these articles as answers to unspoken questions or as ways of meeting the needs of a new audience, it becomes apparent that the journal's readers possessed fundamentally different tastes and prior experiences: readers for whom book-purchasing advice was insufficient, who may have needed guidance understanding the music they heard or played but who would also have happily kept up with Marx's unapologetic Hegelianism. We might imagine them to have been educated readers of Hegel's lectures without significant musical backgrounds or simply a music-loving public looking for a journal that spoke to the style and substance of their intellectual environment.

An expansion of the journal's readership served two ends: first and most obvious, it increased the commercial profitability of the enterprise. Second, however, that expansion was something Marx saw as vital to the growth of the art of music altogether, as its present and future built on its past: "In our view from the perspective of music in our times, it was urgently necessary to work not only for artists and art experts but for the whole public of educated friends of music."[38] This aim to engage more than a small cohort of experts called for the interpretive guidance Marx repeatedly provided—refining, broadening, and enriching his readers' views of music.

The idea of reaching "the whole public of educated friends of music" is important, and it provides a means of tying together the various threads I have singled out. If the music-loving public was growing, adding members with leisure and means but not a depth of expertise, purveyors of the journalism they might read were faced with a choice in how to approach them. They could change nothing and assume that readers already possessed what knowledge they needed. This approach excludes those not already well versed, effectively creating a barrier against new arrivals. Or they could use a small cadre of arbiters who would have judged music and informed readers of their opinions, guiding their taste by edict—it is for writing in this vein that Marx characterizes critics as "vocalizers" (*Stimmgeber*) and complains on several occasions about the Leipzig *Allgemeine musikalische Zeitung*. Marx himself chose a third road in the *Berliner allgemeine musikalische Zeitung*, one that stemmed from important fundamental beliefs he held about music, education, and their role in society. For Marx, learning was not just about the acquisition of knowledge but also about the process and benefits of gaining knowledge. To cling to the standards of the past, to fail to adjust to a new era and a new audience was for him to defend a dying status quo and deny a new generation the chance to explore its world. Pronouncing judgment on the basis of presumed authority alone would have been a means of limiting or controlling readers' intellectual freedom by confining them to a narrow perspective not of their own choosing. Marx therefore felt the acquisition of knowledge without "spiritual enrichment" was "futile and lost." In this context, his fabricated debates allowed readers the freedom to explore the extent of a topic's terrain, while his detailed historical discussions guided them toward understanding not just which music merits their attention but why.

The choice of how to treat these new entrants to the marketplace of journals and ideas was an important one for Marx, not just on principle but because he saw music as one of many fronts in an all-encompassing battle between conflicting ideologies. With Marx's dedication to the freedom of the journal's society of readers and contributors in mind—"may one never lose sight of it," as he exclaimed—this quotation from one of his later writings not only summarizes his view but demonstrates the scale on which he perceived the challenge and the energy with which he believed it should be met:

> What we are concerned with here is nothing other or less than the conflict that engages our era and its most noble powers on all sides: it is the struggle of the spiritual against the material, of free understanding against dogma, of irrepressible progress against standstill and stagnation. This conflict is being fought on all sides and in all forms, in politics as in theology, in the sciences and the arts as in the foundation of all culture, the pedagogical and educational system. Everywhere it is a matter of the spirit becoming free.[39]

Notes

1. Mary Sue Morrow, *German Music Criticism in the Late Eighteenth Century* (Cambridge: Cambridge University Press, 2006); Sanna Pederson, "Enlightened and Romantic German Music Criticism, 1800–1850" (PhD diss., University of Pennsylvania, Philadelphia, 1995); Barbara Titus, "Conceptualizing Music: Friedrich Theodor Vischer and Hegelian Currents in German Music Criticism, 1848–1887" (PhD diss., University of Oxford, Oxford, England, 2005); Robin Wallace, *Beethoven's Critics: Aesthetic Dilemmas and Resolutions during the Composer's Lifetime* (Cambridge: Cambridge University Press, 1986); Wayne M. Senner, ed., *The Critical Reception of Beethoven's Compositions by His German Contemporaries* (Lincoln: University of Nebraska Press, 1999); Stefan Kunze, *Ludwig van Beethoven, die Werke im Spiegel seiner Zeit: gesammelte Konzertberichte und Rezensionen bis 1830* (Laaber: Laaber-Verlag, 1987).
2. *Allgemeine musikalische Zeitung* 12 (July 4 and 11, 1810), cols. 630–42, 652–59.
3. For the rise and growth of the musical middle class, see William Weber, *Music and the Middle Class* (London: Croom Helm, 1975; Aldershot: Ashgate, 2004).
4. Martha Woodmansee raises similar questions with regard to a growing audience of readers in late eighteenth-century Germany: "A rising class of bankers, merchants, and manufacturers who had so recently achieved a modicum of the leisure enjoyed by the aristocracy that they were still in the process of developing ways to fill it." Woodmansee mainly discusses Johann Adam Bergk's *The Art of Reading Books*, focusing on the guidance Bergk offers "predominantly middle-class readers . . . in a craft of reading." While there are suggestive parallels with Marx's writing, too close a comparison would be misguided. Bergk's volume appeared in Leipzig in 1799, while Marx was writing in Berlin in 1824. In the intervening decades, the Napoleonic wars had literally redrawn national boundaries in Europe, and Saxony and Prussia (and, by extension, Leipzig and Berlin within them) had played different roles, especially in the defeat of Napoleon's forces in 1815. Indeed, in defining the purpose of the *Berliner allgemeine musikalische Zeitung*, Marx specifically complains that the *Allgemeine musikalische Zeitung*, published in Leipzig and founded in 1798—just a year before Bergk's book appeared—had failed to shift perspective in twenty-five

years and had not adapted to a new historical era. See Martha Woodmansee, "Toward a Genealogy of the Aesthetic: The German Reading Debate of the 1790s," *Cultural Critique* 11 (Winter 1988–89): 203–4, 210; Marx, "Standpunkt der Zeitung," *Berliner allgemeine musikalische Zeitung* 1 (1824): 444–48.

5. See R. Elvers, "Some Aspects of Music Publishing in Nineteenth-Century Berlin," in *Music and Bibliography*, ed. O. Neighbour (London: Bingley, 1980), 149–59.

6. See Robin Wallace, *Beethoven's Critics* (Cambridge: Cambridge University Press, 1986); Thomas Sipe, *Beethoven: Eroica Symphony* (Cambridge: Cambridge University Press, 1998).

7. Sanna Pederson, "A. B. Marx, Berlin Concert Life, and German National Identity," *19th-Century Music* 18, no. 2 (1994): 89.

8. Celia Applegate, "How German Is It? Nationalism and the Idea of Serious Music in the Early Nineteenth Century," *19th-Century Music* 21, no. 3 (1998): 281.

9. "Preface," in *Musical Form in the Age of Beethoven*, ed. and trans. Scott Burnham (Cambridge: Cambridge University Press, 1997), xiii (original italics).

10. See Patrick Wood Uribe, "Form as Reasoned Freedom: Adolph Bernhard Marx's Theoretical and Critical Writings in the Context of German Romantic Philosophy" (PhD diss., Princeton University, Princeton, NJ, 2011).

11. "Literarisch-artistisch-musikalischer Anzeiger" no. 1 (March 6, 1824): 1–2.

12. Ibid., 3–4.

13. "Einem großen Theile der Leser gelten Beurtheilungen für nichts, als eine höhere Gattung von Buchhändler-Anzeigen, Rathgeber bei ihren Einkäufe." "Ueber die Anfoderungen unserer Zeit an musikalische Kritik," *Berliner allgemeine musikalische Zeitung* 1 (1824): 3.

14. "Wir erkennen alle diese Stimmgeber nicht als Repräsentanten der Leserwelt an und wollen statt jener das wahre Interesse dieser beachten." Ibid.

15. "Jede Bemühung, die nicht auf eine Läuterung, auf Erweiterung der Ansicht, auf eine geistige Bereicherung des Lesers abzweckt, muß dem Schriftsteller für nichtig und verloren gelten." Ibid.

16. "Wer würde wohl an eine Gesellschaft die Forderung machen, daß alle Theilnehmenden sich auf eine durchgängig übereinstimmende Weise benähmen? Oder an einen wissenschaftlichen Verein, daß alle Mitglieder durchaus dieselben Ansichten und Meinungen bekennten? Der Verein der Mitarbeiter und des Redakteurs—man möge es doch nie aus den Augen verlieren!—ist ein so freier, wie irgend eine, wissenschaftlichen oder andern Zwecken gewidmete Gesellschaft." Ibid.

17. "Ew. Wohlgeboren werden sich wundern, statt der mir gefälligst aufgetragenen Recension der 111ten Sonate von Beethoven (herausgegeben von Schlesinger) diese selbst zurück zu erhalten. Ich—kann sie nicht recensiren." "Als Recension," *Berliner allgemeine musikalische Zeitung* 11 (1824): 95.

18. "Die Kunst ist das Leben, ist die vom Menschen wieder erschaffne Welt. . . . Warum soll die Kunst nicht aussprechen, was die Wirklichkeit uns mit eisernem Stempel einprägt?" Ibid., 99.

19. "Mögen Sie, mein Herr Redakteur, den Punkt finden, von welchen aus die Kritik und die allgemein anerkannten Gesetze der Aesthetik gegen diese Neuerungen. . . . Denn wenn die erste Auffassung der Kunstwerke dem Verstande entzogen, wenn es dem Gefühle überlassen wird, den Standpunkt zu fixiren von dem die Beurtheilung ausgehen soll, wenn Werke, die aller unserer Regeln spotten, so feurige Anhänger gewinnen, so verstumme ich." Ibid.

20. Marx later clarifies for his readers that all his contributions are signed with either his full name or the letter "M" unless there's an opportunity for a "playful signature." See *Berliner allgemeine musikalische Zeitung* 48 (1827): 388.

21. "Bekehren Sie sich, junger Mann, ehe es zu spät wird. . . . Es ist ja boshaft, verständige Komponisten und bewährte Theoretiker in der gewohnten Ruhe zu stören und da ich Sie nicht für böse halte, so soll es mich freuen, wenn ich Sie auf den rechten Weg gebracht habe." *Berliner allgemeine musikalische Zeitung* 45 (1824): 384.

22. "So geschah es, daß Kunstwerke die nur dieses Ziel sich gesetzt hatten, weit mehr mit den gewonnenen Erfahrungen und den daraus gebildeten Regeln übereinstimmten, als solche, in denen reichere und tiefere Auffassungen niedergelegt wird." *Berliner allgemeine musikalische Zeitung* 3 (1824): 17.

23. "Die Schwierigkeit, überall Berichterstatter zu finden, die auf die Tendenz unserer Zeitung eingehen, hat nur eine geringere Zahl Korrespondenzen im ersten Jahrgange gewährt." *Berliner allgemeine musikalische Zeitung* 52 (1824): 448.

24. "Das öffentliche Leben in drastischer Weise von der Obrigkeit kontrolliert wurde und die Zensur scharf durchgriff." Florian Edler, "Liberale Programmatik in A. B. Marx' Musiklehre," in *Musiktheorie im Kontext: 5. Kongress der Gesellschaft für Musiktheorie*, ed. Jan Philipp Sprick, Reinhard Bahr, and Michael von Troschke (Hamburg: Weidler, 2008), 418.

25. *Berliner allgemeine musikalische Zeitung* 1 (1824): 3.

26. "Wir erkennen alle diese Stimmgeber nicht als Repräsentanten der Leserwelt an und wollen statt jener das wahre Interesse dieser beachten." Ibid.

27. See note 15.

28. "Ein treffliches Muster hat Felix M. B. sich gewählt; diess glänzende Gestirn überstrahlt alle Neben-Sonnen." *Allgemeine musikalische Zeitung* 12 (March 1824): col. 184.

29. "Möge ihn nie eitle Ruhmsucht und Schmeicheley von der Bahn der Wahrheit und Schönheit in der Kunst entfernen, um dem Mode-Geschmack zu huldigen!" Ibid.

30. "Meeresstille und glückliche Fahrt," *Berliner allgemeine musikalische Zeitung* 46 (1824): 391.

31. "Etwas über die Symphonie und Beethovens Leistungen in diese Fache," *Berliner allgemeine musikalische Zeitung* 19 (1824): 165.

32. "Indem wir nach unsern Kräften das Wesen der Tonkunst tiefer zu ergründen streben, wird, wenn es uns gelingt, mehr und mehr Licht auf die Schöpfungen früherer Perioden fallen. Zu häufig und zu lange sind die Werke älterer Meister in dieser Beziehung vernachlässigt und gleich Leichen nur anatomisch

... durchforscht werden." "Standpunkt der Zeitung," *Berliner allgemeine musika-lische Zeitung* 52 (1824): 447.

33. "Vollständig befriedigend wird die Gegenwart nur aus ihrer Vergangenheit begriffen und wenn auch eine Zeitung zunächst der erstern gewidmet ist, so darf doch der Rath und die Lehre der letztern nicht vernachlässigt werden." Ibid.

34. Ein Kunstblatt muß Auskunft geben nicht blos über das, was geschehen, sondern auch über den Geist, in dem es unternommen und vollbracht worden. Ibid., 448.

35. Other, more neutral choices might be "Sinn" or "Wesenart." The phrase "the spirit of the law," for instance, translates as "der Sinn des Gesetzes."

36. "Haben nicht alle Kunstwerke, die sie uns überliefert, denselben Ursprung, dasselbe Ziel? Hat nicht überall und zu allen Zeiten der menschliche Geist gerungen, mit der Gesammtheit seiner Kräfte im Kunstwerke seine Anschauungen vom Menschen, vom Leben, von der Natur, seine Ideen—sinnlich darzustellen? Für keinen Künstler, für keine Kunstperiode giebt es eine andre Aufgabe. So stellt die Gesammtheit der Kunstwerke eine Geschichte des menschlichen Geistes und seiner Entfaltung zu verschiedenen Zeiten, an verschiedenen Orten, in sinnlichen Bildern dar und wie der menschliche Geist, seine Kräfte entwickelte, sein Gebiet erweiterte, so hat auch die Kunst stets neue Mittel und Werkzeuge sich geschaffen, ist stets zu weitern Gränzen vorgedrungen." *Berliner allgemeine musikalische Zeitung* 3 (1824): 18.

37. See Marx's essay "Form in Music," in Burnham, ed. and trans., *Musical Form in the Age of Beethoven*, 55–90; also Hegel, *Aesthetics*, trans. T. M. Knox, vols. 1 and 2 (Oxford: Oxford University Press, 1974); Hegel, *The Phenomelogy of Spirit*, trans. A. V. Miller (Oxford: Clarendon, 1977; Hegel, *The Philosophy of History*, trans. J. Sibree (Kitchener, Ontario: Batoche Books, 2001).

38. "Nach unserer Ansicht von dem Standpunkte der Musik in unsern Tagen war es dringend nothwendig, nicht für die Künstler und Kunstverständigen allein, sondern für das ganzen Publikum gebildeter Musikfreunde zu wirken." *Berliner allgemeine musikalische Zeitung* 1 (1824): 448.

39. Marx, "The Old School of Music in Conflict with Our Times," in Burnham, ed. and trans., *Musical Form in the Age of Beethoven*, 18.

Chapter Nine

Parisian Opera between Commons and Commodity, ca. 1830

Peter Mondelli

In August 1831, Honoré de Balzac scored a major artistic and commercial success with the publication of *La Peau de chagrin*. One of the "philosophical studies" in his *Comédie humaine*, the novel chronicles the fantastic demise of Raphaël de Valentin. Down on his luck, the protagonist acquires a foreign talisman made of animal hide that will grant his every desire. With each wish it fulfills, however, the talisman shrinks; when it disappears, Raphaël dies. Thus the novel becomes the tale of a man who must desire nothing in order to survive. Surrounded by the lavish material and social trappings of Paris, he fails.

Despite the fantastic elements in its plot, *La Peau de chagrin* has long been understood as a commentary on the excesses of bourgeois materialism couched in ekphrastic descriptions of everyday life.[1] The magic talisman, like the love potion in *Tristan*, is just a prop—the novel still works as a philosophical study without it. Balzac's narrative forces his readers to imagine the impossible task of not wanting anything while living in Paris. Thus even without the supernatural, his novel underscores the unavoidability and potential pitfalls of longing in a material world.

Balzac describes and cautions against a relatively new urban reality—one constructed by and for an emerging bourgeois society in which social and material desires are not satiated but instead beget further longing. Cultural theorists from Karl Marx on have discussed this intersection of desire, status, and goods in relation to the sociology of commodity capitalism.[2] According to this point of view, a capitalistic system forces goods, labor, power, and social standing to enter into a complex network of exchanges in which, in contrast to earlier economic systems, there are fewer definite goals and boundaries; wealth, value, and power are defined by the relativism of a market in which anything could in theory be traded for anything else, so long as one could find a buyer. This results in a material and social system in which one could trade one's way up through reinvestment in the market, and the possibility of acquiring more goods or higher status in turn leads to a desire for more goods and status. The system, in short, makes one want more than one already has.

Yet the decades immediately preceding the publication of Balzac's novel present a different vision of social and material exchange in Paris. This vision— noticeable throughout the eighteenth century and amplified by the French Revolution—eschews the goals of private ownership, favoring instead the cultivation of ideals, materials, and spaces that serve the public good. This idealistic position has been adopted by utopian and socialist political philosophers since Charles Fourier, having reemerged recently as part of the academic discourse on the commons.[3] While most often used to describe land and resources held jointly or publicly, the concept of a commons can also be applied to the media of cultural exchange—to languages, music, architecture, and so forth. According to this logic, a cultural phenomenon such as music is not meant for private consumption and ownership; rather, it should be used for the benefit of as many people as possible. The desire here is not to help oneself but to put oneself and one's resources in the service of others.

Balzac's novel falls chronologically in the liminal space between two historical moments, one seemingly dominated by the ideals of a cultural commons, the other by the reality of cultural commodities. Although these two terms are often cast as opposites, I propose instead that we think of them as two poles, to paraphrase Walter Benjamin, between which we might rethink the oscillations of cultural history.[4] On the one hand, we have the purely commodified society, in which everything is owned privately and exchanged for private gain; on the other, we have the pure commons, in which everything serves the public good and everyone acts altruistically. Each extreme is a fantasy, neither having ever existed. Yet in tracing historical turns from one pole toward the other, we can come to a clearer understanding of how cultural phenomena have been produced, desired, and consumed.

In this chapter I explore one such turn toward commodification through the lens of Parisian opera. Beginning in the 1820s, Parisians reimagined and rebuilt their city according in part to the dictates of the rise of bourgeois capital. At the same time, opera, both in performance and in print, was transformed into a commercial enterprise. A closer examination will show, however, that this apparent privitization of opera was tempered by the logic of the commons. Drawing on the roughly contemporaneous writings of

Charles Fourier and Karl Marx and the activities of Louis Véron and Maurice
Schlesinger, I argue that a broadly conceived history of opera in Paris provides adequate cause to question the historical validity of a separation
between public and private ends, between commons and commodity, in early
nineteenth-century Paris.

Opera as Commons

In what ways might we think of opera as a commons? Although the English
term *commons* originated in the legal discourse pertaining to common land in
a feudal economy, the idea of shared property is much more deeply imbedded
in Western intellectual history. Plato, for example, discusses public gardens
dedicated to the cultivation of fruits and crops necessary to all.[5] In cities, such
shared lands persisted into the early nineteenth century—Boston Common,
for example, was home to a herd of cows until Mayor Harrison Otis banned
grazing in 1830.[6] More recent uses of the term have expanded its purview
beyond land and materials. Michael Hardt and Antonio Negri adopt a more
broadly constructed view, explaining that a commons can encompass "the languages we create, the social practices we establish, the modes of sociality that
define our relationships."[7] According to this logic, opera always functions as a
commons—it provides a shared space and a shared experience. A more useful
question, then, is: to what ends were operatic commons used?[8]

In early nineteenth-century France, the ideal of land, material, and culture held in common formed the core of Fourier's utopian vision. The son
of a merchant, Fourier traveled throughout France after his father's death
in 1781. He worked as a clerk and a salesman until 1816, when he grew
frustrated with commerce and dedicated his time to writing.[9] Rather than
thinking within the norms of existing forms of social organization, Fourier
imagined new communal structures he hoped would circumvent the chaos
and suffering of the world he knew. His goal was to achieve a unified, harmo-
nious society; his means was the *phalange*: a community of 1,620 people—810
men and 810 women (though Fourier himself did not insist on such exact figures)—each of whom represented one of Fourier's 810 divisions in his classification of the passions and affinities of humankind. Each person would
thus perform the tasks best suited to his or her personality and abilities. The
members of these *phalanges* would live together in a *phalanstère*, a massive
building on a tract of common land with a mix of public gathering spaces
and private apartments. Beyond living quarters, everything in the *phalanstère*
would be shared, from food and resources to culture.

Among the common spaces imagined in the *phalanstère* was an opera
house. For Fourier, this was not a space for entertainment, displays of wealth,

or socialization. He was critical of such views of opera, which he considered wasteful: "Opera [in modern civilization] tends only to weaken customs and engage rulers in foolish expenses like the ballets of Novére [*sic*], which put many German princes into debt."[10] Fourier believed opera could serve the common good, and he imagined it having the most positive impact as an educational tool. His rhetoric was ambitious: "Opera . . . will become a source of richness and morality for people of all classes and all ages, particularly for children developing their sense of *perfected unity* [l'unité mesurée], for whom it would serve as a measure of health and a source of skills beneficial to all manner of industries."[11] Fourier's vision of opera in his utopian society is strikingly functional: he saw it as a means for perfecting skills and abilities. He favored it because it could refine multiple traits simultaneously: it demanded precision in singing, rhetoric, gesture, dance, and so forth, thus perfecting voice, speech, and movement.[12] Fourier, moreover, perceived opera as a great equalizer:

> At the opera, no favor can excuse the one whose note is false, whose timing, step, or gesture is off. The prince's child who has a part in the dance or the choir must endure the truth, must listen to the criticisms arising from the masses. It is at the opera that he learns, in every move he makes, to subordinate himself to unitary properties, to general accords.[13]

Within the context of Fourier's *phalanstère*, opera became a commons: like shared land for grazing and farming, opera served a shared symbolic and instructive purpose that would only be weakened through private ownership. It educated children and erased class divisions. Such purposes aligned closely with Fourier's own political values and ideals. For him, opera became a microcosm of the altruism he wished to see reflected first in the *phalanstère* and later across countries and continents. This idealism, however, takes on a more subversive, propagandistic aura if seen through the lens of a different set of values.

Although he was derided as an impractical visionary during his lifetime, Fourier's ideas about opera serving the common good actually reflected the sentiments and practices of his contemporaries in French society from about 1790 to 1830. Examples abound of operas created as instructive allegories, operas received as moral exemplars, opera houses reconceived better to propagate social values, and so forth. James Johnson has discussed at length the allegorical architecture and decor of the Théâtre National when it opened in 1793: no boxes were adjacent to the stage, thus breaking the tradition of placing nobility at the center of the spectacle; and the flattened horseshoe shape of the auditorium positioned viewers at the back of the house closer than usual to the action onstage.[14] The following year, the Théâtre National became the official home of the Paris Opéra, a distinction it held until 1820. The auditorium was altered in 1808 by Napoleon—a frequent opera attendee—with a broad imperial box, thus placing not just the people but also the emperor closer to the stage and making him more visible at performances.[15] The house was demolished in 1820 at the request of Louis XVIII after the assassination of his nephew Charles Ferdinand, Duc de Berry, and a monument was erected in its place. Thus the creation, renovation, and demolition of the Théâtre National were planned not according to purely aesthetic or ideological criteria but according to the status of the house as a symbol of political values. It was a commons, but one whose good was defined all too obviously in relation to the desires of those who held power.

To varying degrees, operatic works themselves followed suit, for the revolutionary and imperial repertory is similarly full of overt symbolism. Indeed, operatic propaganda produced during the Terror stands out in this respect. Gossec's *Le Triomphe de la république* (1794) all but eschews a plot, instead piling allegory upon allegory. In the final scene, a goddess of liberty takes the stage, blessing the new French Republic. A danced finale follows in which the nations of the world come together in harmony before the people of France (both represented onstage and present in the audience) and their newfound republican ideals. Spontini's *Fernand Cortez* (1808) offers a similar, albeit less heavy-handed, example. Premiered on the eve of Napoleon's invasion of Spain, the opera presents Cortez as the just conqueror of a savage people. These works and others like them were not just entertainment: they were intended to fulfill specific instructive purposes within the political regimes of their time. For those in power and their allies, this repertory acted as a commons because it reaffirmed and propagated their political values. Just as a town common was used to grow wheat or graze cattle, this operatic common was used to cultivate republics and empires. According to the ruling ideology, the production and performance of opera served an altruistic purpose. For those who questioned this ideology, however, this repertory would have been not a form of instruction but a form of propaganda.

Such tensions concerning who could define opera's shared purposes continued into the late 1820s, affecting the production of some of the earliest grand operas. The censors of Auber's *La Muette de Portici* (1828) famously confronted the question of whether it was appropriate to depict a revolution onstage by rereading the opera's title character, Fenella, as an exemplar of virtuous behavior in turbulent times: "The contestation of legitimate authority, the popular tumult . . . all is forgotten or blended into the interest inspired by a single personage. It is a woman [Fenella]. . . . It is to her that all hearts are attached. . . . The invention isn't new . . . it's having diverted the attention from a subject that is a little too grave in itself by using an artifice so cleverly."[16] For the censors, it was important that the onstage revolution be tempered artfully so the audience's sympathies would be aligned with the victims of violence rather than with its perpetrators. In short, the censors wanted *La Muette* to serve an instructive, antirevolutionary purpose. As Jane Fulcher has documented, however, the opera's reception could hardly have differed more from the censors' predictions.[17] In Paris after the July revolutions of 1830, the opera's depictions of revolt were on occasion followed by Adolphe Nourrit leading the audience in singing "La Parisienne," a popular patriotic song.[18] In Brussels, the onstage call to arms in Act II was selected to be a literal call to arms in the movement for Belgian independence from the Dutch throne.[19] In each case, *La Muette* was reimagined to serve a common purpose, yet we can see that the purpose of this operatic commons inhered not in the work itself but was instead ascribed from without by those who sought to appropriate it for their own ends.

In each of these examples, what was disguised in Fourier's writings emerges all too clearly: that the cultural commons (including opera) was rarely, if ever, altruistic and that it instead served the ideals and desires of those in power. According to such logic, a good audience was an obedient audience that accepted the lessons and symbols presented without question; such an audience defers its own desires, fulfilling instead those of the ruling class. Yet such an audience likely never existed, at least not in such an idealized form. Throughout the revolutionary and imperial periods, Parisians were drawn to the opera for purposes other than official government edification. Étienne de Jouy, the librettist for Spontini's *Fernand Cortez*, recognized that his opera needed to be more than propaganda to succeed. In 1817 he wrote, "I thought it my primary duty to present the spectator with a natural exposition, and compel him to pity the fate of the Spanish prisoners, in order to soften the odious aspects of their victory later on."[20] Étienne de Jouy realized that his work could not serve its official imperial purpose well if it did not first function properly as a drama. The operatic commons of the late eighteenth and early nineteenth centuries were far from a simple ideological state apparatus in which the government dictated through art the terms of appropriate political behaviors and beliefs.[21] The operatic commons instead reveal the many connections between art and urban life and the myriad ways in which these artworks and spaces could be reused, recycled, and repurposed to serve new ends.

Paris's Commercial Commons, ca. 1830

To understand better the forces that animated Paris's operatic commons, we need to look beyond its repertories and performance spaces. In the nineteenth century, Parisians constructed new urban spaces, making use of new technologies. Many of these spaces and technologies served a different goal: that of bourgeois commerce. Discussing these changes to the city, Patrice Higonnet asserts that the middle decades of the nineteenth century witnessed the rise of "the myth of the urban machine" in Paris: the belief that the old medieval city could be reconceived and reshaped into a more efficient and livable space.[22]

The most famous of these modernizing transformations—Baron Hausmann's demolition and reconstruction of Paris's streets and boulevards in the 1850s and 1860s—has been considered at length.[23] Yet many cultural theorists and historians—especially Walter Benjamin—argue that these processes of urban modernization and commercialization started in earnest a generation earlier.[24] Beginning around 1820, a combination of public and private projects began to provide Parisians with new forms of transportation, new forums for commerce, and new ways of interacting with each other through a growing capitalist market. A closer look at three of these innovations—omnibuses, gas lighting, and arcades—makes it clear that they all functioned as a kind of material commons in their own right, serving not the explicit political ideologies of kings, senators, or emperors but the implicit demands of commerce and industry.

Horse-drawn omnibuses began to navigate Paris's streets in 1828, effectively becoming the city's first form of public transportation. Omnibuses facilitated easier access to stores and goods. They arose in part to accommodate a growing distinction in Paris between domestic and work spaces: the labor demands of certain businesses and industries meant that fewer people could live close to where they worked. This resulted in the development of specialized commercial districts.

Gas lighting systems first appeared on Paris's streets around the same time, in 1822. In 1833 the Comte de Rambuteau, working as préfet of the Département of the Seine, made the switch from oil to gas official. Unlike the thousands of individual oil lanterns of the eighteenth century, gaslight required a civic investment in infrastructure, drawing on networks of fuel and pipes to produce brighter light. Cost proved the crucial factor in motivating the change: once the infrastructure was in place, gas was significantly less expensive than oil. Although fears of accidents were widespread, the benefits for commerce were clear: longer working hours in factories, later closing times for stores and cafés, and the ability to create indoor commercial spaces.[25]

Among these new spaces were Paris's famed arcades. These glass- and steel-covered alleys housed numerous small shops. Most were built between 1822 and 1834 in and around the second arrondissement. The arcades, like the old streets they connected, were often rather narrow, limiting opportunities for socialization. In this sense, they were a marked departure from the commercial spaces of earlier generations. The busiest marketplaces of the late eighteenth century—the Pont Neuf, les Halles, and the Palais-Royal—all featured open-air spaces and were as renowned for their noise and sociability as for their commerce.[26] In contrast, the enclosed, gas-lit arcades encouraged a quieter forum for conducting business.

The shift from one kind of commercial space to another around 1830 must have been sudden and striking. This is apparent in diverging accounts of the level of noise in the city.[27] While the rumbling omnibuses made the streets louder, the arcades provided an aural sanctuary from the sounds of carriages and peddlers' cries. The Marquis de Custine famously took note of this new silence in his 1839 novel *Ethel*, in which he wrote that "the street cries of Paris are [now] the sounds of pens scraping against paper."[28] Walter Benjamin and others interpret this new, quiet commerce of the arcades as the raison d'être of the alienated but imaginative flâneur culture of the mid-nineteenth century, defined in part by the everyday silences between strangers on the street.[29]

These three kinds of civic projects catered to the emergence of the bourgeoisie, creating an environment in which any Parisian of modest means could have easier access to all of the city's goods and services. For vendors, these changes not only increased commercial volume but also amplified competition by placing shops with similar goods in close proximity.[30] For consumers, the very fact that more material was easily accessible created a greater desire for those goods. In this sense, these projects were a commons in the service of business, designed to benefit all by increasing access to commodities and profits.

But such benefits came with social costs. Karl Marx famously claimed that these capitalistic modes of production alienated workers from one another by undervaluing their labor and fetishizing the commodities they produced. Social relationships, he argued, now existed among objects, as people developed material relationships with each other through commodities.[31] These ideas have been developed in Marxist scholarship over the past 150 years, yet their origin was closely tied to mid-nineteenth-century Parisian culture and its idiosyncratic blend of utopian idealism and commodity capitalism.[32] As Isaiah Berlin has argued, Marx's move away from neo-Hegelianism and toward critiques of political economy coincided with his stay in Paris from 1843 to 1845, where what he read and saw around him suggested hitherto unexplored modes of inquiry.[33] In this sense, Marx, too, was a product of Paris's new commercial commons, as his ideas were thoroughly entangled in the lights, wheels, glass, and steel of the 1840s. We can recognize, then, that these new commercial commons did not determine in a simplistic way the reactions of those who used and observed them. A complex social space like an arcade inspired a range of reactions. To a bourgeois financier, the arcades were an engine for profits; for a social critic like Marx, they were an engine for commodity fetishism. In both cases, the space itself did not determine but rather delimited the terms of the debate by redefining the shape (both literal and metaphorical) of commerce.

Such disparate reevaluations of the same spaces also allow us to recognize more clearly the underlying affinities between shared and private property, between commons and commodities in the early nineteenth century. Among them is the idea that both commons and commodities could serve as modes for transferring the desires of others. According to some cultural theorists, the underlying logic in both cases was similar: both commons and commodities served as the material conduits for the transfer of a dominant ideology.[34] Both functioned by forcing consumers not just to accept but to believe that they actually desired this ideology. But such a top-down view of the structures of Paris's politics, culture, and economy—in which those with power make decisions and those without it abide by them—is not universally accepted. Other cultural theorists have argued that there are no true mandates, no cases in which one group can always tell another what to believe, and that power is therefore properly understood as a negotiation.[35] In such a model, commons and commodities would still transfer desires, but they could do so in multiple directions, thus transforming these objects and spaces into sites of negotiation rather than sites of control. To understand how these twentieth- and twenty-first-century models apply to the historical situation in nineteenth-century Paris, however, we need to look beyond mere materiality and consider in detail how these objects and spaces were produced, used, and discussed.

Opera as Commodity

Although histories of French opera are strewn with references to commercial successes and failures, there are few thorough accounts of how opera was produced, sold, and purchased as part of a broader urban commercial landscape.[36] From the 1820s on, commercial considerations played an especially important role in the discourse surrounding operatic production, exhibiting a broader cultural turn away from the commons and toward commodification in Paris.

Standard accounts of the creation of French grand opera manifest this trend.[37] This story—worth revisiting in this context—invariably starts with the aesthetic and financial troubles of the Paris Opéra in the late 1820s. The house continued to run on an antiquated monarchist-imperialist model: it was fully funded by the state and thus was expected to act as its political and ideological standard-bearer. The bourgeoisie, however, favored lighter entertainment. They preferred the spectacle of the boulevard theaters and the showmanship of Rossini's productions at the Théâtre Italien, and not without reason: these smaller venues attracted the attention of the press and the literati. Journalists covered their exploits. Virtuosi composed variations on their musical themes. Publishers oversaw numerous arrangements. These smaller theaters turned profits while the state continued to fund revivals of Spontini and Méhul at the opera—at great expense. In 1828 the opera tried something different with Auber's *La Muette de Portici*, achieving a fair degree of success. Auber's opera was famously modeled on its competition—drawing together elements of Rossini's explosive musical style with the drama and effects of the boulevard theaters. The Opéra, it seemed, was giving the audience what it wanted. More important, *La Muette* refocused the attention of reviewers, composers, publishers, and booksellers on the Opéra, making it much more likely that the house could continue to cultivate its audience by catering to its tastes.

Examined in the context of Paris's newly emerging commercial commons, the financial and aesthetic success of grand opera seems to have been thoroughly integrated with the city's new social and material realities.[38] The commercial commons built in the 1820s and 1830s facilitated interactions between an old institution and new audiences, helping to establish positive perceptions of the genre and making it into a desirable, marketable commodity. Almost immediately after these initial successes, entrepreneurs in both opera production and publishing began to reimagine the relationship of the genre to the urban commons and the capitalist market. The story of opera's commodification is, in a sense, the story of a small group of businessmen requisitioning these new commons for their own gain.

One such entrepreneur was Dr. Louis Véron, director of the Paris Opéra from 1831 to 1835. Véron was the first to take up the challenge of running the Paris Opéra "at his own peril" after King Louis-Philippe opted to transform it from a state-run affair into a highly subsidized, for-profit venture.[39] Having made his name and fortune in medical patents, Véron brought a business model to the institution. During his relatively brief tenure, the house's production values changed dramatically.[40] Internationally renowned singers were brought in at great expense, and production costs doubled as set designs grew more elaborate and spectacular. Moreover, he continued to cultivate a relationship between the house and the press. His contacts and clout as the publisher of the *Revue de Paris*, a literary magazine, no doubt helped in these efforts.

Heinrich Heine understood Véron's methods and motivations more clearly than most. Heine, who lived in Paris after 1831, wrote reports on the city for the *Allgemeine Zeitung* in Cotta. His characteristically biting comments merit citation at length:

[Véron] himself has remarked that Franconi's circus gave him more pleasure than the best opera; he convinced himself that the majority of the public shared his feelings, that most people go to the grand opera out of convenience, and only then do they take delight if beautiful settings, costumes, and dances capture their attention so that they completely disregard the unpleasant music. The great Véron got where he is by the ingenious idea of satisfying the public's desire for show to such a degree that the music could no longer annoy them, so that they would take as much pleasure in opera as in Franconi's circus. The great Véron and the great public want to understand each other: the former wanted to make the music harmless and gave under the name of "opera" nothing but magnificent spectacle; the latter—the public—could take their daughters and their wives to the grand opera, as befitted their social rank, without dying of boredom. America was discovered, the egg stood on its end; the opera house was full every day, Franconi was outbid and went bankrupt, and Véron is now a rich man.[41]

Heine recognized Véron's thorough grasp of the nature of public desire. Both Heine and Véron understood the unique competitive edge held by the Paris Opéra itself. The house had, through more than a century of association with political power and prestige, acquired a social standing that made it practically unavoidable for Parisians who held or hoped to attain any form of power. Véron took advantage, in other words, of the Opéra's enduring position as a political and cultural commons. To attribute Véron's success to a collection of individual audience members each deciding rationally that grand opera was his or her entertainment of choice is to miss a crucial point; the bourgeois audience was going to the Opéra because of its history and status, because they were supposed to want to go there, and because there were still considerable social benefits in doing so. Véron simply tried to transform its offerings into something that looked more like the kinds of things they actually wanted to see, specifically the kinds of staged shows produced on the Boulevard du Temple.[42] In doing so, he effectively branded and commodified a cultural commons. While the Opéra's purpose remained a matter of public interest, its management and profit now also served private ends.

Theodor Adorno explored the idea of performance as commodity in his essay "On the Fetish-Character in Music," a polemical meditation on the effects of commodity capitalism on music in the twentieth century. Adorno's assessment is grounded in Marx's explanation of the commodity fetish. In the first volume of *Capital*, Marx argued that a commodity's "socio-natural properties" resulted from the gradual transformation of person-to-person relationships into object-to-object relationships through the alienation of labor from the means of production.[43] Interactions took place through the market. As a result, perceptions of value and status came to be established and cultivated not according to individual judgments or traditional political systems but according to material possessions. "This," writes Adorno, "is the real secret of success." He continues:

> It is the mere reflection of what one pays in the market for the product. The consumer is really worshipping the money that he himself has paid for the ticket to the Toscanini concert. He has literally "made" the success which he reifies and accepts as an objective criterion, without recognizing himself in it. But he has not "made" it by liking the concert, but rather by buying the ticket.[44]

Adorno's assessment can aid our understanding of the Paris Opéra under Véron. The bourgeois audiences of the 1830s and 1840s turned to the Opéra in part because it provided the means to affirm and cultivate social status. Indeed, the building itself quantified status as no other venue could. The ticket one could afford defined one's position in the social field. If one managed to get ahead in the capitalist economy, one could literally better one's position at the Opéra. It is no coincidence that Flaubert references such vanity in describing Emma Bovary's arrival at a performance of *Lucia di Lammermoor* in Rouen:

> Her heart began to beat once she was in the foyer. She smiled quite obviously, out of vanity, seeing the crowd rushing down the corridor to the right, as she was climbing the stairs to the dress circle. She took a childish delight in pushing open the large upholstered doors with her fingers; keenly she breathed down the dusty smell of the corridors, and, once she was sitting in her box, she arched her back with the insolence of a duchess.[45]

The heroine uses the opera as an opportunity to posture, quite literally, as a person of higher rank.

Many nonfictional attendees were similarly opportunist. In 1842 Richard Wagner wrote a provocative, cynical review of Halévy's *Reine de Chypre* for the *Dresden Abendzeitung*. He started the review not by recounting the opera but by describing members of the audience:

> And do you see that young musician there, with the pale face and the hungry expression in his eyes? He is listening to the performance with anxious concern, greedily snapping up the success of every single number. Is that enthusiasm or envy? It is neither, alas—but a concern for his daily bread: if the new opera catches on, he can hope for a commission from the publisher to arrange fantasies and airs variés on its "favorite melodies." . . . And over there you see the representatives and plenipotentiaries of the various provincial opera managements: they are intently studying the staging of the great wedding procession and trying to distinguish how much applause is coming from the paid applauders and how much from the enthusiastic amateurs.[46]

Wagner's physiognomy of the audience members highlights their self-centered interests all too clearly. We should not, however, be too quick to read this as a blanket condemnation of such motives; the description of the "young musician" earning his living by making arrangements is a self-portrait. Wagner's review ultimately highlights the extent to which the entire operatic experience had been transformed by the commodification of the genre. There is no talk here of opera as an altruistic, edifying commons, only of opportunism. The spectators he describes—from impressarios to the claque—attended because they stood to profit from the Opéra's activities.

Much of this profit was tied to music publishing, and few publishers were as eager to exploit Paris's unique print culture as Maurice Schlesinger. The son of a Berlin bookseller and music publisher, Schlesinger arrived in Paris in 1815. The decades after his arrival witnessed an exponential increase in the volume of printed material produced in the city.[47] By 1838, Hector Berlioz could describe "a rain of albums, an avalanche of romances, a torrent of airs with variations, a sprout of concertos, and rondos romantic, fantastic, frenetic, fanatic, and fluoric."[48] These volumes of material gave publishers tremendous influence, and no publisher was more eager to exploit his influence than Schlesinger. Many sources attest to his ruthlessness in business. Heinrich Probst, for instance, a representative of Breitkopf und Härtel in Paris, constantly complained about his practices. In a letter dated January 9, 1838, for example, he writes:

> He [Meyerbeer] has got this slander from Schlesinger whom you can now consider an all-out foe. . . . Maurice is becoming more arrogant all the time. He claims to have the press under his control. He gives balls and soirées and spends 40[,000]–50,000 fs [francs] a year to get the Legion of Honor. At the same time no banker here will accept a draft of his for as little as 1,000 fs.[49]

Like Véron, Schlesinger recognized the value of branding and publicity, spending lavish amounts of money to secure the prestige needed to bargain successfully. (The amount cited was on par with the scenery budget for a typical production at the Opéra.) As for the press, Schlesinger adopted a strategy that would become fairly common in the nineteenth century: he founded his own music journal in 1834 (the *Gazette musicale*) and purchased another the following year (Fétis's celebrated *Revue musicale*), combining the two shortly thereafter into the *Revue et gazette musicale*. As Katharine Ellis has shown, Schlesinger exercised tight control over the journal, using it when he could as a promotional tool for his other publications.[50] In addition to cultivating prestige and controlling the press, Schlesinger tried another strategy to edge out his competition: introducing cheap musical publications. In 1834 he introduced a series of classical music for amateurs "à bon marché"—designed to pique interest in his products and, of course, outsell his competitors.

Just as Véron had cultivated a modern bourgeois opera house, Schlesinger cultivated a modern bourgeois publishing firm. His goal was not simply to sell the public what it wanted but rather to make the public want what he was selling. Doing so required more than just advertising. It required a calculated effort to develop a brand that balanced two opposing ideas: on the one hand, Schlesinger's firm needed to know what the public seemed to enjoy most, and on the other, it needed to ensure that the public always associated what it enjoyed with the firm. The result is a kind of capitalist tautology akin to that described in Slavoj Žižek's *The Sublime Object of Ideology*: Schlesinger publishes good music; therefore, if Schlesinger publishes it, it must be good.[51] Audiences went to the performances they thought they ought to see and purchased the music they thought they ought to own, just as impresarios and publishers produced what they believed their audiences wanted. In all cases, judgments of taste were deferred to a broader cultural consensus of laws, traditions, trends, and customs. What this kind of commodification of music may have offered, then, is not a democratization of taste in which entertainment was produced to provide what most people wanted to see but rather a capitalist dialectic of taste in which nobody really knew what anybody else wanted. Producers and publishers would try to make the public like what they presented, while audiences under varying degrees of manipulative pressure from this new culture industry would make their judgments in accordance with prevailing fashions and trends. The constant deferral between the two groups, fueled by markets and commodities, produced a mercurial musical culture whose aesthetic norms were grounded not in individual tastes but in a collective understanding of shared desire.

This was the model of commodity capitalism Balzac critiqued in *La Peau de chagrin*, one in which the desire for wealth and status was completely unavoidable because its mechanism fell outside the control of any one person. Balzac was, moreover, thoroughly aware of the position of opera in this system. Consider, for example, his description of Raphaël's coach en route to a Rossini performance at the Théâtre Favart:

> Do you see that luxurious coach, a carriage painted brown, on the panels of which shines the coat of arms of an old, noble family? As it passes quickly, all the *grisettes* admire it, coveting the yellow satin, the rugs from *la Savonnerie*, the embroidery as fine as grains of rice, the soft cushions and well-fitted windows. Two footmen grip the back of this aristocratic coach; but inside, on the silk cushions, rests a feverish head with tired eyes, the head of Raphaël, sad and deep in thought. Fatal image of wealth! He crosses Paris quickly like a rocket, arriving at the peristyle of the Théâtre Favart. The pedestrians get out of his way; the two footmen help him down as an envious crowd looks on. "What has this guy done to get so rich?" asks a poor law student who, for the lack of five francs, cannot listen to the magical music of Rossini.[52]

Balzac here presents the entire activity of opera-going as an object of desire. The *grisettes* covet the material luxury of the coach they cannot afford; the law student envies Raphaël's wealth and status. In this description, Rossini's opera (later identified as *Semiramide*) acts as a proxy for the social status signified by the material objects that surround it. The opera acquires an aura of luxury not solely through its own merits or its fashionable popularity but through its attachment to the coach, to displays of wealth, to the perceived importance of those in attendance. Only in this thoroughly interconnected position can it become an object of desire. Its value is relational and thus can only be manipulated en masse: without the coat of arms, the footmen, the peristyle, and so forth, Rossini's work would hold a less prestigious position in this cultural economy.

It was this richly interconnected urban milieu that truly placed opera between commons and commodity. Although the discourse after 1820 tended to value the genre in terms of commercial success, the context for that success reflected not only monetary goals of individual producers but also a complex set of social expectations defined and redefined in a swiftly changing urban environment. No single impresario, director, publisher, composer, or musician could hope to control the terms of an opera's reception in such a system; the most successful were simply the best at playing a kind of dialectical guessing game with their audiences. And no single consumer could truly own opera: although presented in commodified form, it remained a commons connected to the public not just by the opera house but also by a publisher's stock of paper or the space in a storekeeper's gas-lit shop.

Notes

1. This tradition of Balzac scholarship spans decades. See esp. Philippe Bertault, *Balzac and the Human Comedy*, trans. Richard Monges (New York: New York University Press, 1963); Herbert J. Hunt, *Balzac's Comédie Humaine* (London: University of London Athlone Press, 1959); Allan H. Pasco, *Balzacian Montage: Configuring La Comédie humaine* (Toronto: University of Toronto Press, 1991); Graham Robb, *Balzac: A Biography* (New York: W. W. Norton, 1994).

2. Karl Marx, *Capital: A Critique of Political Economy*, trans. Ben Fowkes, vol. 1 (New York: Penguin Books, 1990).

3. Charles Fourier, *Théorie de l'unité universelle*, in *Oeuvres complètes*, vols. 2–5 (Paris: Libraire Phalanstérienne, 1841).

4. "Art history might be seen as the working out of a tension between two polarities within the artwork itself, its course being determined by shifts in the balance between the two. These two poles are the artwork's cult value and its exhibition value." From Walter Benjamin, "The Work of Art in the Age of Its Technological Reproducibility: Second Version," in *Selected Writings*, vol. 3, *1935–38*, ed. Howard Eiland and Michael W. Jennings, trans. Edmund Jephcott and Harry Zohn (Cambridge, MA: Belknap Press of Harvard University Press, 2002), 106.

5. Plato, *Republic*, trans. George Grube and C. D. C. Reeve, 2nd ed. (Indianapolis: Hackett, 1992), 416a–17b.

6. For more on Otis's "war on cows," see Lawrence Kennedy, *Planning the City upon a Hill: Boston since 1630* (Boston: University of Massachusetts Press, 1992), 53.

7. Michael Hardt and Antonio Negri, *Commonwealth* (Cambridge, MA: Belknap Press of Harvard University Press, 2011), 139.

8. Ralph Locke addresses a similar set of questions about music's uses in early nineteenth-century utopian theories in *Music, Musicians, and the Saint-Simonians* (Chicago: University of Chicago Press, 1986), 15–23.

9. For an early take on his disillusionment with commerce, see Charles Fourier, "Sur les charlataneries commerciales," *La Phalange* 2 (April 11, 1841): 732–36. This is a reprint of a pamphlet published in Lyon in 1807 or 1808.

10. "L'opéra [en civilisation] ne tend qu'à efféminer les moeurs et engager les souverains dans de folles dépenses comme les ballets de Novére, qui endettèrent plusieurs princes d'Allemagne." Charles Fourier, "Opéra harmonien, ou série pivotale en unité matérielle (*Th[éorie] de l'un[ité] univ[erselle]*) 1822,*" in *L'Harmonie universelle et le phalanstère, vol. 2 (Paris: Libraire Phalanstérienne, 1849)*, 208. Fourier probably meant Jean-Georges Noverre (1727–1810), the creator of the *ballet d'action*, forerunner of modern narrative ballets.

11. "L'opéra . . . va devenir une source de richesse et de moralité pour les individus de toutes les classes et de tous les âges, principalement pour l'enfant, en le formant à l'unité mesurée, qui est pour lui un gage de santé et une source de bénéfices en tous genres d'industrie." Ibid.

12. Ibid., 209–10.

13. Quoted in Walter Benjamin, *The Arcades Project*, trans. Howard Eiland and Kevin McLaughlin (Cambridge, MA: Belknap Press of Harvard University Press, 2003), 647; also in Fourier, "Opéra harmonien," 214.

14. James Johnson, *Listening in Paris: A Cultural History* (Berkeley: University of California Press, 1995), 99–103.

15. See Patrick Barbier, *Opera in Paris 1800–1850: A Lively History*, trans. Robert Luoma (Portland, OR: Amadeus, 1995), 32–36.

16. Quoted and translated in Jane Fulcher, *The Nation's Image: French Grand Opera as Politics and Politicized Art* (New York: Cambridge University Press, 1987), 30–31. The original document is in the Archives nationales, AJ [13] 1050.

17. Ibid., 36–46.

18. Discussed in Patrice Higonnet, *Paris: Capital of the World*, trans. Arthur Goldhammer (Cambridge, MA: Harvard University Press, 2002), 256.

19. Sarah Slatin, "Opera and Revolution: *La Muette de Portici* and the Belgian Revolution of 1830 Revisited," *Journal of Musicological Research* 3, nos. 1–2 (1979): 45–62.

20. Quoted in Anselm Gerhard, *The Urbanization of Opera: Music Theater in Paris in the Nineteenth Century*, trans. Mary Whittall (Chicago: University of Chicago Press, 1998), 49.

21. The term *ideological state apparatus* is borrowed from Louis Althusser. See his "Ideology and Ideological State Apparatuses (Notes towards an Investigation)," in *Lenin and Philosophy and Other Essays*, trans. Ben Brewster (London: New Left Books, 1971).

22. Higonnet, *Paris: Capital of the World*, 177–204.

23. The political economy of Second Empire Paris is considered in detail in David Harvey, *Paris: Capital of Modernity* (New York: Routledge, 2006).

24. Walter Benjamin, "Paris, the Capital of the Nineteenth Century," in Benjamin, *The Arcades Project*, 3–26.

25. For more on gas lighting, see Jean-Baptiste Fressoz, "The Gas Lighting Controversy: Technological Risk, Expertise, and Regulation in Nineteenth-Century Paris and London," *Journal of Urban History* 33, no. 5 (2007): 729–55.

26. These spaces are discussed in Robert Isherwood, *Farce and Fantasy: Popular Entertainment in Eighteenth-Century Paris* (New York: Oxford University Press, 1986).

27. This topic is considered in detail in Aimée Boutin, *City of Noise: Sound and Nineteenth-Century Paris* (Urbana: University of Illinois Press, 2015).

28. "Le cri de Paris, c'est la plume qui gratte le papier." Quoted in Philip Mansel, *Paris between Empires: Monarchy and Revolution, 1814–1852* (New York: St. Martin's, 2003), 307.

29. For more on flâneur culture, see Walter Benjamin, "The Paris of the Second Empire in Baudelaire," in *Selected Writings*, vol. 4, *1938–40*, ed. Howard Eiland and Michael W. Jennings, trans. Harry Zohn (Cambridge, MA: Belknap Press of Harvard University Press, 2003), 3–92; Mary Gluck, *Popular Bohemia: Modernism and Urban Culture in Nineteenth-Century Paris* (Cambridge, MA: Harvard University Press, 2005).

30. In music publishing, a sheet music district existed in the nineteenth century on and around the Rue St. Honoré. A complete list of publishers' addresses can be found in Anik Devriès and François Lesure, *Dictionnaire des éditeurs de musique française*, vol. 2 (Geneva: Minkoff, 1979).

31. Marx, *Capital*, 1:164–65.

32. For Marxist theorists who have developed such a conception of commodification, see esp. Theodor Adorno, "On the Fetish-Character in Music and the Regression of Listening," in *Essays on Music*, ed. Richard Leppert, trans. Susan Gillespie (Berkeley: University of California Press, 2002), 288–317; Frederic Jameson, *Postmodernism, or, the Cultural Logic of Late Capitalism* (Durham, NC: Duke University Press, 1992); Slavoj Žižek, *The Sublime Object of Ideology* (London: Verso, 1989).

33. Isaiah Berlin, *Karl Marx: His Life and Environment*, 4th ed. (New York: Oxford University Press, 1996), 61–88.

34. This view of the "culture industry" is developed in Theodor Adorno and Max Horkheimer, *Dialectic of Enlightenment: Philosophical Fragments*, ed. Gunzelin Schmid Noerr, trans. Edmond Jephcott (Stanford: Stanford University Press, 2007).

35. On power as negotiation, see esp. Michel Foucault, *The History of Sexuality: An Introduction*, trans. Robert Hurley, vol. 1 (New York: Random House, 1978). Foucault's ideas have been thoughtfully applied to early nineteenth-century French opera in Mark Everist, "Music of Power: Parisian Opera and the Politics of Genre, 1806–1864," *Journal of the American Musicological Society* 67, no. 3 (2014): 687–736.

36. The following come the closest: William Crosten, *French Grand Opera: An Art and a Business* (New York: King's Crown, 1948); Hervé Lacombe, "The Machine and the State," in *Cambridge Companion to Grand Opera*, 21–41; Hervé Lacombe, *The Keys to French Opera*, trans. Edward Schneider (Berkeley: University of California Press, 2001); Anselm Gerhard, *The Urbanization of Opera: Music Theater in Paris in the Nineteenth Century*, trans. Mary Whittall (Chicago: University of Chicago Press, 1998). This is not to say that other scholars are blind to the influence of commerce—far from it—although I suspect we may have internalized twentieth-century high art's prejudices against commerce and collaboration as somehow cheapening the resultant works.

37. This story is retold and critically reconsidered in Fulcher, *Nation's Image*, 11–23.

38. For my thoughts on the role of print culture in the transmission of grand opera, see Peter Mondelli, "The Sociability of History in French Grand Opera: A Historical Materialist Perspective," *19th-Century Music* 37, no. 1 (2013): 37–55.

39. The phrase is taken from the "cahier des charges" issued to Véron on February 28, 1831 (Archives nationales, AJ [13] 180). Discussed in Fulcher, *Nation's Image*, 54–64. For Véron's own account of his tenure as the Opéra's director, see Louis Véron, *Mémoires d'un Bourgeois de Paris, comprenant la fin de l'Empire, la Restauration, la Monarchie de Juillet, la République jusqu'au rétablissement de l'Empire*, vols. 1–5 (Paris: Librairie Nouvelle, 1856).

40. See Lacombe, "The Machine and the State."

41. Quoted and translated in Thomas Kelly, *First Nights at the Opera* (New Haven: Yale University Press, 2004), 147. For the original, see Heinrich Heine, *Über die französische Bühne und andere Schriften zum Theatre*, ed. Christoph Trilse (Berlin: Kunst und Gesellschaft, 1971), 114–15.

42. Nearly every grand opera after *La Muette de Portici* borrowed a plot or theme that had enjoyed prior success at another theater. Benjamin Walton has examined in detail the many adaptations of William Tell performed in Paris before the conception and premiere of Rossini's opera in 1829. See Benjamin Walton, *Rossini in Restoration Paris: The Sound of Modern Life* (New York: Cambridge University Press, 2007), 257–64. Both of the Meyerbeer grand operas conceived during Véron's tenure similarly had operatic predecessors. *Robert le Diable* (1831) shares thematic similarities with Castil-Blaze's adaptation of Weber's *Der Freischütz* (presented as *Robin des bois* at the Odéon in 1824). *Les Huguenots* (1836) had a forerunner of sorts in Hérold's *Le Pré aux clercs* (Opéra-comique, 1832).

43. Marx, *Captial*, 1:164–65.

44. Adorno, "On the Fetish-Character," 296.

45. Gustave Flaubert, *Madame Bovary*, trans. Geoffrey Wall (New York: Penguin, 1992), 179.

46. Richard Wagner, "A First Night at the Opera," in *Richard Wagner Writes from Paris: Short Essays and Articles by the Young Composer*, trans. Robert Jacobs and Geoffrey Skelton (Sydney: Allen and Unwin, 1973), 163–64.

47. Discussed in Mondelli, "Sociability of History in French Grand Opera," 48–51.

48. Quoted in Arthur Loesser, *Men, Women, and Pianos: A Social History* (New York: Simon and Schuster, 1954), 392.

49. Quoted in Hans Lenneberg, *Breitkopf and Härtel in Paris* (Hillsdale, NY: Pendragon, 1990), 31.

50. Katharine Ellis, *Music Criticism in Nineteenth-Century France: La Revue et Gazette musicale de Paris, 1834–1880* (New York: Cambridge University Press, 1995). We can also note the extent of Schlesinger's control by comparing Wagner's review of Halévy's *Reine de Chypre* (for which Schlesinger had purchased the music copyright) in the *Dresden Abendzeitung* (discussed above) with his much more anemic review for Schlesinger's paper later that year (*La Revue et Gazette musicale*, February 27, 1842).

51. Žižek, *Sublime Object of Ideology*. Žižek seeks to understand capitalism through the lens of Lacanian psychoanalysis. He argues that real satisfaction—*jouissance*, in Lacanian terms—falls outside the purview of what is actually attainable within a system of deferred identity and deferred desire. Satisfying one want simply changes one's position in the social field, making one want something else. Žižek insists that such a psychology of desire underlies modern capitalism.

52. "Voyez-vous cette fastueuse voiture, ce coupé simple en dehors, de couleur brune, mais sur les panneaux duquel brille l'écusson d'une antique et noble famille? Quand ce coupé passe rapidement, les grisettes l'admirent, en convoitent le satin jaune, le tapis de la Savonnerie, la passementerie fraîche comme une paille de riz, les moelleux coussins, et les glaces muettes. Deux laquais en livrée se tiennent derrière cette voiture aristocratique; mais au fond, sur la soie, gît une tête brûlante aux yeux cernés, la tête de Raphaël, triste et pensif. Fatale image de la richesse! Il court à travers Paris comme une fusée, arrive au péristyle du théâtre Favart, le marchepied se déploie, ses deux valets le soutiennent, une foule envieuse le regarde.—Qu'a-t-il fait celui là pour être si riche? dit un pauvre étudiant en droit, qui, faute d'un écu, ne pouvait entendre les magiques accords de Rossini." Honoré de Balzac, *La Peau de chagrin: Roman philosophique*, vol. 2 (Paris: Gosselin, 1831), 135–36.

Contributors

GLENDA GOODMAN is assistant professor of musicology at the University of Pennsylvania. Her work appears in the *Journal of the American Musicological Society*, the *William and Mary Quarterly*, and *Common-Place* and has been awarded prizes from the Society of American Music, the American Society for Eighteenth-Century Studies, and the Society of Early Americanists. She is writing a book about the material culture and social history of amateur music-making in postrevolutionary America.

ROGER MATHEW GRANT is assistant professor of music at Wesleyan University. His research focuses on the relationships among eighteenth-century music theory, Enlightenment aesthetics, and early modern science. His first book, *Beating Time and Measuring Music in the Early Modern Era*, was published in 2014 by Oxford University Press.

EMILY H. GREEN is assistant professor of musicology at George Mason University. Her work on dedications and the marketing of published music has appeared in a variety of outlets, including *Eighteenth-Century Music, Current Musicology*, the *Journal of Musicological Research, NewMusicBox*, and the *New York Times*. She is also active as a performer on historical and modern keyboards.

MARIE SUMNER LOTT is associate professor of music history at Georgia State University. She is the author of *The Social Worlds of Nineteenth-Century Chamber Music: Composers, Consumers, Communities* (University of Illinois Press, 2015), and she has published articles about the music of Johannes Brahms, Clara and Robert Schumann, Carl Czerny, Jan Dussek, and Louise Farrenc in edited volumes and peer-reviewed journals.

CATHERINE MAYES is assistant professor of musicology at the University of Utah. Her research on exoticism and national styles in music of the late eighteenth and early nineteenth centuries has been published in *Eighteenth-Century Music, Music and Letters* (Westrup Prize), and *The Oxford Handbook of Topic Theory*.

PETER MONDELLI has served as an assistant professor of music history at the University of North Texas since 2012. He is completing a book project titled *Opera, Print, and Capital in Nineteenth-Century Paris*. He has presented his research at conferences across North America and Europe, and it has been published in *19th-Century Music*.

RUPERT RIDGEWELL is curator of printed music at the British Library and honorary lecturer in music at Cardiff University. His research interests encompass the history and practice of music publishing in the eighteenth and nineteenth centuries, the technique of music bibliography, and musical life in eighteenth-century Vienna.

PATRICK WOOD URIBE is an independent scholar and a former assistant professor of musicology at Boston University. His primary research explores music and the history of ideas in the nineteenth century, particularly the music, music theory, and aesthetics of early Romanticism. He is writing a book about the music theorist and critic Adolph Bernhard Marx.

STEVEN ZOHN's research focuses on the music of Telemann and the Bach family. Among his recent publications are volumes for the Telemann and C. P. E. Bach critical editions, the book *Music for a Mixed Taste: Style, Genre, and Meaning in Telemann's Instrumental Works*, and an essay on the *Tafelmusik* tradition for *Oxford Handbooks Online*. He is Laura H. Carnell Professor of Music History at Temple University.

Index

Page numbers in italics refer to examples, figures, and tables.